Prostitution Narratives is a compelli
in the brutal prostitution market i
the way prostitution destroys a pe.....
them without safety or a rightful place in the world. The world owes a debt of
gratitude to these women for their courage in speaking out against the most cruel,
organized economic system in the world. These narratives should serve as a
rallying cry for action to end this modern-day slave trade.

> – Donna M. Hughes, Professor & Eleanor M. and Oscar M. Carlson
> Endowed Chair in Women's Studies, University of Rhode Island

Whatever your stand on prostitution, it's the first-hand stories of women that have
to be listened to. These accounts are among the most unsettling you will ever
read, dispelling the comforting fairy tales our society has built around 'sex work'.

> – Steve Biddulph AM, author of *The New Manhood*

Prostitution Narratives is a call to revolutionary action. In these pages you will
graphically understand that prostitution is the degradation of and cruelty to
women. You will be sickened. You will be enraged. You will be filled with disgust
that this sexual violence and enslavement of women and girls not only is allowed
to continue but is facilitated by governments and even so-called human rights
organizations. Most of all, you will be inspired by the courage, resilience and
fortitude of these survivors. You cannot read this book and say "I didn't know."

> – Kathy Sloan, feminist advocate and author specializing in the sexual and
> reproductive objectification of women

Prostitution Narratives reveals the shallowness of the 'prostitution-is-a-choice'
mantra that supporters of the sexual exploitation industries peddle. The real
choice lies with men: stop participating in the sexual use and abuse of women that
is at the heart of prostitution, pornography, and stripping.

> – Robert Jensen, University of Texas, Austin, author of *Getting Off:*
> *Pornography and the End of Masculinity*

In this book, brave articulate prostitution survivors describe the myriad forms of
violence they suffered in stripclubs, web-camming, pornography and other forms
of prostitution. At last their voices join those of other women survivors, of rape,
child rape, violence against women in the home, whose knowledge and activism
inspired feminist campaigns and changes in the law. It is hard to believe anyone
reading this book could still seriously say that prostitution is a job like any other
and that it should be called 'sex work'. This book is an invaluable foundation for
defining prostitution as a form of men's violence that should be outlawed in law
and culture.

> – Sheila Jeffreys, Professorial Fellow in the School of Social and Political
> Sciences, University of Melbourne, author of *The Idea of Prostitution* and
> *The Industrial Vagina*

An antidote to the hollow cant that prostitution is inevitable, a choice, and just a job like any other. These are the voices that tell the truth about prostitution. These are the voices that the media ignores. These are the voices that Amnesty International rejected when it resolved to decriminalize pimps and prostitution users. A heartrendingly frank and honest account about the brutality of prostitution from the women who have been there.

– Janice Raymond, Professor Emerita, University of Massachusetts, and Board of Directors, Coalition Against Trafficking in Women (CATW)

How precious the voices of women! Those trying to end male violence against women are confirmed by this truth-telling. Their valiant endurance and escapes confirm what we theorized: that prostitution is best understood as an institution of men's dominance of women, its methods as violent and oppressive as any right wing dictator's death squad.

– Lee Lakeman, feminist activist, front line anti-violence worker at the Vancouver Rape Relief and Women's Shelter, Canada

Reading these generous Survivor Narratives is a humbling experience for any man. Hearing this 'common language' may be the key to substantive solidarity with women, against profiteers and politicians.

– Martin Dufresne, Tradfem translation collective, anti-sexism activist, Canada

These survivors of prostitution are the leading edge of the abolitionist movement; their voices are the bedrock on which our movement is built. Like slave narratives, prostitution survivors' truths are compelling, revealing, and deeply disturbing.

– Melissa Farley, PhD, Executive Director, Prostitution Research & Education

This book is courageous and lucid truth-telling about a global industry that anyone who is remotely thoughtful or ethical would know is saturated with extreme forms of exploitation, crime, violence and systemic corruption. Their voices are a wake-up call to all of those who claim to defend human rights.

– Abigail Bray, academic, author of *Misogyny Re-loaded* and co-editor of *Big Porn Inc.*

Prostitution Narratives sunders any notions we have that the majority of 'sex workers' have full choice, full bodily autonomy, in the sex trade. Their voices are powerful, disturbing, complicated, honest and extraordinarily brave. Listen to their words. And pass them on.

– Victoria A. Brownworth, columnist, Pulitzer Prize nominee, author of *Lost in America: The Story of Juvenile Prostitution.*

Powerful and painful. Read it and weep. This book is an essential tool in the fight for freedom.

– Danielle Strickland, anti-trafficking advocate and author

Caroline Norma, PhD, is a lecturer in the school of Global, Urban and Social Studies at RMIT University and a member of the *Coalition Against Trafficking in Women Australia* (CATWA). She is also the author of *The Japanese Comfort Women and Sexual Slavery during the China and Pacific Wars* (Bloomsbury Academic, London and New York, 2016).

Melinda Tankard Reist is a Canberra author, speaker, commentator, blogger and advocate for women and girls. Co-founder of *Collective Shout: For a world free of sexploitation,* Melinda's books include *Getting Real: Challenging the Sexualisation of Girls* (2009) and *Big Porn Inc: Exposing the harms of the global pornography industry* (2011, co-edited with Abigail Bray).

Other books by **Caroline Norma**

*The Japanese Comfort Women and Sexual Slavery
During the China and Pacific Wars* (2016)

*Police Investigative Interviews and Interpreting:
Context, Challenges and Strategies*
(with Sedat Mulayim and Miranda Lai, 2015)

Other books by **Melinda Tankard Reist**

*Big Porn Inc:
Exposing the Harms of the Global Pornography Industry*
(co-edited with Abigail Bray, 2011)

*Getting Real:
Challenging the Sexualisation of Girls* (2009)

*Defiant Birth:
Women Who Resist Medical Eugenics* (2006)

*Giving Sorrow Words:
Women's Stories of Grief After Abortion* (2000)

PROSTITUTION NARRATIVES

Stories of Survival in the Sex Trade

Edited by
Caroline Norma and Melinda Tankard Reist

First published by Spinifex Press 2016

Spinifex Press Pty Ltd
504 Queensberry Street, North Melbourne, Victoria 3051, Australia
women@spinifexpress.com.au
www.spinifexpress.com.au

Edited in-house by Pauline Hopkins, Renate Klein and Susan Hawthorne
Typeset by Blue Wren Books
Cover Design by Deb Snibson
Indexed by Karen Gillen
Typeset in Berthold Baskerville
Printed by McPherson's Printing Group

Artwork on front cover by Geneviève Gilbert, © 2013 *Legal Slave*,
mixed media on canvas, 3 wooded-framed panels of 30cm × 100cm
Reproduced with permission

National Library of Australia Cataloguing-in Publication data:

Prostitution narratives: stories of survival in the sex trade /
editors: Melinda Tankard Reist, Caroline Norma

9781742199863 (paperback)
9781742199818 (ebook: pdf)
9781742199825 (ebook: mobi, Kindle)

Includes index

Prostitutes–Crimes against
Prostitutes–Social conditions
Prostitution–Social aspects

Other Creators/Contributors
Tankard Reist, Melinda, editor.
Norma, Caroline, editor.

331.76130674

For the women whose words make this book.
For women everywhere who speak out.
For those whose voices will never be heard.

CONTENTS

INTRODUCTION

Prostitution
Survivors
Speak Out

Caroline Norma and
Melinda Tankard Reist

Prostitution Narratives presents powerful stories by women who have survived the prostitution industry. The testimonies collated in this book bear witness to the effects of prostitution on women and girls, and bring to life its dismal statistics.

Such stories are rarely published. Instead, it is the profiteers who are most dominant and influential in speaking and writing about prostitution. This billion-dollar industry seeks to persuade the world that prostitution is a service like any other that allows women to earn vast sums of money, and to travel and enjoy life's luxuries. In large sections of the media, academia, public policy and the law, the sex industry has had its way. With money no obstacle, its polished representatives repeat the mantra: sex work is work, prostitution is a job like any other, and the sex industry should be treated as just another business enterprise.

Right-to-prostitution groups present women in sex busin-esses as 'escorts, hostesses, strippers, dancers, sex workers'. Prostitution is euphemistically described as 'compensated

1

dating' and 'assisted intercourse' with women who are 'erotic entrepreneurs'.[1] But the sex industry's public relations campaign makes little mention of the damage, violation, suffering, and torment of prostitution on the body and the mind, nor of the deaths, suicides and murders that are common. It is in its economic interest to do so. As long-time abolitionist Melissa Farley observes, much of the business must be concealed and denied in order for it to continue:

> There is an economic motive to hiding the violence in prostitution and trafficking ... prostitution is sexual violence that results in massive economic profit for some of its perpetrators ... Many governments protect commercial sex business because of monstrous profits ...
>
> This information [on the harms of prostitution, pornography and trafficking] has to be culturally, psychologically, and legally denied because to know it would interfere with the business of sexual exploitation.[2]

In critiquing the business of sexual exploitation, the accounts in this book sit outside the sphere of mainstream publishing in exposing the prostitution trade for what it is: violence against women. This violence not uncommonly results in female death, like that of a young woman in Australian prostitution, Pippa O'Sullivan, who in late 2015 died through an act of reported self-harm. She was 28 years old, and had entered prostitution at age 17.[3] Social media posts before her death reveal the suffering and torment she had faced. A media report of her death referred to her "struggle to work while battling

---

1   See Melissa Farley (2006) 'Prostitution, Trafficking, and Cultural Amnesia: What We Must *Not Know* in Order to Keep the Business of Sexual Exploitation Running Smoothly', *Yale Journal of Law and Feminism*. Vol. 18: p. 132.

2   *Ibid.* pp. 108–109, 112. This is also discussed in *The Industrial Vagina: The Political Economy of the Global Sex Trade* by Sheila Jeffreys (2009) Abingdon, Oxon: Routledge.

3   <https://radio.adelaide.edu.au/grace-bellavue-set-to-launch-nywf/>: this interview indicates that Ms O'Sullivan entered the industry underage and was not 18 as reported elsewhere.

mental health problems,"[4] and quoted her disclosing the fact that

> ... you turn into a snappy, violent, aggressive person and somewhere along the line you lose yourself ... It isn't the industry per se, it's just accumulated PTSD and constantly guarding your back or screening ... I've had guns put to my head, yelled at too many people, removed people from clubhouses, been approached by lawyers from all sides of the fence, approached to run parlours, watched a lot of people slip and fall in a bath with their throat slit.

Telling the truth about the violence of prostitution is risky and difficult, first and foremost for the women involved, but also for journalists and writers. Just before O'Sullivan's death, a group of sex industry survivors and their supporters, including doctors, academics, politicians and mental health professionals, released a statement calling for better mental health care services for women in the sex industry.[5] The statement cited research showing women in all areas of prostitution had poorer mental health outcomes than Australian women of comparable age. But even this call for the mental health sector to recognise problems faced by people in prostitution was treated by industry representatives as an act of aggression. The journalist who covered O'Sullivan's death came under criticism, with sex industry figures and supporters calling for her article to be taken down or for the mental health section to be deleted. Simone Watson, a contributor to this book and director of the Nordic Model Australia Coalition (NORMAC), was involved in writing the letter. She recalls the response:

> We wrote about the need for tailored support for the prostituted regardless of whether they considered their lives empowering or not ... We asked to go beyond the politics and focus on the reality

---

4   <https://www.reddit.com/user/brothelgirl>

5   NORMAC (2015) 'Sex trade survivors & their supporters call for tailored mental health interventions', Media Release, 14 October. Accessed at <http://tasmaniantimes.com/index.php?/pr-article/sex-trade-survivors-their-supporters-/>

that the sex trade kills women, and insisted on support for all of us. The sex-trade propaganda lobby lashed out in droves against an article about [O'Sullivan's] death that quoted us ... They harassed the journalist ... lashed out at me for having spoken and called us opportunistic, when in fact our comments were not made about Pippa's death, but happened at the same time.[6]

O'Sullivan's sad death and the backlash against the journalist who tried to tell her story is illustrative of the current political landscape where the harmful realities of prostitution go untold. This is why we wanted to publish the testimonies in this book, which tell a different story. In compiling the book, we aim to redress the imbalance in mainstream publishing on the subject of prostitution so that the voices of those who have survived this reality can at last be heard. We also wanted to produce a written record of prostitution that can be used to tackle the policies, practices and bottom-feeder industries that keep it going.

Prostitution Narratives renders visible a collective record of harm in the testimonies of twenty survivors of the sex industry from seven countries. This harm is often glamourised and romanticised. In 1997, prostitution survivor and feminist theorist Andrea Dworkin insisted that prostitution is not a discussion of ideas but an enactment of a very real harm:

I want to bring us back to basics. Prostitution: what is it? It is the use of a woman's body for sex by a man, he pays money, he does what he wants. The minute you move away from what it really is, you move away from prostitution into the world of ideas. You will feel better; you will have a better time; it is more fun; there is plenty to discuss, but you will be discussing ideas, not prostitution. Prostitution is not an idea. It is the use of a woman's body for sex by a man, he pays money, he does what he wants ... It is the mouth, the vagina, the rectum, penetrated usually by a penis, sometimes hands, sometimes objects, by one man and then

---

6   Personal correspondence with Simone Watson 12 January, 2016.

another and then another and then another and then another. That's what it is.[7]

Writers such as Kathleen Barry, Janice Raymond and Sheila Jeffreys have already provided expert theoretical frameworks for its discussion. The stories in *Prostitution Narratives* go back to basics and counter the myths promulgated by the sex industry about itself. These myths overwhelm the ability of many women harmed in prostitution to tell the truth of their experience. Powerful political, economic and cultural forces operate to make unspeakable their violation, suffering, torment, and death. Former co-executive director of the Coalition Against Trafficking in Women (CATW), Janice Raymond, provides a compelling explanation of how this happens:

> Initially, many women in prostitution will deny the exploitation and violence that has happened to them for various reasons including: to tell the truth about their experiences could be dangerous; they come from backgrounds of sexual abuse where the sexual exploitation they are subjected to is accepted as sex, not as violence; they see violence as part of the job and as an occupational hazard; and they have survived the violence done to them in the sex industry by dissociating from it.[8]

Some women never get to tell the truth of their experiences in the sex trade. They are often erased with the same callous cruelty and indifference as are their lives. In 2008, for example, two Chinese women who had entered Australia and become entangled in the sex industry were murdered. Only two months after starting 'work', they were found lying side by side in a tiny shared flat with their necks slashed. The other women with whom they were living claimed to have seen and heard

---

7   Andrea Dworkin (1997) 'Prostitution and Male Supremacy' in *Life and Death: Unapologetic Writings on the Continuing War against Women.* New York: Free Press, p. 140.

8   Janice Raymond (2013) *Not a Choice Not a Job: Exposing the Myths about Prostitution and the Global Sex Trade.* North Melbourne: Spinifex Press, p. xiii.

nothing. Debt bondage to pimps was suspected in the still-unsolved case. A notorious Sydney pimp was heard on the day of their murder boasting that "Bad things happen to people who upset our people."[9] Terrible stories like this are not rare. Women involved in street prostitution in the UK and Europe are 60 to 100 times more likely to be murdered than women outside of the industry. The average age of death of prostituted women is estimated to be just 34 years because of violence, trauma and disease.[10] This is the reality of how women live and die in prostitution.

Survivors who do manage to speak out about such realities are subjected to threats and violence. Rachel Moran is a survivor, author and activist from Ireland, and wrote the Prologue to this book. Since coming out as a survivor in the early 2000s, Moran has been the subject of constant attack, ranging from smear campaigns to threats against her life. Her work made a major contribution to the passage of the legislation in Northern Ireland along the lines of the Nordic Model. This legislation criminalises the purchase of sex while decriminalising its sale and providing support for women to exit the industry.[11] But after Moran testified at a 2012 US Department of Justice hearing the abuse escalated:

9   Natalie O'Brien (2009) 'Police baffled by prostitute murder mystery', *The Australian*, 31 January <http://www.theaustralian.com.au/archive/news/police-baffled-by-prostitute-murder/story-e6frg6o6-1111118716217>

10 Stuart Brody, John J. Potterat, Stephen Q. Muth and Donald E. Woodhouse (2005) 'Psychiatric and Characterological Factors Relevant to Excess Mortality in a Long-term Cohort of Prostitute Women,' *Journal of Sex Marital Therapy*, Vol. 31, No. 2, pp. 97–112. Also see C. Gabrielle Salfati, Alison R. James and Lynn Ferguson (2008) 'Prostitute Homicides: A Descriptive Study', *Journal of Interpersonal Violence*, Vol. 23, No. 4, pp. 505–543 who provide a detailed description and analysis of how women in prostitution are murdered more often, in different ways, and for different reasons than other female homicide victims murdered by men, in both sexual and non-sexual cases.

11 See *Human Trafficking and Exploitation (Criminal Justice and Support for Victims) Act (Northern Ireland) 2015* <http://www.legislation.gov.uk/nia/2015/2/contents/enacted>. At the time of writing, the Republic of Ireland is on the verge of passing similar legislation.

[E]very legal milestone myself and the many other women globally who are fighting for this legislation achieve, we must pay for by becoming victims of an organised campaign of abuse and intimidation. Those campaigning against the laws I'm fighting for have got hold of my home address, bank details and personal email. Now the abuse lands straight into my inbox as well as my blog, and I have had portions of my home address tweeted at me in a 'we know where to find you'-style threat.[12]

Moran wrote about her own survival of prostitution in *Paid For. My Journey through Prostitution* (2013) which is both a first-person account of prostitution and a work of feminist theory. She wrote of her experience that "It hurt like sexual assault. It damaged like sexual assault. It degraded like sexual assault. It *was* sexual assault … prostitution *was* abuse – *paid* sexual abuse."[13] Moran's determination to maintain awareness of this reality, even while she was suffering its consequences, is described in her Prologue, which pleads for survivors and their supporters to resist the reframing of prostitution as 'work'.

Earlier Voices

Feminists have long understood the importance of recording women's experiences of prostitution. In 1971 (revised in 1976), Kate Millett published two long interviews with women who had survived prostitution in the US.[14] A French-language collection of interviews with six survivors was published in 1975.[15] In 2004, Jody Raphael presented an extraordinary account of the life of a survivor named Olivia whom she had

---

12 Rachel Moran (29 May 2015) 'The life of an anti-prostitution campaigner' *Irish Times* <http://www.irishtimes.com/life-and-style/people/the-life-of-an-anti-prostitution-campaigner-1.2230971>

13 Rachel Moran (2013) *Paid For.* North Melbourne: Spinifex Press, pp. 111–112.

14 Kate Millett (1976) *The Prostitution Papers: A Quartet for Female Voice,* 3rd ed. New York: Ballantine Books.

15 Claude Jaget (1980) *Prostitutes, Our Life.* Bristol: Falling Wall Press.

interviewed over some years.[16] Raphael interspersed Olivia's narrative with social science research setting out the bigger picture of prostitution as a system and its impact on women and girls. The value of such testimony lies in its revealing of the sex industry's strategies of female exploitation and manipulation.

Published *collections* of survivor interviews and testimonies are still few. Some individual prostitution survivors have bravely and lucidly written about their experiences in the form of autobiographies or memoirs. One of the more harrowing of these accounts was *Ordeal* written by Linda Marciano under the name 'Linda Lovelace' in 1980.[17] An even earlier first-person account published in English translation in 2003 describes a woman's experience of prostitution in pre-war Japan. Sayo Masuda published this memoir in Japanese in the 1950s, but its depiction of prostitution is similar to contemporary accounts despite the vast difference in time and space. Other critical accounts include those of Sara Priesley (1997) and Suki Falconberg (2008) who document two different contexts of prostitution. Priesley was in the Australian industry and Falconberg was in US military prostitution but they record similar experiences of violence, degradation and hardship. Other accounts are less critical of the sex industry, but still reveal important and harrowing facts about systems of prostitution in different parts of the world, such as the published memoirs of Kate Holden (2005), Carla van Raay (2006), Sarah Katherine Lewis (2006), and Geena Leigh (2014).

There is, of course, also a genre of writing contrived as individual recollections of prostitution or 'sex work' that is conveyed in a sexualised and glamourised way. The origins of this genre can be traced back to the 18th century 'erotic

---

16 Jody Raphael (2004) *Listening to Olivia: Violence, Poverty, and Prostitution.* Boston: Northeastern University Press.

17 Linda Lovelace & Mike McGrady (1980) *Ordeal.* Secaucus, N.J: Citadel Press. Linda Marciano was prostituted by her husband into the making of pornography. Her story also illustrates the intermeshing of pornography and prostitution in the sex industry.

novel' *Fanny Hill: Memoirs of a Woman of Pleasure*, written by a man, John Cleland. A well-known contemporary example is the two 'London call girl' books published in 2005 and 2006 that are celebratory of the UK sex industry and the author's experiences within it. These books are vastly different from those by Moran and other survivors: they draw little meaning out of the experience of prostitution beyond titillation and entertainment for readers.

'Slave narratives' in the history of anti-slavery abolitionism

We borrowed the title *Prostitution Narratives* from an old literary genre used by the movement to abolish the trans-Atlantic and American slave trade in the 19th century. In this movement, the word 'narrative' was used to describe the testimonies of slavery survivors that were compiled for reading by the public to raise awareness and to mobilise resistance. These 'slave narratives' played a significant role in the abolitionist activities of freed slaves and their supporters. From this time, and continuing for over 100 years, hundreds of first-person accounts by former American slaves were transcribed, often by supporters and government researchers.

This affinity with a genre of the old abolitionist movement is deliberate. There are shared values among the anti-slavery and anti-prostitution movements, and activist women have played a part in both of their histories.[18] This convergence is reflected in the contemporary writing of Melissa Farley and Sarah Deer who have described the historical relocation of Native American women in North America as a practice of trafficking. They also compare the abolitionist movements against prostitution in the contemporary age with slavery in the 19th century and note their similarities in terms of opposition

---

18 Cahal Milmo (23 August 2015) 'How women's key role in abolition has yet to receive the attention it deserves', *The Independent*. Accessed at <http://www.independent.co.uk/news/uk/home-news/slavery-how-womens-key-role-in-abolition-has-yet-to-receive-the-attention-it-deserves-10467431.html>

and resistance.[19] It is often forgotten that enslavement in the American South and elsewhere took the form not only of forced labour, but of systematic sexual assault, particularly of women and girl children. Abolitionist women such as Ida B. Wells recognised that central to the US slavery system (and its aftermath) was the unfettered use and abuse of black women by white men.[20] Senator Charles Sumner was beaten on the floor of the US Senate in 1856 after describing slave ownership as rape.[21] The old abolitionist movement sought to end not only forced labour, but the holding and exercise of the rights of sexual ownership.[22] So do we, the new abolitionists.

Contemporary narratives

There are already important collections of testimony from women who have survived *military* prostitution, including *The True Stories of the Comfort Women* (1996) and *Chinese Comfort Women: Testimonies from Imperial Japan's Sex Slaves* (2014). In 2011, the South Korean Durebang (with Eunice Kim) published a collection of both first-and second-person interview accounts from 17 military prostitution survivors.[23] However there is no comparable literature of women surviving systems of prostitution organised in 'peacetime'.

---

19 Melissa Farley (2015) 'Slavery and Prostitution: a 21st Century Abolitionist Perspective' in Bonnie Martin and James F. Brooks (eds) *Linking the Histories of Slavery in North America and Its Borderlands*. Santa Fe: School for Advanced Research Press.

20 Ida B. Wells (1901/1977) 'Lynching and the Excuse for It', in *Lynching and Rape: An Exchange of View*, Bettina Aptheker (ed) New York: American Institute for Marxist Studies.

21 William Hoffer and James Hull (2010) *The Caning of Charles Sumner: Honor, Idealism, and the Origins of the Civil War*. Baltimore: Johns Hopkins University Press.

22 See Akhil Reed Amar and Daniel Wildawsky (1992) 'Child Abuse as Slavery: A Thirteenth Amendment Response to DeShaney', *Harvard Law Review*, 105, pp. 1368–1372.

23 Durebang (2011) *The Stories of the Women of Durebang*. Uijeongbu: Durebang.

In the context of the contemporary anti-prostitution abolitionist movement, there exist very few volumes of collated first-person testimonies of women who have been prostituted in the global sex industry. One recent volume, published in 2012, features first-person accounts by survivors of trafficking in the United States, presented within a broader narrative about ways to assist victims.[24] What does exist are significant collections of interviews with survivors. In 2001, the Women's Education, Development, Productivity and Research Organization (WEDPRO) in the Philippines published a collection of interviewer-recorded testimonies from eight survivors of prostitution or marriage trafficking. The editors compiled the accounts because, they said, "the human rights discourse needs to be challenged," and because we "cannot argue against torture without the same fervor against trafficking and sexual exploitation."[25] Some stories by survivors do exist in digital form, though. There is an Equality Now collection, and a French-English bilingual web-based collection of published accounts from survivors that includes more than 200 interviews and testimonies.[26]

Survivors Taking Action

As testimony, *Prostitution Narratives* aims to contribute to campaigns directed at stopping the sex industry as an enterprise that inflicts the trauma described by our contributors. The collection thus aligns itself with Kate Millett's *Prostitution Papers*, which was written as a work that

... directs itself to action. Cries out for, was created for, this end:

---

24 Mary Frances Bowley (2012) *The White Umbrella: Walking with Survivors of Sex Trafficking.* Chicago: Moody Publishers.

25 Flor Caagusan (ed) (2001) *Halfway through the Circle: The Lives of 8 Filipino Survivors of Prostitution & Sex Trafficking,* 2nd ed. Quezon City: Women's Education, Development, Productivity and Research Organization, Inc. (WEDPRO), Aida Santos (Introduction), p. xii.

26 <https://fr.pinterest.com/ressourcespros/survivantessurvivors-english-french/>

that it would *do* something. Do something more than it would say ... [it] has always been aimed squarely at *direct action.* 'Organize, organize' this book calls out ... Because I wanted desperately to see something happen. And because, in the end, a book can only incite, be a catalyst, jog a nerve, echo a perception already present or potential in the reader. And because the real organization is one I can only *aid* and *assist.* It must be *accomplished* by others: the prostitutes themselves [her italics].[27]

Since Millett wrote in the early 1970s, political organising by survivors in their own right, and on their own behalf, has gotten well underway. Survivor-led movements like Space International, Moongchi, and the Organization for Prostitution Survivors now speak, write and campaign against prostitution and the deregulation of sex industries worldwide. These organisations and others, like the Irish abolitionist group Ruhama, provide access on their websites to face-to-camera survivor testimony, lectures and TEDx talks describing personal experiences of prostitution, such as those by Mia de Faoite and Barbara Amaya, and the European Women's Lobby's co-production with the Coalition Against Trafficking in Women of the 'Not for Sale' documentary.[28] These filmed testimonies are extraordinary in their detail and eloquence.

Like the 19th century abolitionists, supporters today find ways of bringing individual survivors and their articulated experiences to public attention in order to promote awareness and social change. We similarly envisage *Prostitution Narratives* as 'aiding and assisting' such activities of abolitionist campaigning.

---

27   Kate Millett *ibid,* p. 6.

28   <http://www.womenlobby.org/EWL-campaign-clip-Not-for-sale-2006-EWL-CATW>. See also the anthology *Not for Sale: Feminists Resisting Prostitution and Pornography*, Christine Stark and Rebecca Whisnant (eds), (North Melbourne, Spinifex Press, 2004) which includes contributions by sex industry survivors Andrea Dworkin, Chong N. Kim, Taylor Lee and Christine Stark. The book also mentions WHISPER (Women Hurt in Systems of Prostitution Engaged in Revolt), an early organisation and oral history project for prostitution survivors established by Evelina Giobbe.

We also follow in the footsteps of South Korean women's groups who put together the first volume of 'comfort women' testimony in the mid-1990s, mentioned briefly above. The so-called 'comfort women' were sexually enslaved by the Japanese military in the Asia-Pacific region during the China and Pacific wars. It took more than forty years for survivors of this war crime to be heard publicly, but their testimony sparked the formation of a social movement in support of recognition and reparations. In 2000, their supporters held a citizens' trial in Tokyo to deliberate on the wartime responsibility of the Japanese military and government, at which 60 survivors spoke out about their experiences. Their testimony was distributed throughout the Asia-Pacific. This enabled global mobilisation in support of the 'justice for comfort women' movement to spread worldwide in the 1990s, especially in South Korea, the Philippines, Japan, the United States and China.[29] Hee-Jung Serenity Joo explains that

… first-hand testimony has played an invaluable role in bringing awareness to the comfort women's history, including providing legal witness accounts in the face of scarce, classified, or compromised documentation. In fact, testimony was imperative in decentering a focus on Japanese documents and severing a reproduction of colonial hegemony that decided what were historical events and facts.[30]

29 Caroline Norma (2015) *The Japanese Comfort Women and Sexual Slavery during the China and Pacific Wars.* Bloomsbury Academic, London.

30 Hee-Jung Serenity Joo (2015) 'Comfort Women in Human Rights Discourse: Fetishized Testimonies, Small Museums, and the Politics of Thin Description', *Review of Education, Pedagogy, and Cultural Studies,* 37 (2–3), pp. 166–83, also pp. 167–178. Even in countries like Australia, the testimony of women like Jan Ruff O'Herne has brought the problem of wartime military prostitution to contemporary attention as an injustice requiring remedy. O'Herne's testimony of her time in Indonesia under the Japanese Imperial Army reveals a human rights atrocity that occurred in the past but that endures today as unfinished business for feminists and justice campaigners in terms of righting an historical wrong.

In its call to action, this book follows in the footsteps of pioneering feminists who opposed prostitution and the sex industry worldwide. One of the earliest of these women was Kathleen Barry in her 1979 publication *Female Sexual Slavery* which led to the emergence of an international feminist anti-prostitution movement. Barry's groundbreaking book saw prostituted women as "victims of female sexual slavery" in cases where they were "sexually exploited, physically abused and [could not] get away." Barry called for feminist action on prostitution, which she saw as a "pervasive practice [that] cuts across all lines of race, class, and culture ... [and] is the subject of entertainment in pornography and ultimately affects all women."[31]

We hope *Prostitution Narratives* will be read as contemporary evidence of 'female sexual slavery', as Barry defined the sex trade. Prostitution in 'peacetime' is rarely understood as enacting women's sexual enslavement, except perhaps in circumstances of trafficking or the prostitution of children. But the ordeal of sexual enslavement that lies at the heart of systems of prostitution is reflected in many passages of *Prostitution Narratives*. United States survivor Autumn Burris recollects, "After once being beaten beyond recognition – my eyes were black and blue and bloodshot from the blows and my body covered in bruises – I was later that night picked up by men, and not one of them asked me if I was all right or refrained from purchasing my body" (p. 138). Burris's testimony recalls that of Korean 'comfort' station survivor Yun Tu-Ri who was enslaved in the China War in the 1930s. She recalled that a Japanese soldier bashed her and, even after "the wound on my bottom festered and I had such a high fever that I could

---

31 Kathleen Barry (1979) *Female Sexual Slavery.* New York: New York University Press.

not even lie on my back[,] ... I was forced to keep receiving soldiers."[32]

The broad similarity of experiences found in the testimony of prostitution survivors around the world, whether their experiences are those of wartime or the time we call peace, is an important reason to work to spark recognition of an old and persistent human rights violation. Making the harms of prostitution culturally visible involves a victim recalling her personal endurance and courageous survival of these harms, the retelling of which often brings emotional pain and suffering. Survivors repeatedly explain in their chapters in this collection that they nonetheless decided to tell their stories for the sake of other women and girls. 'Charlotte', for example, states:

> To anyone reading this who is still involved in the sex industry – you are so much more than your body and your ability to provide sexual gratification. You are worthy, important and loved. You deserve so much more. The world is out there waiting for you. You will survive this (p. 185).

Reflections like this make *Prostitution Narratives* a conversation among survivors about their common experience and the need to join together and collectively resist prostitution. The 'unspeakable' nature of the reality of prostitution for victims is a barrier to social change that first-hand testimonies by survivors may overcome.

The contributors

We have included in this volume only testimony from women who have survived prostitution in the so-called 'first-world': the industrialised countries of Australia, Canada, Denmark, Ireland, New Zealand, the United Kingdom, and the United States. Our decision to include only accounts relating to the

---

32 Korean Council for Women Drafted for Military Sexual Slavery by Japan and the Research Association on the Women Drafted for Military Sexual Slavery by Japan (1996) *True Stories of the Korean Comfort Women*, p. 34.

sex industries of the rich, industrialised world was motivated by a desire to show that, even in jurisdictions imagined to have 'better', more regulated and 'safer' systems of prostitution, such as Australia, which has had legalised prostitution in some states for decades,[33] women's experiences of violence and degradation are still extreme. It is common to see government agencies and academics writing about rich-world sex industries as fundamentally different from those of countries such as India in which girls are 'born into brothels'.[34] It is widely believed that legalised prostitution in rich, westernised countries offers women a different and better experience of sexual exploitation. For example, the Resourcing Health and Education (RhED) organisation which is a government-funded Australian body supporting 'street sex workers', submitted to a 2009 Government Inquiry the opinion that a "lack of working visa arrangements available for migrant sex workers who wish to work in Australia for the legislative, health and occupational health and safety benefits of Australian sex industry laws, brings about situations where few options exist other than to go through traffickers."[35] This is a commonly expressed opinion that implies that the money and wealth involved in rich societies somehow makes the sex industry less violent, corrupt and criminal, and makes the experience of prostitution itself more psychologically and physically tolerable. The accounts presented in this book provide a strong rebuttal to this view.

---

33 In *Making Sex Work* (North Melbourne, Spinifex Press, 2007), Mary Lucille Sullivan showed how the legalisation of prostitution in Victoria in 1994 did not make it a safer place for prostituted people. For every legalised brothel, there are now three illegal ones.

34 See the novel *Town of Love* by Anne Ch. Ostby (North Melbourne, Spinifex Press, 2013) which is based on events in a village in the state of Bihar where girls are born into prostitution, and includes an Afterword by Indian abolitionist Ruchira Gupta.

35 Drugs and Crime Prevention Committee (2010) *Inquiry into People Trafficking for Sex Work*, October, Parliament of Victoria, Melbourne, Australia, p. 127. Accessed at <http://www.parliament.vic.gov.au/57th-parliament/dcpc/article/965>

We hope that, if the harm of rich-world prostitution is better understood, readers might turn their minds to how the normalisation of prostitution in rich countries contributes to the maintenance of sex industries in poor or developing countries. Taking Nigeria as just one example, researchers wrote in 2005 that:

> The impetus to take up sex work among Nigerian girls and women has been reinforced by the whirlwind of globalization, which has initiated intense political and economic changes as well as social transformation worldwide. More social mobility, newer systems of values and lifestyles which favour consumption, early sexual initiation, and access to explicit sexual materials, have caused changes in the everyday behaviour of peoples all over the world. ... the changing images of the practice of sex work resulting from the liberalization of private life, the commercialization of sex via sex shops, pornographic materials, escort agencies, internet sex sites and orgies, the disappearance of semi-formal limitations and sanctions from state institutions, and the changing value system which has increased materialism, make sex work one of the acceptable ways of getting money for consumer goods.[36]

Certainly, the situation for prostituted women and girls in countries such as Nigeria is more dire than that of women in rich countries in some respects, especially with regard to rates of HIV transmission, mortality and the extent of their social exclusion. Girls born into intergenerational family-based systems of prostitution in countries such as India are also harmed in an extreme way that is different from other circumstances of prostitution. However, in editing this collection of testimonies from prostituted women in 'first-world' sex industries, we aim to support women's organisations such as Apne Aap in India that tackle prostitution. We need to also look at the systematic

---

36 C Otutubikey Izugbara (2005) 'Ashawo suppose shine her eyes: Female Sex Workers and Sex Work Risks in Nigeria', *Health, Risk & Society*, Vol. 7, No. 2, p. 144.

harm of prostitution in our own backyard.[37] This awareness is crucial to slowing down or stopping, as the Nigerian example shows, the further globalisation of cultural and commercial forces that make women and girls in poor countries vulnerable to the slavery of the sex trade.[38]

Those who defend prostitution in rich westernised countries carry significant discursive and material power to influence the governments and civil society organisations of poor countries. Only recently, Amnesty International (based in the UK) passed a policy to support the decriminalisation of pimping and buying sex worldwide. In their ideological and policy activism, western sex industry advocates like these are fundamentally connected to the brutal prostitution we see in poor countries. This connection arises directly through globalised practices like sex tourism, 'mail order bride' buying, and cross-border trafficking, but also indirectly through political advocacy and ideology formation. The task of dismantling systems of prostitution and their rhetorical justifications in rich industrialised countries is therefore an urgent one.

---

37 A powerful illustration of this is found in the experience of award winning American filmmaker Libby Spears, director of the film *Playground* about the trafficking of girls within North America. She had documented the exploitation of girls and young women in the Philippines and Cambodia before coming to realise "that the trafficking of children for commercial sexual exploitation is every bit as real in North America" <http://nestfoundation.org/playground-the-film/>

38 Julie Bindel also observes the connections between prostitution in developing countries and prostitution in the west in a recent piece in the *New Statesman* in the lead up to publication of her 2016 book *The Pimping of Prostitution: Abolishing the Sex Work Myth* (London: Palgrave Macmillan). "Wadia is far away from the legalised sex industries of Nevada, Germany and the Netherlands, but it has something fundamentally in common with those prosperous nations. Where prostitution is seen as part of the economy and a job like any other, and men are given free reign to treat women's bodies as a commodity, gender equality will remain a distant dream" <http://www.newstatesman.com/politics/feminism/2015/11/inside-tiny-village-gujarat-riven-sex-trade>

The stories in this book also illustrate the dire lack of exit programs for women who want to get out of the industry and pursue work and study options that don't cause them harm. Even though the United Nations Protocol to Prevent, Suppress and Punish Trafficking in Persons, Especially Women and Children (2000) requires ratifying states to "consider implementing measures to provide for the physical, psychological and social recovery of victims of trafficking,"[39] very few countries provide the practical assistance necessary to assist women in this way. For example, in Australia, there are no programs to assist women's exit from the sex industry that attract ongoing government funding. Meanwhile, sex industry lobby group Scarlet Alliance receives hundreds of thousands of dollars from the federal government to address trafficking while stating openly that trafficking of women into prostitution is not an issue.[40] This is a wholly inadequate situation in a country with more than 20,000 people in prostitution, and not in keeping with the country's obligations under the UN Protocol.

'Jade', who was prostituted in New Zealand, describes how she wanted to get out but was given no help (p. 47).

> After five years I wanted out of the sex industry. Twice I tried to go to school … I wanted to be a youth worker. But I couldn't study due to drugs and sex work. None of the sex work advocacy agencies ever offered a contingency to get me out of the sex industry. They supplied lawyers, health checks, lube, condoms and dams but nothing to help me get out.

---

39 United Nations Protocol to Prevent, Suppress and Punish Trafficking in Persons, Especially Women and Children (2000) <http://www.osce.org/odihr/19223?download=true>, pp. 3–4, see also Melinda Tankard Reist (2013) <http://m.smh.com.au/comment/we-must-help-women-escape-prostitution-before-more-lives-are-lost-20131214-2ze76.html>

40 <http://melindatankardreist.com/2015/03/the-scarlet-alliance-says-trafficking-is-a-myth-it-opposes-penalties-for-brothels-selling-trafficked-women-and-exit-programs-for-women-who-want-out-so-why-are-we-funding-them/>

Testimonies and Commentaries

Prostitution Narratives begins with, as mentioned, Rachel Moran's Prologue where she identifies the ideology of 'sex work' as a dehumanising force that conceals the reality of prostitution and makes a passionate plea for not using the term 'sex work'. The survivor testimonies which follow then unpack the reality of commercial sexual exploitation.[41] From the streets to strip clubs, to brothels and escort agencies, from web-camming to the filming of prostitution for the pornography industry, from underage girls groomed for prostitution through child sexual abuse, to young women caught up in a criminal world of gangs and drugs, to students, artists, and single mothers desperate to survive, the chapters of this book have a unifying thread: their contributors survived, got out, and want the world to know what being prostituted was really like.

Following these testimonies – the heart and soul of the book – there are three commentary pieces. The first is an account by Jacqueline Gwynne who worked as a brothel 'receptionist' during her university days. She recalls in detail the suffering she witnessed, and comes to grips with the fact she had, in reality, worked as a pimp. This is followed by a piece on the johns and punters who buy women by Caitlin Roper of the Australian-based activist movement Collective Shout: For a world free of sexploitation. Caitlin's contribution describes the men who are the customers of the global industry, because it is these men who perpetrate the harms of prostitution – aided and abetted by the pimps, brothel owners, strip clubs and the porn trade – against women and girls. It is they who carry ultimate responsibility for its crime. Last is a list of Frequently

---

41 Some of the contributions include raw language about men who prostitute women, including negative comments about personal characteristics. But the central experience of women in prostitution is unwanted sex. So while these epithets might stand out, we retain them as a less significant indication of the harm of prostitution than the descriptions of violence, humiliation and hardship that bleed through every word of testimony in the book.

Asked Questions compiled by Meagan Tyler on arguments and rebuttals about why prostitution is not a form of 'work' for women, and how we can contribute to worldwide efforts to implement the Nordic Model.

In order to better understand and respond to the global human rights violation that is prostitution, we must comprehend what the sex industry looks like and does to the girls and women most affected. For this, first-person accounts by survivors are the best way to begin.

May the women speaking out in *Prostitution Narratives* be heard.

The Dangerous Denialism of 'Sex Work' Ideology

Rachel Moran

The first thing we humans do in any intolerable, inescapable situation is erase our subjective reality. We evade and avoid accepting the nature of the situation itself. People will have different levels of skill, be able to cultivate different levels of conviction, in the business of lying to themselves. Perhaps I was never very good at it, and perhaps it's a skill I was better off without. The business of deceiving ourselves out of a fuller acceptance of an oppressive situation is useful, but only to the extent that it protects us in the short term. It will also store up more hurt for the future, much like using painkillers to mask the ache of a decaying tooth.

I got out of prostitution in 1998 and I am glad of the timing for numerous reasons. One of them is that the nonsense ideology of 'sex work' did not exist in the Ireland of the 1990s. With the advent of this ideology, women have been handed a whole new set of tools with which to deceive themselves and others. In this mythology, the sale of sexual access has been cast as the sale of sex, and the remuneration of that abuse has been reframed as the sale of labour. It is both interesting

23

and saddening to imagine how women in prostitution today navigate the emotional and psychological minefield of processing prostitution while steeped in a self-protective defensive ideology that denies the existence of its trauma in the first place. As they deny it to themselves, they deny it to everyone else, and in turn 'sex work' dogma destroys our capacity for empathy and sympathy, because, in this narrative, there is nothing to empathise with and nothing to sympathise about.

Psychological manoeuvres to protect ourselves during the 90s were commonplace, but they were never under such assault as technology has exposed the women to in prostitution today. Prostitutors – that cohort of men who prostitute women – studiously avoided each other in all areas of prostitution prior to the advent of the internet. These days, they form what they refer to as 'communities' online, where they endorse and condone the same predatory behaviour they once couldn't even look at in each other. Social media, having removed them from the physical presence of one another, has removed them also from the reality of what they are doing. Prostitutors are utterly exonerated by the ideology of 'sex work', which schools them to assert that prostitution is only a service therefore there is nothing wrong with accessing 'it'.

A language particular to this 'community' has evolved, much of it designed to minimise and deny the harmful nature of its members' actions. The men who populate it have come to refer to themselves as 'hobbyists', as though their paid abuse of women were just a mere 'hobby', and really, in the English language, is there a more benign word than that? Meanwhile, prostituted women must suffer indignity upon indignity funnelled and channelled through modern technology. A prime example of this is the men's practice of reviewing the women they buy access to. Everything imaginable is up for 'review' in this practice, from the women's physical selves, to their attitudes and behaviours, to the 'services' they provide and those they refuse to provide. Belligerent comments abound, many of them centred around the attitudes of those women who appear as though they consider what they are doing to be a job. Here again we see exposed the lie of 'sex work'. Men do not want women to approach these encounters as 'work', and it is exactly this male denialism which spawned the uber fantasy of 'The Girlfriend Experience'. It is male denial of prostitution's very nature that this form of prostitution caters to. There are, however, many forms of denial practiced in the business of prostitution, and those on both sides are willing to deceive themselves.

I remember sitting with my younger sister once in a Chinese restaurant in Dublin. We were sixteen and thirteen at the time. She had just come to live with me after spending several months in residential care following a placement in a foster home. When she had first left our mother's house I had been incarcerated in a juvenile remand centre following my arrest from a brothel, so I hadn't been able to take care of her. When I got back to Dublin she moved in with me and that evening, as we sat eating our dinner, I tried to explain to her why I was in prostitution because I knew it upset her. I wanted to try to make sense of it for her, and, in all likelihood (though I wasn't aware of it at the time) also for myself.

I was insensitive enough to use our current time and place as an example of why I was in prostitution. I remember telling her, "I wouldn't be able to come in here and buy dinner if I wasn't on the game." It never crossed my mind that this example might leave her with a sense of guilt for eating her own dinner. It didn't occur to me either that the trading of my dignity might be better defended by the example of something other than a chicken curry.

My point, of course, was that I couldn't negotiate my own life in any sense without making that trade off: prostitution for poverty. I was considering my position in the world taking into account exactly the paltry options available to me, and while

I was very aware of the unfairness of that restriction, like most sixteen-year-old girls I was not questioning my position on a political level. It was a poisonous message that I was giving my own sister, and I can only forgive myself for it because I was little more than a child myself.

What shocks me these days is listening to grown women frame the same basic argument I was framing almost twenty-five years ago, without ever having moved from the conclusion "This is the world as we experience it" to the question "What do we intend to do about it?"

A certain level of consciousness beyond the understanding of our own place in the world has to exist before we will challenge the forces that placed us there. We have got to understand, firstly, that there are forces that placed us there. The basic understanding of people's oppressed position has existed as a starting point for every social justice movement in human history, and the most dangerous element in 'sex work' ideology is that it reframes the social position of prostituted women in such a way as to make revolt illogical and unnecessary.

Can anything that shields us from the full acceptance of a negative situation ever be truly positive? I doubt it. In Dublin of the 1990s, we would hide from the truth routinely and as a matter of course. We would hide from the truth, most obviously, by not telling it to each other. But, conversely, we would inadvertently acknowledge it regularly by showing it to each other. It is important to clarify that we never lied to each other about prostitution, but the truths we shared usually stopped short of utterly candid declarations about our desires to escape it.

The barriers between women and honesty today are many times more difficult to surmount, and the damage of the dogma some of them subscribe to, and propagate, cannot be overstated. 'Sex work' ideology shields women currently in prostitution from accepting the actual reality of their situation; it gives men full licence to use them and it lies to society about the reality for both parties. It legitimises the sexual subordination of women in society, making both the immediate goal of women's liberation and the end goal of gender equality twin impossibilities. It also funnels those already socially vulnerable to prostitution straight into it by reframing prostitution so as to gloss over its damage and degradation and by agitating for the wholesale decriminalisation of sexual and financial exploiters such as brothel keepers, punters and pimps.

'Sex work' ideology acts as a dehumanising force on numerous levels. It dehumanises sex, firstly, by telling us sex is just a service. The ramifications of this standpoint perfectly reflect, hall-of-mirrors-style, the original dehumanising perspective. If sex is just a service, then rape is just theft. If sex is to be equated with any other service, then we cannot complain about the rape of a woman in prostitution any differently than we could complain about someone having their sink fixed and not paying the plumber. Rape is disappeared here. In 'sex work' ideology, we are dealing with theft, not rape.

We are consistently told that when framing prostitution legislation we should consider those most directly affected by it. Indeed we should. We should also make sure we are not duped about who they are. Those in the front lines of the effects of prostitution legislation are not only those who are currently in prostitution; they are also those most vulnerable to it. Many children and adolescents who are currently living the hellish experience of broken homes, family dysfunction, violence and alcoholism, severe neglect and sexual abuse will have the future direction of their lives dictated by prostitution legislation. This is not only about those who are in prostitution; it is also about those who are currently being corralled into it.

I have said that the first thing we humans do in any intolerable, inescapable situation is erase our subjective reality. I believe I got out of prostitution relatively emotionally healthy because I did so little of that. The erasure of my subjective reality I did collude in was at the locus of a surface level pretence, enacted purposefully to protect me from the attitudes of other people. It was never for my own sake. In other words, I lied to others about what prostitution was; I did not lie to myself.

If a subterfuge is consciously constructed it is much easier to identify, and therefore to deconstruct. My deepest compassion is with the women who must mine deeply within themselves to uncover that subterfuge, go through the pain of examining its shapes and edges, and find a way to squarely look at the thing it was designed to conceal. In this process, they must acknowledge the carnage of their own complicity.

The denialist mentality of men who use women in prostitution has never been so utterly fed-to-bloating as it is by the ideology of the 'sex work' lobby. There has perhaps never been an ideological framework in history that so thoroughly condones and emboldens the practice of oppression by the oppressed. It says, simultaneously, "Continue to abuse us please" and "Be at rest that there is no abuse going on here." Women who espouse this view owe it to every other woman to abandon it. They are traitors to their sex and to themselves.

Women who must cut through the 'sex work' ideology face confronting a reality that has been purposefully and aggressively hidden, and they must first acknowledge their own collusion with that concealment and abandon the psychological safety it affords. This is doubtlessly painful, but few things are so utterly necessary. The 'sex work' ideology must be deconstructed, and that starts at the individual level. The alternative is unthinkable for us all.

Rachel Moran is a women's rights activist from Dublin, Ireland. She is the founding member of SPACE International – Survivors of Prostitution-Abuse Calling for Enlightenment <www.spaceintl.org> – and author of Paid For. My Journey Through Prostitution. *She holds a BA in Journalism from Dublin City University and an MA in Creative Writing from University College Dublin.*

TESTIMONIES

Saved by Horses

Linda

My name is Linda. I am employed in the thoroughbred racehorse industry in Australia, as an exercise rider. I am 37 and a recovering addict with occasional lapses. I thank my love of horses for saving me, as I tried many ways of exiting the sex industry and none offered me any hope at all – none of the rehabs or the 12-step groups. I began getting fit in my late 20s. I ran and went to the gym as a way to try to rebuild my health after years of stress, depression and addiction.

I was a prostitute from 18 to 28. I worked in many segments of the industry – from brothels, where I would have to pay the pimps and owners half my money and work very much on their terms – to high-class escort work, where I built my own webpage and worked on my terms, meaning I did not pay anyone to look after me and I kept all the money. Like most women starting out in prostitution, I had to begin at the bottom and learn in order to make the experience survivable, as I could not have lasted long otherwise. The work is very hard. I often saw 12 to 15 men per eight-hour shift. There are drugs everywhere and you are exposed to a very fast-paced, adrenaline-filled environment. The money becomes your sole focus, and most of the women I worked with were addicted to something. At 18 I was addicted to money and freedom. Later I became addicted to cosmetic surgery in an effort to stay young, and after that to hard drugs, which I injected. Being infected with Hepatitis C at 28 meant my retirement from the industry and complete breakdown. I could not work knowing I had a virus that could be spread (I have since received treatment and am no longer infected).

I was affected by depression at about 11, as my family had disintegrated, and my mum had remarried a man I didn't like. My stepfather watched pornography, and I remember being exposed to porn that I was aroused by, but being so young I was confused and became sick and depressed. My stepfather was abusive and my deepest fear was that he would kill me. My mother basically left my younger brother and me with him after the wedding, as she was not around much. I hated the girls' school I attended, though my marks were high. I noticed that the only way I could fit in was if I looked 'hot'. I started wearing a lot of makeup. When I looked sexually attractive my stepfather was less likely to hit me or my brother, so makeup became my mask, my persona. I wore heavy eye makeup and looked anything but myself, dyeing my hair bleach blonde at 14. I did all I could to get out of my house and escape my family. It was hell being at home.

During my time in brothels I asked many of my working girl friends about their childhoods and many were similar to mine: broken, with mum or dad gone, abusive but often not extreme. Looking back on my adolescence I was in a lot of emotional pain. I had little support, no one to turn to, and these realities made me very strong, a trait necessary for surviving in the sex industry. Girls who aren't habituated to pain don't last in the sex industry. They might last a month or two and leave, but the women who start young, and stay, have all had a hard time and learn to live with it strategically. I remember being really judgmental and turned off by girls using drugs in brothels, as I never used drugs during my first two years in them and felt superior to other girls – I was educated and not on drugs. In fact, if you had asked how I had gotten into the sex industry, I would have told you it was MY CHOICE! I was a very good liar and able to act like I enjoyed sex, even though 99% of the sex was disgusting to me; sex with unattractive, cruel, joyless and married men.

In the rooms, you have to pretend to like the sex. The brothels are so competitive that it is not enough to just lie there. To get clients to return, every girl has to not just have sex, but to really pretend to like the whole experience. When I started I thought I could just lie there until the whole thing was over. But you quickly learn to pretend, usually by your second or third time. Also men cum quicker if you put on the act. I think this is important because it proves that it's not real sex. How can you really enjoy sex with strangers 10 times in a row? The most common physical experience is pain. The best way to avoid pain is to use lube and act and make the client cum quickly.

The only thing I looked forward to was the money and the hope of getting away from them, taking off my makeup and being free.

I got my first shift in a brothel half by accident. I was 18 and had been accepted into law at university. I had left home, just been fired from a job, and was living in a small cheap bedsitter looking through the paper for jobs when I came across the ad for 'models' ... offering '$2000 per week'. At the interview I was amazed at how beautiful the place was, with massive statues and spas. My family survived on social security payments, so I envied nice clean beautiful places. They showed me all the beautiful rooms where it became obvious I would be having sex with strangers. I was not a virgin, I'd had plenty of sexual experiences. Not boyfriends really, just sex with boys, but always a letdown. Like so many other girls I secretly thought, "Why not get paid for it?"

My experience of sex with boys before the brothel was always awkward. Many times I got myself into situations where I was going to get raped anyway and so had sex. Many of these guys didn't want to use condoms. I learnt how to do sex through watching porn. I looked like the attractive women in porn, so I knew that you had to moan. I knew how to pretend, since I felt numb and dead sexually around men. I could simply act. I knew that women in porn were acting because penetration had always been painful for me, and I knew I was normal! I slept with three men on my first shift. It was humiliating, they were so much older than me. However, none of them objected to condoms which was good. I was very young and attractive and that helped me have some power in the rooms. When you're young, you are always popular ... really popular! This experience was in Canberra, where the brothels are very quiet. When I later travelled to Sydney and Melbourne I saw that many brothels weren't so quiet. I would sometimes have a line of men waiting to see me; the brothels would be packed and there were sometimes 30 clients. I worked at the Gateway Club on Parramatta Road, and also at the Penthouse and Tiffany's, among the busiest brothels in Sydney. The going rate was about $150 per hour (that was my cut) so I could very easily make $800–$900 per shift.

I later worked at the supposedly upmarket Madam Fleiss where the pay is higher. But in my experience escort work is very dangerous, as apart from a phone number and a credit card, you have no idea who you are going to be meeting. Also the owner was a complete perve, he didn't give a shit about the girls, and he had rules like you have to kiss the client and do oral without a condom. Sometimes when I was getting undressed he would take a pic of me and post it on his website. The more risks you took at Madam Fleiss, the more you got paid. So if you provided a basic service like I did, you'd get a smaller cut but you'd get an extra few hundred dollars for agreeing to sex without a condom.

I guess I learnt to condition sex to money. After that first night in Canberra, I didn't go back for six months. I went to university, got a boyfriend. He wanted me to watch porn with him. I started to hate him, my depression was intense, and I just felt used and like a sex object for everyone. My family had heard of me having worked in a brothel and I got a reputation for being a 'hooker' even though I was at university studying. That first experience tarnished me in the eyes of others.

It would not have mattered whether I did well at uni, I would always be thought of as a prostitute it seemed. I broke up with my boyfriend and started going out with a second guy, who stole my money one night and left me homeless. It was at that point that I started to think about going to Sydney to get some more money. I was homeless and desperate and scared. I drove to Sydney, answered a new ad in the paper and began working in busier parlours. The atmosphere was fast and I met many girls who were really nice and the brothel itself was always beautiful. I often stayed at the houses of other working girls, where I was slowly introduced to ways of coping. I took medication for Attention Deficit Disorder (ADD), and sleeping pills. I earned $4000 in two weeks. I bought a stereo system for my car, later a sports car. I was able to save $20,000 in about two to three months at the brothels. This was starting to become normal.

You can imagine how addictive the money is and how a normal job like a cleaner, nurse, or even being a receptionist would be unappealing to someone trying to leave the industry but cannot adjust to a comparatively low income. Also some women are addicted to the attention. I know I was. I loved being picked over everyone else when I was young and post-surgery. That's why I think the legal age for prostitution should be raised to 25, not because I think it should be legal at all, but because young girls have absolutely no life skills on exiting when they start young. Eighteen is too young because you have not yet experienced life and you really can't make such huge decisions at such a young age, there are also no exit programs for women in the sex industry who want to get out.

I liked that none of the men could see the real me. I was always an aberration of myself, wearing tonnes of makeup and acting sexy, to get the bookings over other girls. I liked that I was very popular and that other girls were jealous of me. I liked that I could always demand that the client wear a condom. What became very obvious was that I had to stay young and beautiful to get booked. I noticed the older girls and the Asians would often get abused and cry after their bookings. One of my friends was an attractive 36-year-old Australian woman and she got choked in a booking. Her client had also shat in the spa; it was terrible. I had a lot of power only because I was young and pretty. The guys can cum quicker when you're young, they feed on vulnerability. I slept with hundreds of men in those first few months and I don't remember any of the faces. I recall bursting into tears a few times because I was tired, sore and over it. I would return home to Canberra when I couldn't take it anymore, and then return when I had more energy. The nature of the work depletes your energy. You have to pretend to be sexy while you are in pain. I was always afraid of getting raped anally, as men, especially the young drunk ones, would try and slip it in.

The violent porn broadcast throughout most brothels put us all in danger. A lot of men wanted re-enactments straight from pornography. It was harder to get booked unless you agreed to re-enact porn and offer anal. Most of the gang sex is requested by military men and by Lebanese and Chinese men, but rarely white Australian men, except the military! What people don't understand is that the foreign men have been exposed to heaps of degrading Western porn and they think Western women are asking for it since the Western men also abuse Western women in porn. With regard to popular American porn, one girl told me that a lot of the gang scenes are by military also, they call the scene a 'mission' and take heaps of Viagra and cocaine to last, and if the girl is lucky she will get Xanax or heroin to help with the pain.

What has always surprised me about men who pay for sex is that they are often physically unattractive, yet they feel no shame in taking off their clothes, where I would only be bought on the condition that my body was perfect. They would take off their clothes and just lie there … so it was always up to me to initiate the sex. I developed a routine that felt safe.

I would first massage them ... then put the condom on, then I would suck the condom, then they would have sex with me. But doing this routine eight or nine or ten times is exhausting. You are trying to hold back everything that makes you human, like saying, "I'm not enjoying this, I don't like you and I don't like being here." A lot of them seem hypnotised, like they don't know that the whole thing isn't real. A lot of them say 'I love you'; a lot seem normal, but not many realise that you are there because you were initially desperate and then you just got lost in the money or drugs or whatever. It's inconvenient for them to think about our circumstances.

Most men (you would be surprised how ordinary they are) are married, but you do see a lot of military men, police and even priests. I saw priests, particularly in Canberra, and in private work, which takes place during the day, not at night like the brothels. I saw about ten priests in Canberra and Sydney. One would tell me he 'forgave me' after we had sex! Police clients were common, and they were always aggressive and self-righteous.

A fair percentage of private clients in Canberra were newsreaders, politicians, public servants, and embassy men. The politicians and media people had a thing for anal sex and little girl role play. With diplomats their people would call me (they'd solicit me through my newspaper ads) and offer me big money if I agreed to meet them somewhere and have a chat. So I would meet maybe the handler or bodyguard at a café. Once we had done some small talk, the handler would call the official and say that I was "OK, young enough, pretty enough." The guard would tell me that I was to call the client by a different name and I had to sign a disclosure saying I would not talk of this incident publicly. On the night of the escort I would be driven to an embassy and told of a special route that I had to follow to gain access to the building. Sometimes I was literally crawling over balconies and through windows to get into the bedroom.

I had one booking at Madam Fleiss, the guy was unshaven and really rude and disgusting, he wanted anal, and I refused to do it, so he called another girl, and she said, "Oh my god it's [name redacted]" ... I had no idea who that even was, I was 19, but he was a complete dick. To this day I can't watch his movies.

I had to sleep with many disabled men. I was working with four other friends at the Gateway Club in Sydney. Management told me that if I didn't take this one client who was physically and mentally disabled, I would be asked to leave the establishment. They threatened to segregate me from my friends if I didn't see him. The client had been waiting a few nights to see me, his carer would wheel him in as he had no legs. I'd try to make out I was too busy to see him but management threatened me. I felt sick in the room having to get on top of a man who was clearly mentally disabled, plus he was really physically disfigured. I guess I felt like I was a perpetrator of sorts because I couldn't really understand if he wanted this interaction, he seemed too mentally disabled to be engaged by the experience. I can't even remember if he came. I have slept with many men with missing limbs, but it's worse when they are mentally disabled, and there are a lot of these sorts of men who are brought in by their carers.

I had a pimp rape me in Melbourne. He pushed me into a room and stuck his penis in me without a condom. I was so angry about it. I drove back from Melbourne and had a car accident that night. But there always seemed to be another reason why I had to return to the sex industry. What I didn't realise, because you can't see it when you're going through the experience, is that it would ultimately be impossible for me to get out of the sex industry. I had become conditioned to money equaling sex; I had become used to earning well over $700 per shift; I had never worked for a normal wage and I was only 20. I could only work for a few weeks or months before I'd get exhausted and have to go back home or back to a boyfriend's place to have time out of the brothels. The only way you can really last in brothels is to do drugs. I experimented with cocaine and uppers many times, and they did give you the energy to get through those shifts.

At 20 I was a regular user of valium to keep my anxiety at bay. I was also unable to sleep a lot of the time. And some brothels required you to work during your period. Doctors and prostitution go hand in hand. Brothels often have their own doctor to send girls to. A girl in the industry can basically get whatever drugs she wants off a doctor, like Duromine for energy and weight loss, and also Xanax and morphine are dead easy. There are many products you can buy for vaginal pain, like numbing cream. Most girls use a combination of numbing creams. The best numbing agent is Xanax and Valium, with alcohol. I've seen many women spaced out on heroin, the ultimate number if you can try and hide the effects from clients. I've never used heroin, but if I'd been forced to stay I would have. Xanax worked the best for me and it's taken me ten years to slowly wean myself off it.

Time between clients was spent perfecting makeup, shaving and sometimes talking to the other girls, who were usually pretty busy. The few times I did try to get a 'normal' job were hard. I started hairdressing, but when the other hairdressers found out what I used to do, I had to quit. I also started my own business selling wigs and hairpieces, but retail would exhaust me quickly, and I found myself swinging between prostitution and retail. I also had bad panic attacks in my own shop and would be forced to leave. I was using pills to sleep and sometimes I'd snort speed for energy. Looking back I think everything I had to do in the industry was causing me health problems.

I opened a small business at 22. I was having a lot of problems dealing with people. I couldn't concentrate, I'd get panicky and I started using pills like Xanax and Valium to deal with anything that stressed me out. I was starting to feel like I just couldn't deal with reality and I was working a little bit in the private market in Canberra, seeing clients. I could charge sometimes $500 per client, and when my website went up I could sometimes charge $800. The only difference was the marketing of myself – I was doing the exact same routine as I did in the brothels. I kept having severe relationship breakdowns, with men stealing my money. These men acted like pimps. I guess I used them as body guards to look after me. Even in motel rooms, I'd have a boyfriend stay and pay him to look out for me. I began to see that you could make a lot more money privately, and you didn't have to stay up all night and you didn't have to compete with anyone. Also the clients for some reason seemed to be of a better ilk. In my experience, the higher your rates, the more respectfully you get treated.

But this was all on the condition that you were young. By 22 I looked old and I felt older. So I had cosmetic surgery – a combination of massive lips, stretched back eyes and cheek and chin implants. You get a pretty constricted look. I looked freakish. Not once did I have a sympathetic surgeon – they all made me feel I needed more work. I had my third nose job at 21, paid for by prostitution. I was always plagued by low self-esteem. I was pretty but only with my armour of makeup. And I was never perfect enough in my own mind. I would get fixated with problems and try to fix them, sometimes spending $20,000 on plastic surgery. But I could hardly talk or smile because of the cheek and chin implants. I'd take Xanax to talk, it hurt that much. So five years later I went to Thailand to get them removed as it was cheaper there. It was uncommon not to have a boob job at exclusive clubs, you cannot work at Sydney's Penthouse on Pitt Street unless you have your boobs done. The addiction to multiple plastic surgeries is really common among prostitutes, and brothels are extremely competitive to work in. You can't make money if you're not extreme in your looks.

I was so bored and depressed by men. I could get by working one week per month. With my website up, I could

earn $10,000 per week and then take a few months off. I did
have regular clients, but it was always an exhausting act for me.
If I had to go on holidays with men, I'd take speed or cocaine
with me to work and put up with them. By my mid 20s I'd
had further facial and breast surgery, which ended up making
me look quite bad, and immediately I noticed a big difference
in the way I was treated. Men were becoming more abrupt
as I aged. I had to get out of the industry. I was no longer
motivated by money. I had also seen enough of male nature
that I was sure I would never want to have kids, I would never
want to get married. To this day I have only boyfriends, I am
not interested in marriage after spending so much time with
married men.

There was no support to get out. I've had to do it myself.
I did go to one place when I was 25. It was a terrible place
full of drug addicts who exposed me to more drugs and I was
very vulnerable. I learnt how to use heroin. I was having such
a bad time at this rehab that I started working in motel rooms
then going back to the rehab. I did 12 steps, but no one wanted
me to talk about my life in prostitution. I started smoking
ice. So I was beginning to prostitute for drugs. I had many
bad relationships where I was physically abused. Ice became
the love of my life. I moved to Kings Cross, booked a room,
smoked ice and saw clients. I started overdosing on drugs,
I was an absolute mess. I knew if I couldn't get out of the Cross
I'd be dead within a few months. I was 27 and completely out
of options. I also had a tonne of psychiatric medication that
I carried around with me. I'd get high on drugs during the day,
and use the meds to sleep. I started getting very edgy and I
would steal from my clients. Sometimes I'd turn up, wait until
they gave me the cash, then leave. I was only interested in ice.

In desperation, I tried a few more rehabs. I had a few
positive experiences, but they involved being with a whole lot
of men, often men from prison. I swung between rehab and
working. 12 steppers and rehabs are happy to hear about crime

and drugs, but not so much about prostitution and surgery and more strange addictions. I was beginning to have money problems, so found myself in women's refuges, and some of these were quite good. They gave me the chance to take a break from bad relationships and work, and drugs. I was 28 and occasionally I would go to Brisbane and do an escort job, as I tried to work out how to get out of this mess.

There was no other option for me. I had tried many different jobs at 28, but none lasted. So I stayed on social security in refuges for as long as I could. I was in a bad state physically, just skinny and always felt unwell. I started to walk, seeing exercise as a way to help myself. At 29 I was a regular at the gym, doing body step and learning how to dance. I had ruined my cognition through stress and addiction, so I was always looking for ways to reverse the damage. I was told I was positive for Hepatitis C at 29. I was sort of relieved because I knew I could never go back to prostitution. I got treatment in Brisbane. One great help in getting me out of the industry for good was Centrelink and the pension. I got the DSP (Disability Support Pension) at 30 for depression and Hep C, and I could finally get my own place without worrying about money for a while. I went home to mum for a holiday when I was 32 and started riding horses again on a dairy farm. I've always loved horses and was very good at riding as a kid. I started having hope. I progressed from the dairy farm to breaking in racehorses. Eventually I ended up at Randwick doing track work for the top trainers. I have found horses to be my only hope. By 30 I was beginning to detox off all the psychiatric drugs, and the horses got me sober, as you are not allowed to use any drug while galloping horses.

Looking back now, it was the horses that saved me.

Linda lives in Sydney, Australia, and travels to various towns doing track work. Her loves in life are horses and dogs, and she hopes one day to run a rescue home for them.

The Fake You

Jade

I never met my dad. Mum had me when she was only 17, she was young and not supported enough by her family in New Zealand to bring up a child, and so I grew up with a lot of negative self-belief. Mum left me with my nanna when I was ten, and I didn't live with mum again until I was 14. By that stage I had started drinking heavily.

When I moved back with Mum we all moved into a house where the previous tenant had had his head blown off in the toilet for a botched drug deal. Police found his body in a park across the road stuffed in a drainpipe. This normalised crime to me. Kids at school heard there was a quarter of a million dollars of drug money somewhere in my house, so my entire high school years were spent looking for the rumoured money. I never found it, but in the process I found out what drugs were. My school friend's parents were drug dealers and her dad had recently tried to leave a gang, who in turn slit his throat. We had easy access to prescription morphine pills and so at 14 I was popping pills at school. At 15, we moved away to another city.

I started a new school there, but I soon got suspended because I had no understanding of how to behave properly. My next school was an adult learning facility, and it was there I gained access to pot and started drug dealing. At 16, I discovered one of my friends had Attention Deficit Disorder (ADD), and so I would swap a $20 stick of pot for their medication and sell it to a neo-Nazi gang for $120. I tried to get straight and get youth service counselling but I ended up just convincing them

I had ADD too so I could get meds. They soon found out and I stopped going to counselling.

I tried to be 'normal' and get a job, but it didn't last long because I was heavily addicted to prescription speed. I was 17 when I first started working as a prostitute. I had recently been fired from a job as a waitress for being drunk and stoned. My 'friend' told me she knew a way to make money fast and easy. At this stage of my life I had been a drug addict for four years. Everyone seemed to have given up on me, I had no mentors or people in my life I trusted to help me with decisions so I went with her.

We hitchhiked to Auckland, and about half-way there we scored a job with a team on the V8 car-racing circuit where men were happy to molest us with oversized sex toys for a couple of hundred bucks and a few beers. It was my first experience of selling sex. Arriving in Auckland, my friend gave me her identity card (because I was underage) and dropped me off at a brothel while she went to another. The madam was an overweight middle-aged woman who talked with me at the bar as I sucked on a lollipop. She barely glanced at my ID. She seemed pleased with the fact I looked about 14 and put the word out that I was young.

My first client in the brothel was into paedophile fantasies. He was in his 50s and wanted me to recount things from my childhood so he could get off, such as my first sexual encounter. The younger I pretended to be when I lost my virginity the more he enjoyed himself. From then on I had night after night of paedophile types – clients who would ask me to role play as a child or would say really perverse things to me about children. Men would often ring around the brothels asking for new young girls, so when one was in, it was like a feeding frenzy. The madam had convinced me to keep my money safe by putting it away with her and the club (I was living in the brothel for convenience). She said I could access it whenever

I wanted. When I did request it she gave it to me in bags of crystal meth. I had never tried meth before, but she said it was easy, "just like smoking pot".

Another working girl noticed I had meth and somehow we became friends. We started hanging out and she introduced me to a bikie gang who manufactured meth. I was given a lot of drugs. I was used as their sex slave. I couldn't leave, as I was scared that I knew too much. I had heard too many stories of women going missing for talking to the wrong people and things like that. They rented an apartment, I assumed so they could cook meth, and I was moved in there in between cooks. One night they told me I had to be out but I fell asleep. This made them angry as I think I stuffed up an operation. So one day when no one was around I took off. This was risky because I knew a lot and they were smoking thousands of dollars worth of meth a day (their drug empire was the biggest in New Zealand at that time) and were highly paranoid. But I had to leave. I had gone from 80kgs to 40kgs in three months due to not eating and because of the volume of drugs the gang was pumping into me.

I flew home and managed to dry out for a couple of weeks while I had my eighteenth birthday. Because I was now legal and had such an overwhelming hunger for meth, the only option I believed I had was to continue working as a prostitute. Conveniently my first friend was back in our home city again and offered to take me to a new place. Since I was legal we could work together. And so off I went, again.

There's no 'how to' when learning to be a prostitute. I was at the mercy of the clients who would take advantage of my lack of personal boundaries. I would be left with bruises all over my body from the rough sex, men always wanted to imitate hard core porn, acting out the sexual violence they were feeding on. The drunker they were, the angrier they would get until they were in hateful rages. Those were the times my vagina would bleed from the trauma. I had no one to tell or to help me as we (the girls) were all experiencing the same thing. We fixed it by numbing out with drugs and alcohol.

Over ten years I estimate I have been raped at least 30 times and suffered about 2500 severely violent attacks. I never got any medical treatment. One time I went across the road to use a cash machine for a client. On the way back I slipped and broke my tail bone. Unaware of the seriousness of the damage, I told the madam that I had really hurt my bum. She scowled at me and told me to get back on the floor as we were busy. I did a 14 hour shift in seven-and-a-half-inch stiletto heels. I had sex with ten drunk men, most of whom I had to wrestle to stop them kissing me or holding me down and causing bruising. One client I punched in the face so hard he fell off the bed; he had ripped off the condom and had held me down to force himself inside me. The pain from the fall had made me aggressive. He complained to the madam about my behaviour. I found out about the severity of my injury only when I woke up the next day unable to walk. I went to the doctor and they prescribed two weeks of bed rest and a heap of pain relief. But less than a week later I was back at work in the stilettos. My drug abuse was such that it numbed all pain, even that of a broken tail bone. Two years later I finally got an x-ray. The continual trauma had caused slippage of five discs in my back, and led to scoliosis of the spine. My tail bone had fused to my hip bone. The physical intensity of working as a prostitute was like experiencing a car crash every single weekend.

Mentally, your identity is messed with, you get another name, you become another person in prostitution. You shift from real you to fake you. I was disassociated from reality, I had Post Traumatic Stress Disorder [PTSD], I walked around as if in a dream.

I started to move from brothel to brothel, town to town, as seems to happen with the more regular prostitute girls. One time while working and living in a brothel I remember there were Asian girls there. They were kept separate from us and we tended to stay away from them even though sometimes we shared a dressing room and smoking area. An Asian guy would always sit in front of the doors to their sleeping quarters. I realise now that these girls were being kept against their will. This revelation is hard to think about now when I remember one of the girls crying in the changing room and begging for it to stop. I shrugged it off at the time thinking we all had those moments. This was in a successful brothel in New Zealand.

I travelled to Australia frequently because in my meth psychosis I would get very anxious and want to go somewhere new. The meth psychosis led to the TV telling me to leave and go to certain cities. I also found being fresh in a new brothel out of town got me lots of work straight away, especially if I told the madams I hadn't worked before. Often the brothel would pay for my ticket over. It was easy to find a club and start working. No one seemed to notice my deteriorating mental health which eventually led to full blown drug-induced schizophrenia.

After five years I wanted out of the sex industry. Twice I tried to go to school – once when I was eighteen and again when I was nineteen. I wanted to be a youth worker. But I couldn't study due to drugs and sex work. None of the sex worker advocacy agencies ever offered a contingency to get me out of the sex industry. They supplied lawyers, health checks, lube, condoms and dams but nothing to help me get out.

I remained in the sex industry for another five years. During this time I even became a madam myself. This came naturally as I had been in the game long enough to know well the tricks of the trade on both sides of the desk. I managed to convince young women to start careers as prostitutes. This is hard for me to reflect on now as I wonder where they are. I remember a well-known paedophile coming into the brothel. I was under strict instructions from the owner to make sure he was taken care of. He sat at the desk asking me perverse questions about the girls. After a while he asked for me to pick one of the girls for him. I chose the girl without any children herself, because

I felt that would minimise the damage as it would affect only her, whereas the other girl had a two-year-old daughter. A job like this would likely affect both of them. In the moment we all just take it as a hazard of the job but this act has haunted me since. I wish I had told him to get lost and told my boss to stick it, but instead I sold a young woman to a predator. I hate myself for that.

It didn't take long before I was working again, the lure of money for drugs was too much.

It is important to understand the links between the psychological trauma which results from prostitution, followed by the introduction of drugs either by a client, staff or other prostituted women and how this combination is the noose that tightens and traps girls like me in 'legal' sex work. The constant bombardment of trauma and the drugs to escape it creates an inability to function outside of addiction, hence the need for quick cash through sex work, reinforcing a cycle that is not easy to break. So women get literally trapped in the industry.

But I still desperately wanted out.

One night a client had the audacity to open the Bible to me, as we stood naked after he had taken his fill of me. While his hypocrisy is easy to see, this experience led me to becoming a Christian, which has changed my life. I have been rebuilt as a human being. It took 18 months of intense residential treatment to overcome the trauma of sex work, then a further two and a half years of living in supported accommodation before the fear and anxiety of participating in everyday life was overcome. I still have regular counselling; the psychological effect of sex work has had an incredibly debilitating effect on my life. It is hard to maintain relationships after you have been treated night after night with contempt. It is hard to value yourself when you've been sold for as little as a packet of cigarettes.

I don't know why or how prostitution can be legal, and I believe there needs to be more support for women in the industry to leave and get specialised counselling. I spent a decade in the sex industry and count myself as one of the rare and blessed survivors to be able to get out. Too many do not.

Jade is working towards a career in health promotion in New Zealand.

Prostitution Sounded Like a Life of Adventure

Annabelle

I was sexually abused as a child and a teenager growing up in Melbourne, Australia. My mum had a mental illness so there was a lot of instability at home which made life difficult. When I was rejected at age 15 by the young man I lost my virginity to, I started to care less about myself. After falling asleep from drinking too much at a party, I woke up with a man raping me and a group of men watching. At 20, I was raped at knifepoint by a stranger while visiting a friend in Adelaide. My childhood sexual abuse and the rapes I experienced set me up for the sex industry. Once you have been violated in this way there is a sense you can never get back what was taken. It's like an invisible force pulling you in.

I worked as an accountant after doing a traineeship when I was 18 and was quite successful in my job considering my emotional instability, my sexual behaviour and the drugs and alcohol I used to manage my feelings. At 27 I was hit by a car while riding my bike to work and broke my neck. I was off work for six weeks and became addicted to opiate painkillers and sleeping pills. When I returned to work things became very difficult due to my slipping performance and a lack of support in my workplace. I had started a relationship with a man who led me on for six months and then suddenly rejected me. This continued a pattern of rejection in my life. I remember one day having the thought, 'I would be better off if I was getting paid for sex'.

I had a friend who had started working in the sex industry two years earlier. When she told me about it, I hadn't considered it for myself. But I did ask her many questions. Eventually I called her to ask if I could start at the brothel where she worked. She gave me some literature from the Scarlet Alliance, which I understood to be some kind of advocacy group that was there to support sex workers, offer support and connect you with services so that you could live an empowered life and have a successful career as a prostitute. The literature was laid out 'comic book' style. It made life as a prostitute seem like an exciting adventure. There were cartoon-like pictures of sexy women in stockings and even the name Scarlet Alliance made me feel excited about the industry. The word 'Scarlet' made me think of being 'sexy and desirable' and a bit 'risky and exciting'. The word 'alliance' made me feel like I would become part of something, and I would experience some kind of sisterhood and moral support.

I started to wonder what the women would be like to work with and what the men would be like. I wondered how much like the movies it would be. My attitude changed from just wanting to go into the industry because I felt used, to an anticipation of this amazing new life I was going to have. Reading the Scarlet Alliance literature helped me finally decide to become a prostitute. I liked the way they called prostitutes 'sex workers' because it sounded like it really was a profession: the 'oldest profession' was how they put it, and that was exciting too. I would be embarking on this journey into a life that people looked down upon only because of stigma and lack of understanding.

When I said I was ready, my friend took me to her work. It was a small, legal brothel in Collingwood, an inner-city suburb of Melbourne. It was glamorous, just like the comic suggested. It had chequered black and white floors, tall hallway mirrors, and women lounging around in robes in the staff area. At first I was too afraid – I turned down the first client who tried to book me. But once I got the courage I said yes to the second. When I saw the money in my hand I felt a power that had been missing all my life.

I was distorted in my thinking about what I was doing. I thought I was doing something good for myself – paying myself back financially for all that had been physically and sexually stolen from me – and something good for society – helping lonely men with their problems and saving their marriages so they could continue to love their wives when those women no longer desired sex.

One day a client told me I could make more money in a 'six-star' brothel. So I moved to South Melbourne where there are two very busy 'upmarket' brothels. Now I was making more money in a day than I could in a week as an accountant. I thought I was living the dream: getting paid to have sex, lounge around, sleep and smoke cigarettes. I could buy anything I wanted. But the deception was eventually shattered.

A client came in one morning. He was an African-American man, twice my size. I got a real sense of hatred from this man; I felt afraid of him but didn't know why. He asked me for anal sex and for sex with no condom. I told him that I wouldn't perform anal sex with him and that sex without a condom was illegal. He got angry, started criticising me and pushing me around. He accused me of thinking I was better than him. He told me to turn around and get on all fours. He didn't try to have anal sex with me but was very aggressive and forceful in the way he penetrated me as if trying to punish me for saying no to anal. I told him he was hurting me but he ignored that and finished what he was doing. It seemed as though he was expecting me to tell him how much I had enjoyed myself, but I couldn't.

When he left I felt like I had been raped. I told the receptionist what had happened and asked to go home. She looked at me strangely and said, "Isn't that your job? Can't you just stay for one more client? I've got one waiting for you." I saw that the next client was a young white Australian guy about my age and I thought he'd be nice to me so I agreed. But he became angry with me because I didn't offer kissing. He kept licking my face even though I asked him not to. At the end I realised he had given me $80 less than he was meant to. I was scared but told him if he didn't pay the full amount I could report him to reception and they would catch him on the way out. He threw the money at me, called me a slut, and left. Traumatised, I sat there with thoughts running through my mind: "I haven't been paying myself back, I have just been getting paid to let men rape me." I felt ashamed of myself, went home and didn't work again for a month. I was emotionally shattered, but I was addicted to working, and financial pressures eventually led me back.

I was taking a lot of codeine and morphine pills during work hours to try to numb myself. I took cocaine with clients because it helped me lose my inhibitions and work longer hours. I didn't like using cocaine because we had to clean the room afterwards and it was hard to do cleaning tasks if I was too high. But I was addicted to prescription opiates, and also sleeping pills and Valium. Normally when I arrived home from a shift I would feel as high as a kite (even if I hadn't had drugs) because of adrenalin and anxiety. I would take pills to get to sleep and eventually couldn't get by without them.

I was in the industry only 18 months, but it damaged me severely – emotionally, physically and spiritually. One of the biggest impacts was the isolation and loneliness. I eventually realised that almost everything I told people about my life was a lie. This is a very traumatic experience.

Another very difficult part of the job is that all the women hate themselves and each other, and are constantly picking on their physical flaws, having unnecessary surgeries and trying to alter their often already beautiful appearances. Some are so young it is heartbreaking. Some have young children at home and yet take cocaine with clients, developing expensive habits. They would date clients and get themselves into all kinds of situations. Addicted to the initial glamour of having all this money to buy expensive clothes and makeup, many women work for ten years and become unemployable, so feel trapped. I was grateful knowing that I was finishing my accounting degree and saving my money instead of spending it, but many weren't preparing for their future at all.

There was one young woman, about 20, who had a lot of clients. I suspect she was about 14 when she started. Her dad would drive her to work and pick her up and this made me feel very sad for her. I tried to support her and get to know her a bit because I felt very concerned. She opened up to me a little and told me that her parents had a business breeding racehorses and her dad had made a business error that had cost the family a lot of money. Her parents told her they would lose their house – and by working as a prostitute she could get them out of debt and save her mum, dad and little sister from being homeless. I think after she shared this with me she felt vulnerable. Perhaps she felt it was a mistake and so she refused to speak to me again. It tormented me knowing this young girl was being pimped out by her own family, and I suspected that her parents had lied to her to manipulate her into doing the work and they were simply living off the proceeds. I often wondered how she would ever get out of the industry because she had no opportunity to get a real job or career, and she was brainwashed by her parents, damaged by the industry and investing her spare time learning pole-dancing and stripping instead of getting an education. At the other end of the spectrum were women who had been in the industry since they were her age, and were tired, bitter, worn out and looked a lot older than their ages. As new and young women came in and got all the clients and all the attention, the older women became jealous, hateful and devoid of joy.

Other problems I encountered were with the brothel owners and the reception staff. The owners of upmarket brothels are businessmen who have families and sell women for their livelihood. They didn't like me telling them to keep their hands off me unless they were willing to pay like all the other clients. They believed that because I was a whore I would let them have a free grab or utter a sleazy remark. I felt the need to keep whatever dignity I had left, so was very strict about this. The receptionists were very manipulative. They would always call us 'babe' and give us heaps of compliments about our looks to try to inflate our egos. But if you didn't do what they wanted their true attitudes would be revealed. Their job is to sell your body to men. They put a lot of pressure on you to stay after your sixth or eighth job has ended, saying "Oh I just booked one more client for you", and even asking you to stay double shifts. The longest I worked was 14 hours. I remember sleeping in the brothel change room and being told off for putting a towel on the floor.

Lounge areas for clients were enormous, luxurious and decked out with pool tables and comfy couches, with a bar and juke box like a nightclub. But the lounge rooms for the girls out the back were tiny, just three metres by three metres. Often you will have as many as ten women squashed into them, and sitting on the floor. One brothel didn't even have a lounge, just a 'locker room' with a couple of showers and a toilet. One brothel had interstate or international women (mostly Asian) sleeping upstairs for $60 per night. Some never left the building. It was well understood they were trafficked.

Having to lie about everything every day has a profound effect. You get very good at it out of necessity, to the point where you almost start to believe the lies you make up. You lie to your clients, other workers and outside of work you lie to your family, friends and everyone you meet who asks, "So what do you do for a job?" You lie to yourself and that is soul-destroying.

As for the Scarlet Alliance and other similar 'support groups and services' – they tell you about all the ways they can support you but really it's a very isolating job. I discovered that no services can replace your stolen dignity.

I believe it was a miracle that I got out, because the life is so addictive. I am so grateful that I eventually saw the absolute insanity of the venue, the other working girls and clients. I put myself into rehab where I dealt with my drug addiction and emotional issues – and discovered I was pregnant. I was in shock and confused as I had always been very safe and careful. I had heard about some women maliciously putting pin-holes in condoms to try to get other women pregnant so they would leave the brothel, and so there would be less competition. All the other girls hated me because I was one of the busy girls and was making a lot of money. I kept to myself a lot because they didn't like me. So I wonder if they did that to me. I had an abortion without batting an eyelid. I was so damaged and broken. The abortion seemed like a solution at the time, but I suffer from the guilt and grief of the loss of the pregnancy. Even though I didn't know who the father was, I still regretted having the abortion and needed counselling afterwards.

To say that a woman enters the sex industry by 'choice' is a lie. To make a choice you need to have the facts about what you are choosing. I believe all prostituted women are held captive, not just physically as in the case of trafficked women, but by the lies of the sex industry. The industry knows once you're lured in it's hard to get out. I don't believe any woman would choose to emotionally, physically and spiritually cause herself the amount of trauma that the industry left me with.

Thankfully I got out. I have been freed from my past. But, in my mid-30s, I can see scars in my life that I would like to believe can be healed, but that I accept may be permanent. I have seen a psychologist, and completed a program for post-traumatic stress disorder. Working in the sex industry is hell on earth, and to be free from it is like a breath of fresh air. I am grateful to be free and grateful for my life. I've just given birth to a son, who represents all that is new and good in my life.

Annabelle, 34, lives in Melbourne, Australia, with her husband and son. She runs a small business from home and in her spare time writes about her former life in the hope that other prostituted women will come to find the freedom she now has.

Groomed into Prostitution

Kat

In 2014 in Bristol in the UK, 13 men were convicted of the sexual abuse of girls, including prostituting and grooming them. In 2012, nine men were convicted of similar crimes in Rochedale. The courage of the abused girls in speaking out has been groundbreaking. They have disrupted what has been normalised for decades by naming the abuse that thousands of girls face every day and pointing out that authorities have rarely been able to act or haven't thought it was a problem. There are now far-reaching enquiries into similar perpetration against girls on a mass scale in Oxfordshire. The grooming of girls for sexual exploitation has been normalised throughout all of British society and it is men from all racial and cultural backgrounds who are using their power in order to sexually abuse teenage girls.

We have also seen celebrities, like Rolf Harris and a string of others, be held accountable for the abuse of girls. Society is now acknowledging systemic sexual abuse against us by older men from all walks of life. I feel a sense of optimism that some of the cultural norms that have landed girls in prostitution and sexually abusive situations are beginning to shift. We must keep working to end the systematic abuse of girls and women of which prostitution is a major part.

I was around 13 when I began hanging out with a group of girls, some my age and others a couple of years older. Most were vulnerable in one way or another; either in care, drug addicted or with very low self-esteem. Because of our age and social vulnerability, a group of much older men preyed on our susceptibility by supplying us with drugs and booze. In exchange it was understood that we would be sexually available to them. The times they had penetrative sex with me were awful and agonising. Some of the men were brutal. They even made public jokes about the pain and suffering they caused me. In retrospect it was a form of sexual exploitation, both rape and prostitution, but at the time I would never have thought of it as that. I thought I was cool, cruising around with men twice my age.

At the time I didn't understand the damage the men were doing to me, to my sexuality, my trust, my self-esteem and ultimately my soul. I wasn't a bad kid, but I became a bad teenager and a worse young adult. These men destroyed any chance I had at developing into a normal human being. I can't blame the men entirely, there were other things going on for me in my family household, but I know if I hadn't been repeatedly sexually violated I'd have stood a chance of developing in a significantly healthier way. By the time I'd met my first john I had been groomed into prostitution through culturally normalised child sexual abuse.

I will never forget the first time I was bought with money at age 14. The man really made a fool of me. As if my self-esteem was not low enough, his actions took it to a whole new level. I followed him down a street in my home Yorkshire town not really knowing what would be expected of me. My friend yelled after me, "Make sure he pays you well!" He didn't waste much time, opening his fly and looking at me commandingly. I followed his silent orders. I was never a fan of penises and his made me gag and choke. You'd think this might have put him off, but he seemed to get excited by my suffering on my knees, unable to breathe and on the verge of vomiting. It wasn't as quick as I'd hoped, it probably went on for about ten minutes. It felt like forever.

I asked him for money, not specifying an amount as I had no clue how to negotiate that sort of thing. He scrounged around in his pocket and pulled out two fifty pence pieces. I said, "Oh come on!" and he went back in his pocket and pulled out another fifty pence. He said that was all he had. When I got back to my friend, she queried how much I had been given. When I told her, she burst out laughing and shared the information with the other girls, who joined in the taunting and giggling. "Not even enough for a blast-away lolly!" one girl mocked. The next day at school I had at least three kids who had not been there come up to me laughing and saying, "One pound fifty." I felt awful. Sick and humiliated on so many levels.

It wasn't long after the 'one pound fifty' incident that I got expelled. The school knew that I had a problem with drugs, alcohol and truancy. I am also sure they knew I was being sexually abused by older men – they'd see me out with these men. Truancy officers would pick me up in places where it was obvious older men shouldn't be with a teenage girl. The way the school decided to deal with it was to expel me. I wasn't offered any kind of counselling or support.

After several further expulsions from state schools, my poor parents were faced with the difficult decision of either putting me into a special education school or paying for a private education. At age 15, after a period of being out of school altogether, they opted to pay for a private education for the last year of my school life, which I'm now grateful for. We weren't badly off, my father worked in local government and my mother in administration. But I know they had better things they could have spent their money on. If they hadn't chosen to support me I would never have finished school. They also decided to give me the opportunity to board at the school. I was expelled from the first boarding school after only three weeks for possession of a large quantity of amphetamine and a supply of bourbon, which I'd stolen from the supermarket. By then I was psychologically dependant on drugs and alcohol.

Remarkably, I was accepted into a second school. I knew this was my last chance to finish school and I made a decision to turn my life around. I stopped taking drugs and started to study. It was the first time that I felt safe. I loved the school, I loved that there were no older men preying on me, no prostitution, no bullying. I started to explore my sexuality, I even dated a nice boy of my own age for a while, but ultimately I realised that I actually wanted a girlfriend, not a boyfriend. I realised I didn't want men like my previous 'boyfriend', a 27-year-old loser who repeatedly committed statutory rape against teenage girls. My first lesbian relationship while at the school was with a gorgeous 19-year-old woman who lived down the road. Worlds apart from the men and the abuse. It was the first time I had enjoyed sex and intimacy on any and every level. I loved her but I couldn't keep her. The heavy consequence of being prostituted and sexually abused meant that I couldn't trust people and I couldn't exercise a healthy form of intimacy.

She left me on my sixteenth birthday. Devastated, I went straight back on the drugs and manipulated a local GP to supply me with 80 mg per day of Temazepam, which I was allowed to self-administer (and hand out to other students). I went home at weekends, back to my old life and on occasions I was bought for sex. I needed the money to fund my substance dependencies, to cope with the realisation that I had become unlovable, or at least that's how I felt. I lived in two worlds, one beautiful life with healthy friends my age, laughing, joking and getting into low-level trouble; the other filled with drugs, rape, nightclubs and prostitution. I knew I was financially fine at home and at school; I never starved and never needed anything, but drugs and alcohol cost money.

On my last day of school a friend and I jumped on a train to London. We felt like we wouldn't belong anywhere in the world after leaving school. We stayed in a cheap hostel in

Paddington. My friend returned after a week but I decided to stay. I was 16 and a half, which was old enough to leave home. One night I went home with an older woman. I told her I was desperate for a place to stay and she offered to introduce me to her friend who she thought might let me stay with him for a couple of weeks. I was delighted as I thought it meant I'd have a girlfriend and a place to stay until I could get a job or some money. We met up with her friend at an East End pub the next day. He was friendly but very creepy. I tried to think positively about him because he did offer me a place to stay.

When I got to his house it became apparent that he and I would be sharing a room. He constantly harassed me for sex. I'd wake up with him touching me, sometimes trying to penetrate me while I slept. I thought that I'd been selfish and naive to expect a place to stay for free. He gave me somewhere to stay. He paid for me to go to nightclubs and sometimes gave me cash. He was in his 40s, I was 16. My body wasn't fully developed and I didn't desire him sexually. He often took naked and sexualised photos of me. I've never known what he did with them.

The sexual development of a human being is so important; the destruction and abuse of a young person's sexuality is toxic to their development and detrimental to their ability to form healthy adult relationships. For a young woman being able to trust another human being sexually is crucial. We are so sexually vulnerable as girls, we can be harmed in a really sensitive part of our body. We can be impregnated, treated like an object (or worse) and easily injured physically. When men choose to prostitute us, they cause extensive and irreparable harm.

Men are conditioned to sexually enjoy this vulnerability, and to make the most out of any opportunities they have to pleasure themselves at our expense. This is what pornography teaches many men to get off on. This man was an addicted porn user and only had sexual interest in girls or young women. The woman who had introduced us had also been prostituted by him, or that's what he told me. I asked her about it one night and she turned on me, accusing me of cheating on her with him and being his 'whore'. I think she was trying to avoid facing up to what he had done to her when she was younger. He also confessed to me he'd been a pimp to young women and asked me if I wanted to go to Soho to make bigger money out of prostitution and pornography. He said he had connections and offered to protect me. I declined that offer, but I did agree to be prostituted by some of his friends, for which he 'managed' the money.

After some weeks of dealing with him, I went to the dole office in Stratford in East London, but they couldn't give me access to either the job seeker's allowance or housing benefits without confirmation from a parent that I was estranged. My parents gave this statement, but it was months later. They were going through a break-up and it was unclear where any of us would be living. I think their assumption was that I would return to Beverley. I did go back there to start college, very briefly, before moving out with a new partner at age 17. But I still regularly visited the john in the East End. He would pay for my train ticket and give me money, and sometimes pay for friends I'd take with me.

On one occasion, I witnessed him prostitute another young woman. He paid her for sex and then penetrated her when I was in the room, she was clearly distressed and in pain. Witnessing this and relating it so strongly to my own experiences caused me immense trauma.

This incident was different from the 'regular' trauma I had endured as a result of other incidents of sexual abuse and prostitution. For over a year I had flashbacks and bad dreams. I couldn't sleep and felt like I was going to die. Still I went back a few more times. He would pay me for a night or sometimes the weekend. This didn't stop until I was almost 20. I had started university and the first library book I borrowed was Andrea Dworkin's *Letters from a War Zone*. That put things clearly in perspective and I didn't go back to him after connecting deeply with Dworkin's writings. She was a sister and a survivor and her words validated my own trauma so articulately. I still live with the trauma, it manifests mostly as an intense psychosomatic anxiety.

When we talk about prostitution, it is mainly girls and women who are put in the spotlight, and expected to justify why we ended up in prostitution. Men are not asked to explain why they do harm to girls and why they use the bodies of girls and women in prostitution. When I was at school I was often asked by other kids, who were better adjusted than me, why I was such a mess, why my behaviour was so extreme and why I was allowing myself to be sexually used by men. Some other young girls in my situation had good reasons, or what were considered legitimate 'excuses'. I didn't have an excuse. My parents weren't poor or alcoholics or sexually abusive. They were unhappy and I was lonely. I had also been sexually violated on a day-to-day basis by a boy at my school from when I was four years old. But none of that ever felt like a good enough excuse to justify the level of trouble and the harmful situations I put myself in.

Now I know I do not need any justification for the way men treated me. They preyed on me, they sexually harmed me, it was not my responsibility and I do not need to explain why I was prostituted and sexually abused by men. They need to explain why they prostituted and sexually hurt a girl. It is never the fault of the girl and it is never the circumstances a girl is in that led to her being prostituted. It is the choices that men make because they have the power to make those choices because of cultural norms, lack of education and harmful legal frameworks. This is the real reason girls and women are prostituted.

A survivor movement has emerged around the world, with women speaking out against prostitution and talking about the harms. These voices are backed up by research undertaken by Melissa Farley and others, which show that the average age of a female when she is first prostituted is 14. The majority end up with PTSD and most do not want to be prostituted. There is a stack of evidence that the sex trade is incredibly harmful. The sex industry does not accept this evidence and instead the advocates of the industry go out of their way to silence women and girls who speak out. Men also try to silence women, particularly family members, boyfriends and the perpetrators themselves.

I came out as a prostitution survivor very publicly and had my father publicly deny it. He thought it would be career limiting, show him up as a bad father, as well as bringing shame and embarrassment to the family. I know other women who have had their partners try to deny their experiences, afraid that it would bring shame to their reputations. Again, this is the attitude towards women who have been prostituted, that it happens only to girls and women who have justifiable circumstances, that no 'good' girl would ever do those things and that it is the girls and women, and by extension their families and friends, who need to be shamed. This is the one thing, and probably the only thing, that I vaguely agree with the neo-sex trade lobby about. We should not ever judge or shame women in the sex trade, whatever their analysis of the industry and its impact.

All girls deserve a childhood safe from sexual predators who would exploit their vulnerability and use their developing bodies for sexual gratification, causing untold harm. I deserved a childhood that was free from sexual exploitation. While prostitution exists as a concept and institution which justifies men's right to buy access to female bodies, making women and girls into commodities that can be bought and traded, girls will not be safe. They will be objects with a market value. The younger the girl the easier to exploit.

I hope for a world where women and girls have this basic requirement for freedom.

Kat is active in campaigning for legislative change toward the Nordic model and the rights of people who are prostituted to report their buyers. She is a member of Amnesty International and lobbies internally for change to their prostitution policy platform.

Didn't Come to Hear Bitches Recite Poetry

Rhiannon

Canberra in the Australian Capital Territory, where I grew up, has Australia's most liberal laws on prostitution. It's also the place where parliament sits; these two facts are not coincidental. The industrial suburb of Fyshwick is essentially Canberra's 'red light' zone; this is where virtually the city's whole sex industry is licensed to practice. The brothels and strip bars there report their biggest annual spike in business during parliamentary sittings when politicians, lobbyists and the like fly into the capital.

One thing I can say about growing up in Canberra is that the city's lack of legal restriction on the sex industry and its reputation as 'the sex capital' seemed to make it more socially acceptable for men to buy sex than in other states. Boys in Canberra tended to see visiting brothels and strip bars as a right of passage upon turning 18; they said since it was legal they were doing nothing wrong. Most boys I went to high school with discussed their exploits openly and for that reason it was widely known how many underage girls worked in the sex industry. Due to Canberra's small population, almost every boy I knew who had visited Fyshwick had seen at least one underage girl they recognised. I used to find this disturbing in itself; more disturbing was some did so with a smirk.

Canberra is known for its highly regulated sex industry;

the strict regulations that are seen to accompany a legalised industry are supposedly intended, and widely believed, to make conditions safer; but the large number of underage girls who work in brothels and strip bars don't bear that out. Women are legally required to show identification to prove they are 18, but unless a brothel is raided, which rarely happens, this is not enforced. Punters are unlikely to report the employment of underage girls, trafficked women, or other illegal activities they see to police; it's the punters who create the demand for those things in the first place. Buyers tend to seek the youngest women possible and will pay more the younger she is. Occasional spot checks hardly ensure compliance with regulations.

The legality of the sex industry made it a more visible and viable option for young women who needed work – almost everyone knew a story of a girl from their class at high school who went to work at what was callously referred to as the 'Fyshwick fish market'; the difference was, unlike the young men I knew who visited Fyshwick, the women who went to work there were invariably the 'troubled' girls, the ones labelled 'sluts' at school, the ones with known histories of childhood sexual abuse or teenage rape, and the ones from dysfunctional families. The ones like me.

While many women are forced into the sex industry through lack of other financial survival options, this is not always the case. Women from all backgrounds can end up in the sex industry, but the common thread is always some kind of vulnerability that can be exploited. In my case, it was emotional vulnerability, naiveté and mental illness that made me vulnerable to sexual exploitation. Mental illness was made worse by early sexualisation; I was not sexually abused as a young child, and my family dysfunction was not as severe as many. Still, I was emotionally neglected as a young girl, and being especially sensitive exacerbated the effects of that.

My father was very affectionate and loving, and my bond with him was deep. But he suffered from a depressive illness and a drinking problem. My mother also suffered from mental illness. She was self-absorbed and unable to emotionally connect with others, and was abusive to my father. He left our home when I was two years old. I don't clearly remember him leaving, but I remember feeling abandoned by him. I remember deep pain and feelings of defectiveness, I thought there had been something wrong with me to make my father leave. My older sister seemed to view me solely as competition for parental attention. She taunted, bullied, belittled and disparaged me relentlessly. Her merciless put-downs and torment compounded the erosion of my self-worth.

I had the advantage of coming from an intellectual and academic family. My father was a writer and my sister and I were years above our expected reading level when we began school. After my father left I also had a caring and devoted stepfather but, being the sole carer and income earner for four children and my mentally-ill mother who abused him, he simply could not give me the attention I needed.

My biological father's intermittent and unpredictable presence during my childhood and the instability of my care in the early years resulted in my developing a severe attachment anxiety – I was unable to trust that anyone I loved would return. I desperately sought affection from anyone who would offer it – a perfect recipe for my exploitation. While my older sister drew constant praise and attention for her academic brilliance, I was always told I was the prettier one. My grades were very good but not as good as my sister's – she convinced me I was hopeless and there was no point in trying. Being pretty was the only thing I was praised for by anyone other than my father. By the age of 13 I was so desperate for affection that being told how pretty I was by older men approaching me as I walked to the city from high school felt wonderful.

My first sexual experience happened around this time. My mother's alcoholism aggravated her mental illness, and to avoid her abusive behaviour I loitered around the city or the park. Sometimes I hung around with older teenage boys who gave me joints to smoke. One day I was approached by two men in their 20s. They told me I had a pretty name, and told me how beautiful my eyes were. They made me the centre of attention. They made me feel special and wanted. We went to a park near my school where they gave me blueberry-flavoured vodka cans. After a while I felt dizzy and told the men things looked blurry. They led me to a hotel room. It took ten years before I could call the experience that followed rape. I didn't know rape could occur without physical resistance. I was 13, I was drunk, and I was intimidated. But surely it was consensual, I thought, if no force was used? At one stage I cried out in pain, assuming that the man would take it as a sign to stop; it was ok, he said, because my cries of pain turned him on. I blacked out from the alcohol and woke to my body being fondled. I remember feeling violated and running out of the room – the blood from my broken hymen was running down my thighs. I knew there was an immense power imbalance in that hotel room. The girl who came out was not the same one who went in. After that I never felt able to say no to sex no matter how much it was unwanted: not when I was 13, not when I was 18, not when I was 22.

In the years following my rape I continued to suffer sexual abuse. When I was 14 I met an older man who convinced me he loved me. He would give me ecstasy before he used me and I thought I was in love. I didn't know until years later that he had been filming himself with me and selling the films at a Fyshwick shop. I developed bulimia and began self-cutting and burning my skin. I took overdoses of pills and was filled with self-loathing. I was hospitalised after one overdose and later a psychiatrist prescribed me anti-depressants. They helped me function a bit better after graduating from high school. I had become closer to my father, which seemed to improve my emotional state. I volunteered in South America, and returned able to speak Spanish and in a more positive state of mind.

At 21 I moved to Queensland to begin my university degree in a warmer climate.

However, the fact I had learned to depend on men's sexual attention for self-validation never left. Emotional instability and feelings of loneliness crept back in. I attempted to escape these feelings with frequent binge drinking, which often ended in acquiescence to unwanted sex or sex while almost unconscious. I may as well have been a plastic doll. After they had their way I would lose my appeal and they'd dispose of me. So I kept trying to keep their attention for as long as I could without having sex. When I felt used by one man I'd run to another. I had never experienced an orgasm. Even at 21 I was unaware my body had a sexual response. No man had cared about my stimulation. I knew sex could cause me pain, but I didn't know it could give me pleasure.

My father's early death when I was 22 had a heavy impact on me. My early feelings of abandonment returned and became more extreme. My mental illness worsened. I withdrew from my friends, became erratic and dropped out of my classes. I smoked large amounts of cannabis daily to numb my emotions. I returned to self-mutilation, and was frequently admitted to an emergency psychiatric ward after para-suicidal behaviour. My financial situation worsened; the job market had dried up following the 2008 global stock market crash. I received around $200 a week in student support payments but they barely covered my rent. When I got behind in my payments, I received a warning from the landlord and worried that I would be evicted. My housemates became concerned because I was taking food from the university charity cupboard and couldn't pay my bus fares.

When you are a woman, especially a young and attractive one who is struggling to find work, there is one form of so-called employment that is always and ubiquitously available; the sex industry is aggressive in its pursuit. Men constantly suggested stripping and prostitution when I complained about not being able to find a job. Ads promising fast cash jumped out from newspapers. Strip bars had flashing signs out front: 'dancers wanted for immediate start, $$$'. After almost a year of unemployment and the stress of poverty I accepted a job as a bikini waitress. The job required me to travel to taverns and pubs that had booked me through an agency and, dressed in a g-string bikini and high heels, greet the men who entered the bar. I was required to flirt with them, take their orders and bring them drinks. I rationalised that I would be wearing a bikini if I were at the beach, and that being paid more than I would as a bartender just to wear a bikini and serve drinks was almost a good thing. But I couldn't deny the reality that I was being paid to submit to the status of sexual object. I could never escape the deep sickness I felt when the eyes of those men were on my flesh.

I had read the classic feminist literature of the women's liberation movement as a teenager and considered myself a feminist, if not in my actions then at least in my understanding of the world. Women in the university feminist collective used a language of choice to talk about prostitution and stripping: *my body, my choice.* This seemed an extreme misuse of the phrase I had understood as relating to women's rights of reproductive autonomy.

What I was doing did not feel like bodily autonomy – it felt like I was selling my bodily autonomy. When a person is paid for sex they are being paid precisely *because* of the fact the sex is unwanted. Sexual autonomy cannot exist when a person is sexual for any reason outside their own desire, for their own pleasure. The sacrifice of my bodily autonomy was precisely what I was being paid for. I felt ashamed for acquiescing to sexual objectification, but I also felt it wasn't me who had created this situation. Choice was the last thing I felt I had. I was unable to do the job without being drunk and, unlike any other job I had ever had, I was allowed to have the men buy me drinks and to drink as much as I wanted.

Because there were only one or two jobs available a week – with these being only two-hour shifts, and because the agencies took half the fee, I made next to nothing. I still struggled to pay the rent. After a few weeks the agency began to tell me there were no bikini jobs that week and all that was available was lingerie waitressing at bucks' parties. It didn't seem like a huge line to cross, and I needed the money. Walking almost naked as a woman into a room full of drunk, rowdy men, many twice my age, made me feel vulnerable and shaky. They heckled and groped me and tried to photograph me. Some referred to me as 'slut' rather than use the false name I had given. I was always offered extra cash to remove my bra. At first I refused. One man complained his money had been wasted because he had wanted to 'see some tits'. He pulled down his pants and flashed his genitals at me yelling 'suck it, bitch' as I left. I'd consume several drinks before arriving and continue drinking through the shift – this was the only thing that made it possible to endure. After a couple of weeks the agencies told me there were few bookings for women not willing to perform a strip show using vegetables or dildos and the only other jobs they had were for topless waitressing. The offer of more money for being bra-less, and the thought that I wouldn't be hassled and pestered to take my bra off as it would already be off, was enough to make me agree.

Society grooms women long before they enter the sex industry and the industry continues to groom us. After a few times serving men drinks in nothing but stilettos and a g-string, doing so in nothing but stilettos didn't seem like much of a line to cross. One week, when the only booking available was for a nude waitress at $20 extra an hour, I agreed to it. A week after that I was sent to a venue where men had ordered a naked poker dealer. I undressed and accepted a glass of whisky. I woke a day later in pain at Roma Street Parkland with a man's shirt over me and nothing else. My body hurt inside and my thighs were bruised. I had a black eye and a near blank

memory. I didn't think there was any point going to the police
– the men would simply say I was drunk and had consented.
(I had reported a rape to police once before as a teenager
and was told I had little chance of a conviction.) The agency
kept no details of the men who made bookings with them
anyway, and I couldn't have tracked them down if I'd wanted
to. My phone and wallet were gone and the money for the
topless poker game with it, but the agency had taken their large
cut of my fee with the booking so there was no loss for them.

I called an older woman I'd worked with at a few bucks'
nights; she had offered me oxycodone tablets during a worse-
than-usual shift. Up until then I'd refused, but that day I asked
her to meet me. The pills made me feel better. I bought various
drugs from then on. I hitchhiked to Sydney. I wanted to run
as far away from Roma Street Parkland as I could, and I had
decided I would work as an escort. I felt so violated I just didn't
care any more. All I wanted was money for drugs. It is illegal
to be prostituted as an 'escort' in Queensland – prostitution
can only legally occur in-house at a licensed brothel – but
it was legal in NSW. I bought into the illusion that being a
'high-class escort' would be more palatable and highly paid,
and I imagined there would be some kind of glamour in it.
The agency advertised their call-out rates at $600–$1500 per
hour, depending on the rank they gave you, but they took half.
Plus I would need to spend thousands on designer suits and
shoes, hair and beauty procedures including teeth bleaching,
waxing and eyelash implants. I'd probably need breast
implants, too. This was because they usually only dispatched
out-of-work models. I was too short, so I was advised to first
work in less 'exclusive' brothels to save up money for the
beauty procedures.

So I hitchhiked back to Brisbane and went to work in a strip
bar instead. I had convinced myself I didn't care what I had
to do for money any more, I just didn't care about anything
much at all. I could barely sleep due to nightmares. I figured

working at a strip bar would distract me from them. I had also become infatuated with a heroin-addicted man who later became abusive and violent. I needed money to support him.

The most coveted job in a strip bar is that of bartender; she doesn't have to be naked and in some places can be fully dressed. She has a solid hourly rate of about $20 an hour plus tips. Dancers, on the other hand, can gyrate naked against a pole all night and still make no money; the men pay a fee of around $30 to enter but the club keeps all of it – the women are paid only if a man chooses them for a private dance. The dancers have to compete with each other to convince the customers to choose them. The only thing more degrading than having to gyrate naked on the lap of a balding, fat old man for money is to have to beg him to pay you to do so – while he objects that the fee is too high. There is a common myth that men are not allowed to touch strippers during a private dance; the truth is that the private dance usually entails the man putting his hands all over you, and doing almost anything but penetrate you. The dance normally ends with him ejaculating in his pants. The club takes at least half the private-dance fee.

The man who owned the strip bar also owned several others across Brisbane that he rotated us around. I worked with women who had grown up in foster care, women who had fled childhood sexual abuse, women who had lived on the streets, women living with drug dependency, and young single mothers who had no other way to provide for their kids. All of us had been raped at least once, and some of us habitually self-mutilated (punters never seemed to care about the scars on our wrists). We are told of women who 'love' working in the sex industry, but in my time I never met such a woman.

On what was to be my last night at the strip bar, none of the men had paid me for a private dance. I hadn't made a cent despite stripping to nothing and gyrating around the pole. As usual the men refused to give me any tips because they had paid at the door – they didn't care that I got none of the door fee. I sat with a young man who told me he liked to write poetry which he recited to his friend seated beside him (it was terrible), and he chatted about the Australian bush, which reminded me of my father who had loved the bush and wrote beautiful poetry. I imagined it would break his heart to see me now, but I didn't think it mattered much since he was dead anyway. I drunkenly began to recite the Henry Lawson poems he used to read. The man lost interest and chose another woman for a private dance. He told me he wasn't there to "hear bitches recite poetry." In that moment something broken inside me broke just a little bit more. I became increasingly desperate to 'sell' a private dance but all the men said the fee was too much and maintained they would pay it only if I would go out the back with them for full sex. Most were old enough to be my grandfather, which only added to my disgust and feelings of degradation. By about 4am when the bar was closing I handed the red dress we were required to wear to the boss and told him I would not be coming back.

By this point I was drunker than usual and doped up on codeine and Xanax. I stumbled onto the street and a flood of built-up tears that could no longer be contained began to spill out. The more I cried, the more the tears flooded out. A man approached me on the almost empty street and asked if I was okay. I had lived long enough to know that the man who approaches the damsel in distress does not actually care about her. I asked him flat out what he'd pay to have sex with me. He told me he had $200 and I followed him to his apartment. In the world I lived in, the sum of all I was worth was $200. That fact filled me with more pain than I could contain. In his bathroom I took the rest of the pills left in my bag, found his razor and used it to cut my wrists, then removed my clothes and went and lay down on his bed with blood sticking to the toilet paper I had stuck on the cuts. He only had a hundred dollars, he said. It was all he could find. I insisted on clutching the cash while he used me. This man felt it was worth paying a hundred dollars to have sex with a woman who had a tear-stained face and bleeding wrists. It was over in less than a minute. When he was finished I got up, put my clothes on, and calmly said, "You need to call an ambulance now, because I'm going to kill myself." He responded with a blank, stupefied look and kind of shrugged. I walked out of his apartment down the stairs and went outside as I dialled triple zero myself. I could see the Story Bridge across the street and decided that if the ambulance didn't come in ten minutes, I was going to jump off it.

The ambulance did come. I was held at a psychiatric ward overnight; a place I have been admitted to more times than I can count. A psychiatrist told me I had Post Traumatic Stress Disorder alongside the Borderline Personality Disorder I had previously been diagnosed with. I was now eligible for a disability pension under mental health criteria. The pension is enough to live on comfortably while studying full time and, unlike other welfare payments, is reliable and long term. It strikes me as absurd that Australia's welfare system required me to become psychiatrically disabled by sexual abuse in order to be considered eligible to receive the amount of financial support that would have prevented much of the sexual abuse in the first place.

I left my violent boyfriend and after a long time of feeling ashamed to ask him for help, I reached out to my stepfather and moved back to live with him in Canberra. He paid for hours of group therapy sessions and drove me to them. After a year, I returned to Brisbane and resumed my degree. The safety and comfort of being on the disability pension afforded me a sense of security I had never known. Knowing you will never have to have sex with anyone you don't wish to brings such freedom and nourishment to the body. My university attendance is imperfect and I still struggle through many of my days, but I've achieved top marks over the past year.

I'm not telling my story in search of pity; none of us want your pity. I tell it as testimony to the bare truth of what prostitution is, the truth that every day is drenched in lies. I'm telling this truth not for myself but for all the women who are still suffering and all those yet to suffer in this climate of denial. That truth is this: women cannot be afforded human status in a world where prostitution exists; women cannot be afforded human status in a world where prostitution can even be imagined.

Rhiannon is a university student living in Queensland who works for the Australian Greens.

Internalising
the Violence

Tanja Rahm

I was quite privileged, as a 20-year-old girl in Denmark, deciding to go into prostitution. No one forced me, I didn't have a pimp, I didn't do drugs and the choice was mine, and mine alone. I believed I was some kind of high-class whore, not standing in the streets, not doing drugs but instead working in high-end brothels as an escort. I didn't see myself as a victim. Not until I had depression, anxiety and was afraid to go outside, and then began to do drugs – anything to help me endure being a prostitute. I had never been depressed or had any kind of anxiety before I went into prostitution. Instead, depression, anxiety and the cocaine addiction came about because of my experiences in it.

Today I don't believe there is any difference between street prostitution and working in high-class brothels. What you do and what you experience is the same whether you are picked up in the streets or if you are sitting in a brothel with a spa, silk sheets and champagne. You can find drug and alcohol addicts both in brothels and in street prostitution. Actually, it might be easier to comprehend the depression of the situation when on the streets than when you are wearing luxurious lingerie, expensive gold and lots of Gucci.

But the men who buy sex are all the same no matter where they find you. They are men whose needs are more important than the safety of women. They are men who may seem like good men in other aspects of their lives but who let go of all respect and empathy when they buy access to women's bodies. They don't feel any responsibility for their actions, and show as little respect as they wish. They feel entitled to belittle and humiliate the women they have paid to satisfy their sexual needs. They violate them physically, psychologically, sexually, financially and materialistically. There are so many aspects of violence in this industry. And that is what you have to understand, that the violence in prostitution is complex. It's not just being hit, kicked and raped. The violence is so much more.

It is psychological and verbal: It can be expressed through name-calling, insults, humiliation, intimidation, threatening behaviour, threatening body language, and an unpleasant alternation from being sweet and caring to being rude and threatening. It can also be in threatening to reveal your identity.

It is physical: It can be pushing or pulling you, spitting on you, throwing things at you, striking or kicking you, pulling your hair or putting a stranglehold on you.

It is sexual: It can be biting your ear, your lip, your cheek or your nipple. It can be kissing you, licking your face, trying to pull off a condom, putting fingers inside you, or doing more than what was agreed in advance. It can be thrusting himself so hard into you that it hurts physically, so much so that you're not able to walk, dry yourself after using the toilet, or even wear pants.

It is material: He can rip your underwear into pieces, rip your stockings, or break your necklace on purpose.

It is financial: He doesn't want to pay the price, and systematically manipulates you to do things you don't want to, or into giving him a discount. When he is drunk or high, and isn't able to come, he blames you. He calls you a nasty whore, and wants his money back. When you are lying there, naked, feeling threatened, it's easier to give him back his money than take the risk of being beaten up.

When you are in prostitution you internalise the violence.

You hear the same repulsive things over and over when you are being called a slut, a whore, stupid or disgusting. But still, you defend your 'free choice' and say that prostitution is just ordinary work, because realising the truth is so depleting. You dissociate yourself from the men and their actions, because no one has the psyche to be present in the acts of violence in prostitution.

When you understand the complexity of violence, then you understand that prostitution can never be recognised as a profession, but that the only thing to do is to criminalise those who organise, maintain and exploit people in prostitution. This obviously includes those who pay for the sexual violence, which the buying of sex is.

Prostitution and the damage caused by prostitution are the same all over the world. The men who buy sex are also the same. When people travelled to Denmark, from Norway, Sweden, Finland, Germany, England, Scotland, the United States, or from China, Japan or any other country, and bought sex, I had the same experience with them as with Danish men who bought sex. Buying sex means you buy access to masturbate into another person who is only there because she needs the money. And that action in itself is violent.

What I learned from prostitution was that I couldn't trust men. They had hidden personalities, and the worst of them were shown to me as a prostitute. All their violent fantasies, their paedophile fantasies, their anger, their disrespect, their condescending view of me as a prostitute. The way they didn't even try to hide what they thought of me. They made constant attempts to exceed my limits, just because they could. Just to show me how little respect they had.

People always ask me how the criminalisation of buyers would have helped me while I was in prostitution. My answer is this: If it had been a crime to buy women for sexual pleasure then I would have known that what these men were doing was wrong. For a long time I blamed myself, thinking that it was my own fault. I chose to be a prostitute. I gave them the opportunity to buy me. I took their money. How could I blame them? How could I blame anyone else but myself? But I am sure I would have left prostitution much earlier if I the law had been on my side. Because then I would have known that what these men were doing was wrong. I took the blame for their numerous attacks. I felt that I had set up myself in this situation and therefore couldn't blame them. There was no support or help to get out. I'm absolutely sure that a ban on buying sex would have helped me by sending a clear signal that the buyers' actions were wrong. It is no use thinking liberally about prostitution if we want to help women out of prostitution. Because how are prostitutes ever able to open their eyes to the violent structure of prostitution when there is no social or political support for recognising prostitution as being violent and harmful?

I was a prostitute for three years. No one actually forced me physically into prostitution, but I also didn't choose to grow up in a family with a drunken and violent stepfather. I didn't choose to be sexually molested when I was 10 years old by a man in his fifties, touching my body, putting his hands under my skirt and between my legs. Neither did I choose, when I was 11, for a man to follow me up an apartment stairway and put his hands up my skirt, touching me between my legs. I didn't choose to be raped by a boyfriend two years older than me when I was 12 years old. I didn't choose to be sexual molested when I was 13 by a man on a train or in a public toilet, I didn't choose it when I was 14, or when I was 17 years old. All those choices were made by different abusive men.

Growing up in a world where, as a girl or a young woman, you can't feel secure, because so many men think they have the right to abuse children and young women, degrades you as a human being. You are brainwashed into thinking that you don't have the right to say no, that you don't have the right to your own sexuality, that your sexuality belongs to men, whenever they feel the need for it. My 'free choice' in going into prostitution was actually not that free, because I didn't feel like I owned myself or my own sexuality. Abusive men made that choice for me, leading me to think that I was just an object for their satisfaction.

Every time a man came into the brothel, paying me to satisfy him, I felt that I was worth something. Not because of him, not because of what was going on, but because of the money. The money seduced me for a long time. Feeling that I was actually worth something.

My story is not unique. In Denmark we have a lot of former prostitutes who have been telling stories just like mine. Most of them 'chose' to go into prostitution because of sexual abuse in their childhood. Other women in Denmark were sold by their fathers or stepfathers as children.

When you are a child, you have dreams, lots of dreams. You want to be an actress, a singer, you want to work in a candy shop, you want to work in a zoo, in a toy store or maybe you want to be an astronaut and go into space, maybe you want to work in a circus, or be a writer, a dancer or a policewoman. None of those dreams include sexual behaviour. Growing up in a careful, loving and reliable family gives you healthy opportunities. It gives you self-esteem; it teaches you that you have the right to say no, and that you can choose to be whatever you want to be. No healthy family teaches their children to give away their sexuality unless it is equal and pleasurable.

No one wants to be a prostitute because of the prostitution. When people choose prostitution it's either because of the fact of no other opportunities to choose from, because of low self-esteem, an inability to say no, poverty, abuse or because of different psychiatric disorders. When people see prostitution as a choice, or as sexual liberation, or think that women actually like being prostitutes, they see prostitution through a lens of fake illusions.

After one year in prostitution I had been violated in so

many ways that I developed anxiety and depression. I wanted out. But what the system of prostitution did was to neglect my feelings. No one said to me, "Let me help you out of prostitution." What they did instead was to convince me that no one ever gets out. After two years in prostitution I almost couldn't go into the room where the men were waiting. They told me everything would be so much easier if I just had some cocaine. So I did. After three years in prostitution I wanted to kill myself. No one in the system wants to let go of you if you can still make money. As long as you are the profit-making machine that entices buyers to the brothel, they won't let go of you, because in the system no one cares about you as a human being. You are a sex machine, making their brothel a profitable business for the owners.

For decades, the discussion about prostitution has been about the prostitutes. But the only reason why prostitution exists is because men are buying them. Men are the ones who are sneaking around brothels. Men are the ones harming and violating the prostitutes. Men's demands are fuelling trafficking. But it is never about these men. Only rarely does a man admit that he is one of those who buy sex. But a report from Denmark shows that 15.5 per cent of Danish men aged 18-65 years have bought sex. A high number of these didn't care if the woman they bought had been forced into prostitution.

In Denmark prostitution is recognised as a social problem. We actually have exit programs for prostitutes, to help them get back into a normal life. To help them with getting psychological treatment, assistance for different kinds of addictions, access to education programs and to advise them about financial problems. The Danish government has set aside 46 million Danish krone for these exit programs. Do we have exit programs for any other jobs in Denmark? No, we don't. And why is that? Because we know, deep down, that people are being harmed in prostitution. And as long as we ignore the fact that prostitution is violent, and fail to criminalise those who do harm, we won't be able to protect the ones being abused, violated and exploited in prostitution.

Prostitutes may be serving male society, but they definitely don't belong to it, because men don't want to be associated with buying sex. Men who buy sex have no interest in building relationships with prostitutes, because they know that what they are doing is ethically and morally unacceptable. Otherwise, wouldn't they tell people about their actions? Wouldn't all of them just shout it out proudly, that they are the ones buying prostitutes? Wouldn't they tell their wives, their children and their families? Or maybe their colleagues and friends? They know what they are doing is wrong. And that is the reason why the buyer often gets aggressive. Because the shame, and all the things the prostitute represents, reminds him of his own actions. And that feeling can lead him to frustration, anger and violence.

A lot of women around the world have been trying to tell the truth about prostitution and what is going on in prostitution. But when you speak out, you take a high risk. You run the risk of being threatened, hated, being told that you were weak, weren't strong enough, that prostitution isn't for everyone, that you chose it for yourself, that you got a lot of money from prostitution and are therefore a whore. What the pro-prostitution lobby tries to do is frighten women into not telling the truth about their experiences, so that you won't be able to hear the truth.

The fact you don't hear from them very often is not because they are not there. It is because they aren't ready to confront society's neglect of their experiences. Besides that, it takes a really long time to figure out how the system of prostitution manipulated you into thinking that you actually enjoyed letting other people masturbate into you for money. But they are there. You will see that more and more women will stand together, all over the world, fighting for equality and for the right not to be seen as sexual objects who can be bought and sold.

I came out publicly as a survivor in 2011. I had been away from prostitution for 11 years. In that time I had been trying to get a hold of myself. I fought my way through nine years of therapy just to make sure that, when I came out publicly, I would be healed, so that no one could threaten me into silence. It was so important for me that I was able to come out with no tears, no regrets, no hatred, and with the strength to stand up against all the resistance I knew I would meet, primarily from men. I know that other women spend years and years fighting to live a normal life. Some of them never will. Some of them are alcoholics and drug abusers, some of them are fighting with post-traumatic stress disorder, anxiety, depression and suicidal thoughts. Some of them are already dead.

When I was a prostitute I worked in some of the finest brothels in Denmark. Sauna clubs for businessmen and brothels where there was a waiting list to work there. I was a high-class escort, and we used to tell ourselves that what we were doing was so much better than what prostitutes did in the streets and in seedy brothels. But the fact is we did exactly the same thing: having fake sex for money. It didn't make any difference that the sheets were clean. It was the men and their actions that made it seedy and uncomfortable. The men and their actions were all the same. Actually I'm quite sure that the more money the men had, the more offensive and manipulating they became. The more money they had, the more they tried to cross your boundaries, all the while being ice cold and arrogant about it.

The government should have protected me against these abusers. The law should have made sure that I could have received help to get out when I wanted and needed to after one year in prostitution. Legalising or ignoring what happens in prostitution is the same as saying that prostitution isn't harmful. But I have been there, I know. It is harmful.

A letter to my Johns[1]

FOR YOU, WHO BUY SEX

Dear sex customer,

If you think that I ever felt attracted to you, you are terribly mistaken. I have never had any desire to go to work, not once. The only thing on my mind was to make money, and fast. Do not confuse that with easy money, it was never easy. Fast, yes. Because I quickly learned the many tricks to get you to come as quickly as possible, so I could get you off of me, or from under me, or from behind me.

And no, you never turned me on during the act. I was a great actress. For years I have had the opportunity to practice for free. Actually, it falls under the concept of multi-tasking. Because while you lay there, my thoughts were always elsewhere. Somewhere where I was not confronted with you sucking out my self respect, without spending as much as ten seconds on the reality of the situation, or to look me in the eye.

If you thought you were doing me a favour by paying me for 30 minutes or an hour, you were wrong. I would rather have had you in and out as fast as possible. When you thought yourself my holy saviour, asking what a pretty girl like me was doing in a place like that, you lost your halo when you proceeded to ask me to lie down on my back, and then put all your efforts into feeling my body as much as possible with your hands. Actually, I would have preferred if you had just laid on your back and had let me do my job.

When you thought you could boost your masculinity by getting me to climax, you need to know that I faked it. I could have won a gold medal in faking it. I faked it so much the receptionists would nearly fall off of their chairs laughing. What did you expect? You were perhaps number three, or number five, or eight that day. Did you really think I was able to get turned on mentally or physically by having sex with men I did not choose myself? Not ever. My genitals were burning. From lubricant and condoms. And I was tired. So tired, that often I had to be careful not to close

---

1 Tanja's letter to her johns is adapted from <http://www.welt.de/vermischtes/article123793374/Ich-ekelte-mich-vor-Euch-und-Euren-Fantasien.html> where it was first published.

my eyes for fear of falling asleep while my moaning continued on autopilot.

If you thought you paid for loyalty or small talk, you need to think again. I had zero interest in your excuses. I did not care that your wife had pelvic pain, and that you just could not go without sex. Or when you offered any other pathetic excuse for coming to buy sex with me. When you thought I understood you and had sympathy for you, it was all a lie. I had nothing but contempt for you, and at the same time you destroyed something inside of me. You sowed the seeds of doubt in me. Doubt as to whether all men were just as cynical and unfaithful as you were.

When you praised my appearance, my body, or my sexual abilities, you could just as well have vomited on me. You did not see the person behind the mask. You only saw that which confirmed your illusion of a raunchy woman with an unstoppable sex drive. In fact, you never said what you thought I wanted to hear. Instead, you said what you yourself wanted to hear. You said that which was needed to preserve your illusion, and which prevented you thinking about how I had ended up where I was at twenty years of age. Basically you did not care at all. Because you had one goal only, and that was to show off your power by paying to use my body as it pleased you.

When a drop of blood appeared on the condom, it was not because my period had just come. It was because my body was a machine, one that could not be interrupted by a monthly cycle, so I inserted a sponge into my vagina when I menstruated. To be able to continue on the sheets. And no, I did not go home after you had finished. I continued working, telling the next customer exactly the same story that you had heard. You were all so consumed with your own lust that a little menstrual blood did not stop you.

When you came with objects, lingerie, costumes or toys, and wanted erotic role-play, my inner machine took over. I was disgusted with you and your sometimes quite sick fantasies. The same goes for the times when you smiled and said that I looked like a seventeen-year-old girl. It did not help that you yourself were fifty, sixty, seventy, or older.

When you regularly violated my boundaries by either kissing me, or inserting your fingers into me, or taking off your condom, you did it knowing perfectly well that it was against the rules. You were testing my ability to say no. And you enjoyed it when I did not object clearly enough, or when I too often would simply ignore it. And then you used it in a perverted way to show how much power you had and that you could cross my boundaries. When I finally told you off, and made it clear that I would not have you as a customer again if you could not respect the rules, you insulted me. You were condescending, threatening and rude.

When you buy sex, it says a lot about you, your humanity, and your sexuality. To me, it is a sign of your weakness, even though you confuse it with a sick sort of power and status. You think you have a right. I mean, the prostitutes are out there anyway, right? But they are only prostitutes because men like you stand in the way of healthy and respectful relationships between men and women. Prostitutes exist only because men like you feel you have the right to satisfy your sexual urges using the orifices of other people's bodies. Prostitutes exist because you and your peers feel that your sexuality requires access to sex whenever it suits you. Prostitutes exist because you are a misogynist, and because you are more concerned with your own sexual needs than relationships in which your sexuality could actually flourish.

When you buy sex, it reveals that you have not found the core of your own sexuality. I feel sorry for you, I really do. That you are so mediocre that you think that sex is all about ejaculating into a stranger's vagina. And if one is not handy, it is never further away than down the street, where you can pay an unknown woman to be able to empty yourself into a rubber while inside of her. What a petty and frustrated man you must be. A man unable to create profound and intimate relationships where the connection runs deeper than just ejaculation. A man, who expresses his feelings through his climaxes, who does not have the ability to verbalise them, but prefers to channel them through his genitals to rid himself of them. What a weak masculinity. A truly masculine man would never degrade himself by paying for sex.

As far as your humanity goes, I believe in the good in people, also in you. I know that deep down you have a conscience. That you have quietly wondered whether what you did was ethically and morally justifiable. I also know that you defend your actions and likely think that you treated me well, were kind, never mean or did not violate my boundaries. But you know what? That is called evading responsibility. You are not confronting reality. You delude yourself in thinking that the people you buy are not bought. Not forced into prostitution. Maybe you even think that you did me a favour and gave me a break by talking about the weather, or giving me a little massage before you penetrated me. It did me no favours. All it did was confirm to me that I was not worth more. That I was a machine, whose primary function was to let others exploit my sexuality.

I have many experiences from prostitution. They enable me to write this letter to you. But it is a letter which I would much rather not have written. These are experiences I wish I could have avoided.

You of course thought of yourself as one of the nice customers. But there are no nice customers. Just those who confirm the women's negative view of themselves.

Yours truly,

Tanja Rahm

Tanja Rahm was prostituted for three years in different Danish brothels. She managed to extricate herself from prostitution when she was 23 years old. She works as a therapist, sexologist and a lecturer. Her book A–Z Love and Sexuality *was published in Denmark in 2010. In 2014 she obtained a degree in social education from University Sjaelland.*

We Are All Expendable

Christie

there was a little girl
who held a precious pearl
right in the palm of her hand
but it fell from there
and got lost somewhere
in the garden of demands
and the weeds grew high around it
and choked it from the light
and the girl forgot about it
and went on with her life

cruel winds blew
to chill hot blood
and stinging rain did fall
upon her garden deep and lush
in fertile muddy soil
a hazy maze of hedges grew
confounding clearer vision
and filtered rays of sun shed light
upon her verdant prison
but seeds of discontent took root
and rose up to unleash
rebellion
in this mundane muted world of
'aim to please'

a mighty storm erupted in the verdure overnight
a bolt of lightning struck down
with a swift illumine light
whirlwinds tore at anchored roots
(the subterfuge of years)
exposed
the sobbing woman shook
dissolved in bitter tears

dawn revealed the wreckage
of this woman, mother, girl
and in her desolation shone
a single glowing
pearl

I wrote the first verse of this poem during my third year in the Australian sex industry. At that time I couldn't come up with an ending. I was still there, still trapped in 'the garden', confused and blinded by the distorted, damaging beliefs about myself that took root in childhood. By the time the bolt of lightning struck my prison of self-deception, discontent was rife. The fantasy that there was something noble in devoting myself to giving men affection, offering my body to prop up their self-esteem in exchange for money and being grateful for occasional kindness and superficial affection, was wearing thin. Staying was killing me, but the psychological prison walls held tight. The bolt came hard and swift. Police raided the illegal massage parlour where I worked. They burst in on a naked girl and client, guns pointed. Thank heaven I was spared that humiliation – and a police record. The timing coincided with my son leaving school. It was the catalyst I needed. My tiny nest egg became an escape fund. By then I had begun to build a life outside. I had formed healthy friendships, so I organised for my son to live with trusted friends and I moved into the spare room of an old acquaintance in the country. It was all I could afford.

Didn't I have pots of money? Don't women in the sex industry earn a fortune? Ha! The myths! The insidiousness of fast money with zero security or guarantee. The constant overestimation of that cash in hand. Making loads of money one day and none the next, or far less than expected. I wasted a lot of money devising ill-planned means of escape, always keeping myself on the edge financially so I couldn't leave. Every time I fell in love I would quit work. Sometimes soreness or damage done by clients (scratches and bruising in delicate places) or an attack of herpes would keep me from earning money. On three frightening occasions I hemorrhaged heavily for a week because my body was so overused. Pushed too far, not by choice, but by being overbooked. I would come out of a booking to be told that so-and-so was waiting for me. "He's already in the room and, by the way, you'd better be on time because you are booked solid for the next six hours." It was a case of get the client out on time, clean the room, freshen up, walk into the next room with a smile and pretend to be happy to repeat the performance over and over again, surreptitiously cutting short each booking five or ten minutes to keep to schedule. If a client noticed they would be furious. By the end of the day it was impossible to remember who I had 'seen'. Complaints were not welcome: "You girls always complain when you're not busy, then you complain when you are!" There was no recognition or concern for the physical and emotional toll involved. Everyone is expendable in the sex industry. Sometimes I became mentally ill trying to cope with the mind-games clients play, and the regular clients who demanded more and more. From playing the compliant 'girlfriend' who is never demanding and always in the mood. To be in the brothel meant to lie, lie, lie, all day long. "Mmm yes ... that feels beautiful," she moans, looking sexy. "For God's sake, hurry up!" she screams inside her head.

I tried to leave, but to make the resolution stick a body needs something to live on, somewhere to go and someone to help. When you add a dependent to care for, making the 'choice' to leave is harder. The modest rented suburban home, the little luxuries like piano lessons and new clothes would have to go. I didn't want my child to suffer. I wasn't trained for high-paying work. Like many women I met in the industry, I stayed to give my child the advantages of a middle-class lifestyle. The problem was, the longer I stayed, the more socially isolated I became. The mainstream world became frightening: a place where I could be exposed and shamed – my child shamed! No, it seemed safer to keep going and keep to myself, but it was hard to sustain. My heart cried out for leaving, but like women from violent relationships who feel lost and broken inside, I'd return again and again. I often went back out of sheer loneliness. I felt closer to clients and to the women like me whose real names I rarely knew than to anyone else in the world. Walking away was to lose that connection. Going back was like the homecoming I longed for and never got from my family. Within days or hours, I'd be planning my next escape.

When I finally left you might suppose I would have signed on for the dole? "No, I don't have a certificate of leaving … no, I don't have proof that I worked anywhere … no, I don't know the name of the woman I worked for and no, she doesn't know my name either." The dole wasn't really an option. After 13 years in the industry I had suffered enough shame and humiliation. I wanted to start clean, but with no references, no resume, and no work history to speak of, it was tricky. That is where it ended. I will do my best, in this limited space, to explain how it began.

I think I was born at a bad time for my mother. With no capacity for self-reflection, her frustration, loneliness and disappointment at my father's cold indifference made having me seem like the last straw. My sister was only 16 months old. If I'd been a boy, my mother could have had her tubes tied and been done with childbearing (she told me). Instead she suffered further trauma having my brother. My mother told my sister before she died that I was "Demanding from the start". She said that, for the first six months of my life, "I woke her every night to be fed!" How very inconvenient. "You wicked, wicked girl!," she would scream, looming over me as I huddled in a blithering heap on the floor. My crime? To place the sugar bowl an inch from its rightful place in the cupboard. Her parting shot whenever I crumpled under attack was to sneer, "You're such an actress! I *hate* women who use tears!" For some reason this never happened to my sister or brother. They learned to score brownie points by banding together at my expense.

I was branded a sexual deviant by the age of five. I played 'witch doctors' with my friend, a delightful game where we healed imaginary illnesses by pushing plastic bowls and cups under each other's clothes, delighting in the feel of the objects against our skin. There was nothing 'rude' going on, but we were caught and the worst was assumed. I was taken home and shamed, long and loud. I took to wearing layers and layers of underpants. I will never know if anything 'happened' to me back then, but I had terrifying, half-waking dreams that 'ghosts' were sticking 'fingers' into my mouth. I'd try to bite the fingers but there was nothing there.

The problem was always me. "You don't fit in!," "No one could ever live with you!," "You're impossible!" No one in the family questioned this. I was bad, they were good. Being bad led to having my appendix out. My father, convinced I was faking feeling nauseous at age seven, roughly propelled me to the car, shouting, "I'm taking you to the doctor and if there's nothing wrong with you, you're in big trouble!" Terrified, I lay on the doctor's couch. He poked my tummy, "Does that hurt?" I nodded, too frightened to speak. Next thing I was whipped off to the hospital. They took out my perfectly healthy appendix, then poked around looking for something else before conceding defeat, leaving a scar across one third of my abdomen. They found pus in my urine, but nothing more. I was sent home in big trouble. "What a liar! There was nothing wrong with you! You manipulating little actress!" Dad decided to tour some car yards on the way home from hospital. Mum sat in the car and smoked while he dragged me around the car lots. I was in agony. As he spoke to one salesman my nose started to bleed. Blood was pouring out and I cupped my hand to catch it, calling, "Dad, Dad" in a small voice. My father ignored me. The salesman looked on, horrified. He took a hanky from his pocket and handed it to me.

The best thing about the appendix episode was that during my recuperation I discovered books. As I lay in disgrace, I began to read. I learned that I could lose myself. Books became my world. Characters in books became best friends, surrogate family and mentors. Spirituality and books saved my sanity. My life wasn't all bad, more like an ordinary playing field strewn with landmines. Both parents could be charming and funny. There were creative outlets, cousins, visitors and laughs. Photos show a nicely dressed, healthy young girl with dark circles under her eyes. I suffered chronic insomnia, which persists. My mother was a health food fanatic and a fabulous cook. I went to Sunday school, elocution lessons, drama and ballet for a while. I had to leave ballet due to my inability to remember footwork – and farting. It was so embarrassing, a result of chronic tension-induced indigestion. Also, my mother complained nonstop about being a human taxi. She never let me forget that children had 'ruined her life!' The list of what she could have done without us, without me, made me feel guilty.

Our family moved a lot early on, so no long-term friendships were forged. Adolescence was hard. I developed early and grew quite busty. I looked more mature than I was; inside I was naive and innocent. At 11 I wanted to be a nun, dedicating my life to helping others. Then came the Whitlam era of free university. I wanted to be a doctor but this was scoffed at. All right, I conceded, a nurse or a midwife. But my mother wouldn't hear of it. Perhaps I would study literature or be a historian. Not an option. My mother decided that I wanted to be a hairdresser. She could never distinguish self from other. At 14 I was put to work on Saturdays in a local salon. On my fifteenth birthday, I was whisked out of school and apprenticed to a salon quite a distance away from home, which meant long hours and travel six days a week. I was shell-shocked, I had hoped she'd get over the idea. I also felt ashamed because my yuppie peer group was planning grand professions. I had just become comfortable talking to boys at school, having class debates and expressing my opinions. Suddenly it was all gone. Segregation and social isolation are themes that have repeated in my life. At 16 I was cast out of the family home forever.

I got shamed out of home because my parents thought I was having sex with my first boyfriend. I wasn't. I didn't even like him, I was just lonely. I moved into a flat with a 20-year-old girl whose friend raped me a week after I arrived. A few days later, her boyfriend burst into my room in the middle of the night and raped me. I begged my mother to let me come home. She refused. I was raped by four more unknown men in that flat. One did so very sadistically for hours on end; another drugged me. I became bulimic. I was still 16 when I moved next door; my housemates were in their twenties. It was expected, in those circles, to have sex if someone liked you. With no knowledge of boundaries and low self-worth, I had sex with boyfriends or guys who made me feel obliged, in an out-of-body kind of way. I didn't enjoy it, I just did what was expected. I pushed away anyone who got too close, to hide my bulimia and because I believed that if they really knew me they would find out I wasn't worth knowing. If I slipped away first, I could save myself the pain of rejection. I became more severely bulimic. I couldn't stop. The pain and grief were too much. By 19 I was suicidal.

One weekend I took 42 of what I thought were sleeping pills, stolen from my grandmother. (They turned out to be diuretics.) The following Monday I called work, saying, "I'm sorry, I can't come in today. I think I need a week off, I tried to kill myself yesterday and I feel really, really sick." "Oh, all right," was the reply. When I confessed to my mother a few months later, she sniped, "You just wanted attention!" Maybe I did.

I did meet someone who stayed around. I felt loved for the first time and spontaneously stopped being bulimic. Then I got pregnant. We both knew it wouldn't last but we got married. It didn't last. I agonised over the marriage break-up, sharing my thoughts with my mother who seemed to understand, but betrayed me badly later on. I never stopped trusting my parents. I kept trying to prove to them that I was a worthy daughter. I had always worked hard. I tried several occupations after hairdressing, seeking something meaningful. I was well-liked and trusted, but plagued by breakdowns. I worked all through my marriage. After the break-up I was burnt out. I refused to consider a parenting pension because I had been taught, 'people who don't carry their own weight deserve to be shot!' I trawled the paper for jobs. I found 'Masseuse wanted, no experience necessary'. When I called, there was laughter in the background. The receptionist was friendly, "You do realise it's nude massage?" she said. I hung up. Then I called again. I'd give it a try. I felt welcomed by the sex industry, at home among a sisterhood of misfits. Everyone had a back-story akin to mine. I was no longer the odd one out.

I began by doing 'hand relief' massage. This was easier than full sex, but most places were illegal so the risk of trouble was always present. Still, I was smart enough to want to get out as soon as possible. A series of events led to a job falling through in Darwin, where my family was living at that time. I needed a roof over my head for a short time and some help to sort myself out. The roof was denied, my brother introduced me to escort services instead. I never thought to ask for outside help.

Who would want to help me? Escorting is extremely risky, it involves being on a client's turf and turning up to strange places at night. Four hours with a business executive at a ritzy hotel can be followed by an hour in the outer suburbs with a drugged out weirdo who collects guns. If you don't return from a booking no one will search for you. If you are found dead, you're just a prostitute, who cares? I thought, I'm tarnished now, I may as well make it work for me. I continued to escort back in Melbourne until my anxiety rose to such levels I could no longer cope, so I moved on to brothels. When I could take it no longer, I went back to an illegal massage parlour, which was subsequently raided, as I described above. It was a blessing in disguise.

Eleven years on, the girl/woman I was is gone, but the psychological scars may never disappear. I still shudder at the thought of male genitalia, and I am still unearthing harsh, uncompromising beliefs that cause me to keep my distance from love and from physical touch. I am grateful for the knowledge and wisdom I have gained, but the pain is alive just under the surface. It's a work in progress. I am happy with my life. I am growing and expanding, I have a lot to offer. I know I am a good person: a compassionate, caring person, sometimes wise. I have learned to ask for help when I need it, whom to trust and to honour and respect myself.

Christie lives in the beautiful Yarra Ranges of Melbourne, Australia. She enjoys music, writing, recording, performing and study. Trained as a counsellor, majoring in abuse and trauma, she has worked and researched in the fields of family violence, sexual abuse, the commercial sex industry and human trafficking. She is currently writing fiction, studying for a Bachelor of Social Work, and still finds solace between the covers of a good book.

Porn Companies Don't Care if We Live or Die

Jan E. Villarubia

I lay there covered in bodily fluids, saliva and sweat from 25 different men. I was disgusted, sore, defiled, and void of all emotion. A part of me died that day; my soul was shredded and divided up among the men I had just sold my body to.

My journey into the identical industries of pornography and prostitution was justified by my desperate need to feed my three children. I was a destitute single mother prepared to do anything for my children. My first porn scene was filmed in Las Vegas USA in 2006 for an illegally operating porn production company called Sensational Video. It was shot in an apartment. There was no fancy set, no personal changing area, no security, just a rundown, run-of-the-mill hole in the wall. I was told it was a 'test' shoot and that I was lucky to get paid for it, but that if I went through with it I would gain fame and fortune. So I did the scene. In an hour the abuse was over and I was paid $300. As I was ushered out the door and promised more work, the next victim walked in. On my way home, with a knotted stomach, my only thought was that I had just sold my soul for $300 dollars. I vowed never to do it again. But I didn't keep this vow.

Eight months later, I faced the same situation. I was in need of money even though I was working full time. The demands of being a single mother with no help from my ex-husband were too much. A couple of men I knew had seen my first movie and encouraged me to make more. I re-lived the trauma in my mind and wanted to cry, but I needed money fast.

I posted a profile on a sex jobs site and not even five minutes later received what seemed like a million phone calls from so-called producers and agencies, all with promises of grandeur and instant wealth. I got some very sexually perverse calls too. Some men asked if I would abuse them or sleep with underage boys on camera. I accepted a 'gig' from a producer in Compton, California who ran a company called Tiger Media Group. When I got to his hotel I was informed that the producer, who looked shabbier than the room, was also the male performer or 'talent'. I was expected to pleasure him and his female companion. I was taken aback. I had been told it was going to be a boy/girl scene, not a boy/girl and then girl/girl scene. It was double the expected scene for the same original price, but what was I going to do? They knew I was a single mom and needed the money so they took advantage of that.

The producer told me I needed to show him my ID card and sign a model release that contained legal terms I didn't understand. Since I was new and uneducated about the ways of porn production, I naively thought it was for tax purposes. When I asked him if he was going to wear a condom he shoved an AIM (Adult Industry Medicine) test in my face and said we would not be using a condom. He never asked me for an STD test. When the abuse was over I was sore, tired, and disgusted with the others and myself. The producer paid me half of what he promised and said the cheque for the rest would be in the mail. I trusted him because he sounded professional. The cheque never came.

Within days I began to drink heavily and take painkillers I had lying around to treat a previous back injury. I started popping pills, especially when it came time to do a porn movie. The porn industry offered me drugs too – marijuana and alcohol from porn producers and porn stars, and I gladly accepted. I didn't want to feel the pain of penetration from an over-sized penis or from being told to hold poses for still camera shots while being penetrated and choked. Every scene lasted at least two hours because of the need to do painful freeze-frame pics and get good angles and lighting. I was degraded on camera, but had to pretend to enjoy it, or else no pay! I was called names like bitch, whore, and slut, and because I was in the BBW (Big Beautiful Women) niche my weight was used constantly as a form of exploitation and insult, even though I was actually told not to lose weight.

I was also forced into prostitution. Producers sent me to do 'privates' for high-paying clients and my agent got a nice percentage of these profits. I wasn't in control of my life; I had lost my identity as Jan and became Elizabeth Rollings the porn star.

About six months into the porn lifestyle I was offered my own website. A husband and wife team – Ditto and Dutch – who owned pay-per-view sites in Las Vegas, had an idea for a BBW network and wanted me to be their 'top model'. I was promised that if I worked tirelessly on my website I would gain financial freedom. The offer seemed appealing because I did not want to do any more hardcore scenes. Ditto made a contract and convinced me that it was all for my benefit. When I suggested a lawyer read it over, he guilt-tripped me into signing it because of our so-called 'friendship'. He promised he wouldn't keep the website up if we parted ways. I fell for it. What drugged up alcoholic and traumatised woman wouldn't? It wasn't long before Dutch started propositioning me for sex aside from the website work we did together and telling me if I didn't have sex with him it would cost me my site – he would financially break me if I didn't obey. He wasn't the only producer to force me to do off-camera sex acts. Prostitution was a form of manipulation producers used to get off.

One particular producer, Gabor, the owner of Heatwave Video, really loved to use on-the-side sex as a tool of manipulation. He'd tell me how much he loved me and that I was his number one model. He coerced me into believing that having sex with him was a sure way to maintain a steady cash flow. Gabor even sponsored a booth for me at LA Erotica in 2007, where I was billed as the first BBW to ever have a booth. He was happy to do it as long as I 'gave it up' whenever he demanded. He was nothing more than a glorified pimp. I was assured that having a booth would help me gain more exposure and more money. I was a puppet on a string.

As time went on and my thoughts of hopelessness and desperation grew, I felt like I wanted to die. I wanted to sleep and never wake up. Every day was a good day to drink heavily. I hated myself for being a horrible mother and I was desperate – only this time for a way out. The abuse and pain was so bad that I ended up in the emergency room for a nervous breakdown. When I told my web designer I couldn't do it anymore, all hell broke loose. His threats worsened and he refused to take the website down. I reminded Dutch many times of our verbal agreement, but he just laughed in my face and told me he had a couple of thousand to burn in a courtroom while I, on the other hand, was broke.

Hopeless, and facing thoughts of committing suicide, I got on my knees and cried out to God for help. After a couple hours of tearful praying I went online to look for answers. I web-searched 'porn help' and found Shelley Lubben. I contacted her and told her my story. It didn't take long before she was sending me encouraging words from God, gift cards to help feed me and my children, and resources in my area to aid in my recovery. She helped return me to the Christian faith I once knew. It wasn't, of course, all smooth sailing. In April 2008 I felt very ill and reluctantly went to the emergency room. Frightened about what it could possibly be, I was diagnosed with chlamydia and herpes. My whole world came crashing down. I did the right thing by getting out of the industry, but now this? I had always thought I was safe because I was getting tested on a monthly basis through AIM.

It has now been eight years since I left the porn industry. Although it hasn't been easy to constantly relive those painful memories I have done numerous porn convention outreaches, speaking engagements, and radio and TV interviews. I will never stop spreading the truth of the fantasy of porn. I performed in over 40 porn films, including a gang bang scene with 25 men, participated in over 20 pornographic websites including my own and three pornographic magazines. The women in porn are replaceable objects who keep porn companies wealthy while the majority of performers struggle to make ends meet. I want people to know the truth: the porn companies do not care about human value, they do not care if the women in porn live or die.

Jan Villarubia was involved with pornography for two years and contemplated suicide before finding help. Now, eight years later, she works with the Pink Cross Foundation in the United States, and is studying for a Masters Degree in Family Therapy.

A Piece of Me

Kendra Chase

Time heals all wounds. Time does little for scars. They permanently stick to you as a vivid reminder of your vulnerability and the time you faced some form of harm. I carry over 4300 emotional scars with me every day from each man I sold my body to during seven years of prostitution. When I was finally emancipated from sexual exploitation, I had spent over a quarter of my life as an escort, brothel worker and, later, a madam. I am not the extreme story you hear of where a woman is abducted, transported to a random location, beaten, and then trafficked into the sex trade. I am the woman you would walk down the street next to and envisage was probably a college student or someone working a 'square job'. The fake smile I put on each morning will never alert you to who and what I really was, or that my real world was filled with sadness, abuse and loneliness.

I had the textbook middle-class upbringing with a healthy and happy home life. For so long the only undesirable thing I could really recall happening to me was that a boy at my daycare would make me touch his penis during nap time. I was three. A worker there also physically and emotionally abused me. Eventually it was discovered and I underwent counseling for a bit, and was seemingly 'healed'. Immediately after, though, I became very aware of sex and violence, like my childhood innocence had ended right there. I dressed very provocatively once I reached about age nine or ten, began experimenting with chemical drugs at 13, and I lost my virginity just after my fourteenth birthday to an older guy who pressured me until I finally gave in. From 16 I spent three years dating a crack dealer who was emotionally harmful through tactics of belittling and controlling me. He then cheated on me, gave me chlamydia, and eventually began physically abusing me. When I was 20 I met a seemingly nice guy who worked hard and seemed to have his life in order. He eventually became a coke addict and ran me $10,000 into debt through bank fraud on our joint account. By age 22 the financial abuse I experienced in these relationships left me tens of thousands of dollars in debt, despite having spent the previous two years as a single woman working five part-time jobs and averaging 96 hours a week attempting to pay debt off while still meeting daily needs. I did not have the necessary experience or education to secure a solid career with reliable pay. One evening my monthly bills were soon due, I had no gas in my vehicle, I had maxed out my credit cards and had no food in my fridge. In nothing more than an act of utter brokenness and despair I contacted a brothel and enquired about employment.

The madam was extremely cruel and demanding. It didn't matter whether or not I felt comfortable enough to have a session with a client, if he wanted a session with me I was required to service him. I still remember the first john I saw. He forced himself on me. I earned $220 and paid $40 to the house. I had sex with three men immediately after that and can still recall the feeling at the end of the night. I felt traumatized and violated beyond words. I also felt elated about having $720 cash in my hand. I cried that night, but went back the next day, and the day after that, and the day after that.

I never forget a face, ever. I hate that now I am out of prostitution I see all their faces. I see them out in the community, sometimes while with my loved ones. I always thought my 'gift' would protect me in the sex trade: that I would recognise the violent johns from their mugshots in the 'Wall of Shame' maintained by police, but my ability to remember a face did nothing to stop johns abusing me. I have experienced horrific, disgusting, and traumatising things that no person should ever endure. I have had men force sexual acts upon me, and run out of the room without paying (and I still had to pay $40 to the house). I have been violently sodomised, choked, photographed and filmed having sex without my knowledge or consent, and been used so hard by some men that my genitals and anus were left torn and bleeding. I have had men become so infatuated and obsessed they have contacted me hundreds of times a day, followed me home, and randomly showed up banging on my door in the middle of the night. I have been raped numerous times without condoms. Some johns tried to disguise that they were removing the condom while others wouldn't even bother.

In my first few months at the brothel there was a girl working with me who looked out for me and protected me from intimidation and exclusion by the other girls. She was my mentor and friend. A few years ago she was violently murdered and her body dumped in a farmer's field. He discovered her skull while walking his property line one day. I think about her every day.

I eventually worked my way into a 'mistress' role where I specialised in domination. I felt I would not need to have intercourse as often, and it seemed safer and more detached. Yet, even as a dominatrix, the horrifying acts continued. Men would ask me to urinate in bottles for them to chug back or to shit in their mouths or bake them muffins from my fecal matter for them to eat in front of me. One man offered me $10,000 to have sex with his dog on film. Another was so brazen he asked me to role-play his nine-year-old sister who he used to molest as a teenager.

I became popular. Apparently acting was my forte. Every client thought he was my favourite and that I loved my job, and was empowered and happy. I sold the same lie over and over that I loved to have sex for a living. I had to, because I thought that if I told the truth I would have no clients.

Now I know differently, because I don't think any john has any part of him that genuinely cares for prostituted individuals or their wellbeing. The phony pleasantries are only for obtaining sex and for the administration of their power and control. At my peak, I was having sex with upwards of 13 men a day and over the years I earned over $1.2 million. I had 'made it' in the eyes of others. I was booked for weeks in advance, travelled abroad with 'important people', pursued post-secondary education and was an owner of a comfortable starter home (as a single woman under 30). Still, they found me: the men who could make all that 'success' irrelevant once they entered me again. The ones that were overweight, hairy, middle-aged, unhygienic, and dripping sweat into my eyes as they drove themselves into me, calling me a dirty whore, a bitch, or a slut. The ones who would short me $20 just for the fact there was nothing I could do about it. Those were the johns I could not shake. Not only did they take a piece of me, they replaced it with a piece of them that I carry forever. I was numb and depressed every single morning while doing my hair and makeup, fantasising about when and how I would end my own life.

I had trapped myself without even realising it. I now had a large mortgage, tuition costs, and vehicle repayments. As simple as it might appear that I could have stopped at that point, I would have had to sell off all my acquisitions and obtain a government student loan. To me that was regression. What had I already sold my body thousands of times for? I felt I had to stick it out until my goals had been reached, which was mainly graduating from college. To the outside world it probably doesn't matter whether you sell your body one time or a million times, you have already been stigmatised and labeled a 'prostitute'. But I increasingly needed to soothe the harms of prostitution with material objects. In the moment, they seemed to affirm that what I was doing was working in my favour. I medicated with trips, shopping sprees and nights out drinking and dining in upper-end establishments. "Look at me, look what I have. This is success." I couldn't quit, and so I kept the armour on, put my head down and continued on. With all my credit cards now cleared and with a small loan from family, I built a brothel of my own. I saw it as a means of escaping the control and direction of other madams and as a way to provide a safe and happy place for women to conduct their business. I tried to convince myself that my brothel would be different. I learned early that it was no different. I never made any money from the business. My heart couldn't bear to fine the girls when they would fail to show for a shift, or charge them a room rental fee when they had been 'dined and dashed'. I paid out of pocket for a full-time receptionist/security to assist the girls, a cost that I had to cover even if the brothel saw no clients that day. After a year I knew I had made a mistake. I saw a girl come out of a room crying because her client was in his 70s and had been "touching her like an incestual grandpa." I could relate: the oldest man I had intercourse with was 93. I scrubbed myself to the point of being raw for days after that man because I kept getting his scent in my nose and thought it was still on my skin.

Now I was trapped with a four-year lease that would have entailed an $80,000 payout to the landlord should I walk away. I began to run the brothel less and focus more on travelling with affluent men abroad on work trips to offset the losses. One trip resulted in me receiving a ten-year ban on entering the US on charges of prostitution. I was travelling to Las Vegas with a doctor and another escort. I still cannot visit for five more years. After being denied at the border, the other escort later approached me to extort the (married) client for money due to the complications we endured. I refused, but when I did she exposed me as an escort on social media, harassed me for months, made repeated threats of physical violence, and did thousands of dollars of damage to my car outside my house one night while I slept. I began living my life not only looking over my shoulder, but also wondering who knew my 'secret'.

Add to that my constant reclusive tactics to avoid seeing johns in the community, I began to isolate myself. Suicide began to appear even more inviting.

Then it happened. He appeared: my husband. A successful, loving and caring man who had known me since the age of 14, someone who knew me before I was just a set of holes used by men for orgasms, who didn't want anything from me and wasn't looking to use me in any fashion. He had heard rumors of the direction my life had taken, but never judged me. He listened, he empathised, he understood and, most importantly, he accepted me and loved me. With an equal-contributing partner and the eventual sale of my brothel to another escort, I turned my last trick on 19 December 2012. One week off seven years since the first. I graduated from college and, with his support, I now attend university and work part-time as an advocate for other women still involved in the sex trade. We married in 2013 and together brought the most beautiful little life into this world, our son. I live the fairy-tale life that all women dream of, regardless of whether or not they have a history of sexual exploitation.

I try to move beyond my past every day, but I struggle. I have vivid nightmares three or four times a week that wake me in a panic. I worry about my son one day finding out the truth. At least once a day I have an overwhelming feeling of dissociation followed by a squeezing restrictive sensation all over my body. My armour is now damaged and all the shame, guilt and fear I suppressed thousands of times is slowly coming to the surface. I remind myself, though, that the cracks are where the light shines in and that good can prevail in situations of darkness. Still, I feel as though I have so little of 'me' left because I spent so much of my life pretending to be someone else. I still feel like an escort on the inside years later, one that just hasn't turned a trick in a while. The day I received my first legitimate paycheck I broke down sobbing because it was the first bit of money I'd earned in the previous seven years where

I didn't have to lay on my back and spread my legs. The feeling was overwhelming, but it was quickly followed by dismay at the dollar amount, and then by mental calculations that what I earned in two weeks could have been earned in four hours through prostitution. The real world doesn't feel real. I feel at any moment it could all crumble and I will be back in a brothel with man after man lining up to further scar me.

Although my journey through prostitution ends with a seemingly happy outcome, it never really ever fully ends. Just recently the escort who harassed me sent a letter to my workplace trying to get me fired with false accusations that I traffic narcotics. Years after the event she is still targeting me. I still see johns at the grocery store, and they attempt to contact me through my email at work. I feel enraged when I see the continued exploitation of women and girls in the world, and our socio-economic marginalisation. I hurt when I see my trauma flow to my husband who naturally absorbs it. I hurt when I see people viewing prostitution as a victimless activity and shouting loudly for its legalisation. They forget the stark reality of what it does to an individual's soul. It aches when people argue about 'choice' when virtually every sexual service provider only 'decides' to sell sex, at best, due to a lack of better options, or as a means of escaping violence at the hands of someone forcing them to submit to sexual exploitation. More than anything, I grieve at the reality that nothing seems to change. There will always be people placed in compromising circumstances who are desperate for a means of survival, and there will always be those who line up to exploit that vulnerability. Prostitution is the world's scar that never vanishes.

Kendra is studying at university in Canada and works part-time as an advocate for women still involved in the sex trade. She is married with a son.

Goodbye Mademoiselle

'Mademoiselle'[1]

I was a prostitute for ten years. You can call me a sex worker, a call-girl, an escort, a lady of pleasure, but it all means the same thing: prostitution. Initially, being a prostitute didn't really bother me much, but as time went on it wore me down both physically and mentally. It wasn't long before I hated it and the men who paid to sleep with me. I wanted to get out, but I had low self-esteem and was lazy. The money was good, but the price I paid was more than any amount of money could justify. This is my story …[2]

I started out as a very pretty prostitute but the stress and emotional turmoil took its toll. I lost my glossy hair and radiant skin and soon began to look pasty and older than my years. I developed anxiety, which I still struggle with. I hate sex and rarely do it with my partner. Sex makes me feel physically ill. Even though I have left the sex industry, I change my underwear several times a day as any moisture 'down there' makes me feel dirty. As I write this, I have begun to scratch. When I was a prostitute I would scratch all the time because I felt so dirty, like I had the clients' disgusting germs all over me.

I was raised in a normal home environment. I was the eldest of four children (one sister and two brothers). My parents were

---

1   Dedicated to Heidi, Charrlotte and Robin for all their support.
2   This is an excerpt from a longer version of my testimony.

ordinary working-class people. My father worked very long hours and my mother was a housewife. My father was distant but caring in his own way and never harmed me. My mother married young, largely to escape her volatile father, but was deeply in love with my father. She was pregnant within six months of marriage and appeared frustrated and depressed at times.

At age 16 I was performing poorly at school and I was bullied. My parents had a meeting with the head teacher who informed them that there was no point keeping me at school, and that I was a 'waste of money'. So I got a position as a junior office worker in an accountancy firm.

From age 17 to 20, I partied, got really drunk and dated a lot of guys. My parents were disgusted and called me a slut, but in fact I was a virgin. A lot of guys dumped me when I wouldn't put out, and I took this as meaning I was boring and unattractive.

When I was 20 and out with my work friends at a nightclub, I saw the most attractive looking guy I had ever met. His name was Mark and I met up with him for dinner. When he turned up at my door and smiled I felt completely blown away. He was into alternative music and we would watch bands and go to festivals. We spent our time camping, canoeing, fishing and surfing. I was very, very happy and couldn't believe a guy like him could be interested in me. I fell completely head over heels in love and decided to lose my virginity to him. It was absolutely magical for me and I had my first and only orgasm. But afterwards, he surprised me by turning his back and going to sleep. I remember lying next to him feeling hurt but told myself I was just being silly. Mark seemed to change after that. He became critical of me. He would comment on my weight and tell me I wasn't attractive. He also started to call me 'pathetic' and 'narrow-minded', and would get in really bad moods.

Mark dumped me because I was "uninteresting, boring, judgemental and he did not find me attractive." I did not cope with the break-up at all. I felt particularly devastated because I had given up my virginity to him. I felt so ashamed and cheated.

At the office I was promoted to clerk. My duties now consisted of making coffees, cleaning tea rooms and typing up scripts. It was mind-bogglingly boring and I was desperately unhappy. I would spend a lot of my time in my lunch breaks alone and in tears – grieving for the lost relationship, feeling isolated and hating my work. Then a new office clerk started and we became close. One day she mentioned she knew a girl who had done escorting and was paid to go out and have dinner with men and didn't have to have sex with them. She lived in a beautiful apartment and had Chanel make-up. I was desperate to leave home but couldn't afford it on my junior wage. The idea of escorting and being able to live out of home through just going on dates with men for money was tempting. I grabbed a copy of the yellow pages and looked in the escort section. After a couple of failed attempts, I called a place where the lady who answered was really nice. I asked her if I had to have sex, and she said that she wanted to meet me to talk about that. I got dressed up and took a lot of time with my hair and make-up because I thought I might not be pretty enough to do it (little did I know!).

The unit was in a nice area. I was so nervous. The door was answered by a lady in her 30s. She looked pasty with grey-whitish hair and dark bags under her eyes. She was dressed in shorts and a t-shirt and her shorts were so brief that her bum hung out. I tried not to stare but I had never seen anyone who looked like that. She stared back at me and said, "Are you sure you are in the right place?" She then introduced herself as Julie. She had worked for about ten years, mainly in brothels in Sydney. She said she had a few girls who worked for her and that they made a lot of money. Julie said that the work was pretty easy but you did have to have sex a lot. I told her I was worried about the sex bit, because I didn't know if I was good at it because I had only had sex with one guy. She said not to worry because it was like 'riding a bike', and you didn't have to have sex with all of them and when you did, it was often quick. She said that in bookings you mainly talked to them and then quickly had sex at the end: "It's no big deal."

The clients at Julie's were in-calls and out-calls. I remember how disgusting a lot of the men were – smelly and some had fungus. Not one client ever got me aroused, and I focused just on getting the job done. I hated it when they touched me but just tried to block it out. They turned my stomach, but I just tuned out. When they were drunk they couldn't even get hard. One day Julie and I did an outcall where there were two men together. They were horny and very demanding, wanting us to do girl-on-girl action. Instead we both had sex with them. After Julie said we now needed to go, the atmosphere changed. They started getting argumentative. Julie said we would shower and then give them a girlie show. We went into the bathroom, got dressed and ran out the door. We could hear them shouting at us and then they set their dogs on us. Thankfully we were able to get to the car in time.

Julie's house got dirtier and strange people started turning up to buy drugs. One day a group of Asian men were there and Julie swapped me for a drug deal. I felt really uncomfortable and didn't want to see one of them. He was so dirty and had black fingernails and stank. Most clients stink but he was particularly repugnant. He grabbed my nipple straight off so hard. I yelled, expected Julie to do her usual knock and ask if I was ok. She didn't. I ran out of the room naked and Julie was sitting there with his group of friends shooting up and just laughing. His friends were really rough and I felt frightened. I went back into the room and just jumped on top of him. Thankfully, he had a little dick and he came quick. He got up and spat at me and walked out. I had an extra-long shower and cried. I went over to my handbag and my money and headache tablets were gone. I left Julie's house that night and never went back.

Another worker who had left Julie's called me and told me about a place that was really good to work for. This mini-brothel was always busy; it had placed a lot of advertisements. I found it harder to work there because I wasn't used to so many clients and I had to work through my period. I was told to put a sea sponge in my cervix to soak up the blood. I was always worried that I would end up with some sort of infection. It was disgusting having sex with it in. I felt physically sick.

I encountered some rough clients. The receptionist complained to the madam that the clients were complaining about me. The madam told me that if I wanted to work there I had to see any client and let them do whatever they wanted. She seemed quite out of it – not drugged out but just strange and predatory. Apparently she had worked since she was teenager. She had scars on her chest and back but we were too afraid to ask where they had come from. She also wore a wig because the stress of the job had made her hair fall out. One part of me felt sorry for her but another part despised her because she was so difficult to work for and took half my earnings.

I found the number of clients quite hard to deal with. They came one after the other and I felt emotionally and physically exhausted after a shift. I stopped getting into contact with my old friends and would spend my spare time alone in my unit. I was putting on weight and not exercising, and I didn't care. I felt so sore all the time so I stopped wearing underwear and wore loose skirts.

I had started to look pasty and washed out because I was working during the night and sleeping through the day. I was unhealthy and depressed. I started getting headaches so I had strong prescription codeine tablets that I took more and more of. I was also drinking before my shift because I found the number of clients I was seeing really stressful.

The men I saw became a blur. Some were married and would complain about their wives not putting out. Others were single and lonely. Some young men were just horny and wanted someone to pound into and get their rocks off. The odd one was pissed off and wanted someone to jam their dick into as hard as possible. Some were old men who just wanted fresh meat. They came from all walks of life. You could never tell if they were going to be an easy client or someone who would be rough and treat you like a whore. The ones who were really nice were the hardest because when they were nice it made me want to cry (I don't know why).

I turned up a few shifts later and the door was answered by some policemen. I was terrified. They told me to come inside and had a camera on me. I said I was really scared. They formed a circle around me and wouldn't stop filming me and firing questions at me. After what seemed like an eternity but was probably only a few minutes, they told me to go. I jumped into the lift and ran to my car. I found out the sex worker on shift and the receptionist were charged, as well as the madam, for running an illegal brothel. The madam was incredibly angry at getting busted and blamed me. She turned up at my house with her pimp (who I had never met before) and buzzed my unit but I refused to let them in. I don't know how she found my address – she must have looked in my purse when I was with a client and seen my driver's licence. I also found out a few years later they had beaten up girls in the past.

I moved on to another brothel, but one day the old madam turned up and started being nasty. She grabbed me, threw me on the ground and had my head between her legs. She was beating me around the head with punches and with her stiletto shoe. After what seemed like an eternity, the receptionist finally intervened and punched her. I ran into another apartment and a kind old painter let me in and I stayed in a corner of his room crying for hours. He offered to get me help but I said I just needed to stay for a little while. What a kind old gentleman he was to let me in, shelter me and offer to help.

I didn't want to go back to the brothel but I was promised I wouldn't be hurt again. I had nowhere else to go to and was too low in self-esteem and suffering from depression to look for a normal job. The old madam came around to my apartment with her pimp again but I refused to answer the door. The receptionist said she had a friend who could stay with me for a while because I was so scared.

Her friend's name was Greg, and he was a long-term heroin addict. Greg wasn't the most attractive guy but he was funny and I was lonely, so he ended up staying with me. We did become lovers for a bit but I found it difficult to have sex because I was over sex and sore all the time. But he was good company and always kind to me. He had been in jail and one day he told me he was originally in jail for drug offences but while in jail a young bloke had given him shit so Greg and a group of men threw him to the floor and raped him. I was horrified he would do something like that and found it difficult to believe the story.

I smoked some heroin with Greg for the first time. It made me feel relaxed so I started to smoke it regularly. I had had a particularly bad client one day when I was by myself at the brothel. The booking started off normally but he wanted anal sex and when I told him I didn't do that, he punched me really hard in the face. I was stunned so he threw me on the bed and raped me anally without a condom. The receptionist came back and I told her what had happened. She gave me a tablet that she said would make me feel better so I could continue working. I didn't want to work and I told her so but she got angry and said that the tablet would help. The tablet was Rohypnol, which I had never heard of. I don't remember much after that. I remember being in the room naked with a client but nothing more. I don't even know how many clients I saw. The next thing I knew I was being shaken awake and angrily accused of trying to commit suicide because I had eaten a whole box of Panadol (which I had no memory of doing). I went home and had a sleep. For some reason I got out an old doll collection and started playing with them. Greg came in and looked at me really strangely.

It then dawned on me how completely fucked up my life was. I was a prostitute, smoking heroin, getting raped and drugged and was living with a rapist heroin addict. I wondered how my life had gotten this way. I wondered how I was going to shovel my way out of my own living hell. I wondered what had happened to the pretty, social girl who liked to go out with friends and dance all night.

Greg said he had a friend who could get me hostessing work in Japan where I didn't have to have sex. I met with Greg's contact. She had worked in Japan as a hostess and made a lot of money. She informed me that the travel would cost $2000 and she would arrange free accommodation for me for a few weeks with a friend, as well as a hostessing job. She assured me that I didn't have to have sex. She had a lot of money and looked classy and successful. I told family and the few friends I had left that I was going on a holiday to Japan.

When I arrived in Japan I was quite scared and was glad I was met at the airport by an attractive platinum blonde named Mary from Australia. She had lived in Japan for a few years. Originally she did hostessing, and now she taught English and did some modelling. She was easy to get along with and lived with her Japanese boyfriend who seemed wealthy. I was introduced to him as her 'friend's niece'. A day later Mary took me to a hostess club. It was night time and busy with men sitting in groups of about six or eight with one or two western hostesses. I met the 'mama-san' who had a real evil look about her. I couldn't speak Japanese and she barely spoke English. She looked me over sternly, told me to turn around, checked my teeth and examined my face under the light. I was given the position and told I would start straight away.

The mama-san took me over to a table of men where there was an Australian hostess. She explained to me that we had to encourage the men to buy drinks and we had to fill their drinks and light their cigarettes. She said some of the men spoke English and I simply had to try and chat and smile. It was weird that I got paid to do this. I never had to have sex. But I found the work incredibly boring, largely due to the language barrier. Mary spent some time with me but I was alone a lot in her apartment.

After two weeks of working as a hostess Mary came to the club and spoke to Mama-san. They called me over and Mary said that there was a 'sugar daddy' who would set me up with an allowance and I would be his mistress. I was then introduced to this Japanese man who was about 50, called Okami. He could speak about ten words of English. Money was exchanged discreetly between Okami and Mama-san, and also Mary. I was given none of this money. I was starting to feel tense and overwhelmed. I couldn't speak Japanese, didn't know anything about Okami, and was now going to live in one of his flats and be his mistress. Mary told me that I was very lucky but somehow I didn't feel lucky at all. I said to Mary that I had come to Japan to be a hostess and that I didn't want to be a prostitute anymore. But she said I was going to be a 'mistress' and would be very well looked after.

Okami took me by the hand and to a restaurant. I smiled at him and ate the food but we didn't speak. I noticed he wore a Rolex and had a chauffeur. He took me back to an apartment and gave me a key. We had sex with a condom. He was thankfully gentle, with a tiny penis and it was mercifully quick. He didn't touch me which was another bonus. As he was leaving, he left a heap of cash on the table and said 'shopping money'. I was a bit scared he might come back but he didn't. I didn't know where I was but he had left a piece of paper with Japanese writing on it that looked like it might be an address.

The apartment was lovely, quite large with views. However, despite this, I felt miserable, scared and alone.

Early the next day, a Japanese lady showed up at the apartment with groceries. Then she starting vacuuming. The phone rang and it was Mary who was checking in on me. She said that she had modelling work but that Okami didn't want me to model. He wanted me to go to language school. After she hung up I was by myself for several days in the apartment. I felt incredibly lonely and isolated. I was on edge because I had no idea when Okami would turn up again.

After a few days Okami showed up in the evening and we went straight to the bedroom to have sex. Again, the sex was quick and painless. Another couple of thousand yen was left for me on the table.. He returned the next night and we had sex again, and he left me another few thousand. I was alone all weekend in an apartment and couldn't even watch TV as it was all in Japanese. I felt trapped. Mary called me and said that Okami wanted to take me to a Japanese flower festival and to a sumo wrestling match where he had a special box. I was to entertain his clients. I told her I didn't want to do it because I felt so uneasy about the situation. Okami told her he was angry and that I had to do it. He showed up every day or night at different times for a week and left no money. I felt constantly on edge because I wasn't allowed to leave the apartment and felt like he was checking up on me.

On his last visit, Okami and I had sex and he again left a few thousand on the table. Mary called me the next day and said I was going to the festival and wrestling match to entertain clients and that they were all booked. But there was no way I was flying somewhere (I didn't even know where) to do god knows what. I packed my backpack and walked out of the apartment, trying to get the attention of someone who spoke English. One Japanese lady I found could speak English and offered to call me a cab. I didn't tell her any details, only that I needed a taxi.

By the time the taxi arrived I was shaking. I got to the airport and was told there wouldn't be any flights to London for about eight hours. I stayed in the airport the whole time, terrified Okami or Mama-san would find me. It wasn't until I was on the plane that I started to feel half normal.

After I got to London I started to run out of money fast. I decided to call up some escort agencies. The first time I said I was available to work I got a call within an hour. I called a cab and ended up at an Indian man's house. I was scared to go in because I was unsure whether there was only one person in the house. The booking went okay – normal sex and I was out of there within an hour. The rate was quite high and I had to give only 30 per cent to the agency. I worked roughly one day or night a week and saw about six clients a day.

I had a booking with a wealthy Swiss man named Richard. The booking went normally – the sex was quick – and he didn't touch me or demand anything. He was well known to the agency and frequently took girls away to his Swiss chalet for weekends. He offered to take me and I accepted. I met him at his townhouse in a wealthy suburb with my backpack. He actually went through my backpack, which I found very rude. He then took me to his dead wife's wardrobe and told me to put on her clothes. They were old fashioned and way too big for me. He told me I was to wear her clothes during my time at the chalet. I felt so embarrassed wearing his dead wife's ugly clothes. He also made me wear her underwear, which I found really disgusting.

We went to the airport and flew first class to his chalet. He took me shopping and bought me jewellery. The sex was hard because he had forgotten to pack his drugs to give him an erection. He became angry and blamed me and made me suck his floppy old dick for hours. He said that I "didn't do it properly," and became moody and distant with me. His daughter turned up who was older than me. She looked at me with disgust. It was really bizarre to talk to his daughter wearing her mother's clothes. The whole situation was starting to wear me down. Richard was getting angry with me because of his limp dick and I said I just wanted to go back to London. He said no, so I walked off and started to cry and his daughter asked me what was wrong. I told her I wanted to go back to London. Within an hour, she went through my backpack and searched me. Then she took me to the airport and I organised and paid for a flight back to London. Naturally Richard complained to the agency about me and I was fired. I didn't really care because I didn't like doing outcalls – I was always scared that someone would attack me (luckily no one did).

After this I got back together with my Australian boyfriend in London, a guy called Chris, and returned to Australia. We had no money and lived with his parents. I don't think his mother liked me much and once said to him, "She is too pretty and will end up leaving you." I was still a bit of a glamour girl and spent hours doing myself up. But my self-worth was so low that I thought that was all I had to offer. I think she saw me as vain and shallow. Chris got a job on the Sunshine Coast so we decided to move there.

Chris was getting depressed and spent all his spare time watching TV and smoking weed. This had been ok when we were overseas but I was getting really bored with it. I was also trying to get work but was not having any luck. I decided to go back to prostitution on the side for a little while, until we had enough money to afford our own place and get a car. I looked in the local paper and rang up an escort. She arranged to meet me at a café. Her name was Natalie and she was about 34 years old, slim with frizzy black hair and glasses. She told me she did in-calls and out-calls, and had two girls working for her. She seemed ok so I arranged to work for her one or two days a week while Chris was at work. I told him I had a job temping.

Times were pretty quiet, and one day Natalie said a buck's night needed an escort. I was hesitant because that would mean there would be a lot of drunk men and things could get out of control. She assured me that she knew the groom-to-be, and there would be adequate security. I felt really pressured, so went along. Natalie's boyfriend drove us both to the house where the party was held. We sat down and the organiser announced that they were going to raffle off a prostitute. Natalie told me to stand up. I had never felt so humiliated in my whole life. I felt like a piece of meat. I looked down at the ground because I was so ashamed. The raffle went ahead and I went into the room with a middle-aged man. He was normal and sensed my embarrassment, so was nice and gentle with me. He sensed I was unhappy, and I told him there was nothing else I could find as work. He mentioned study but I told him I hadn't yet finished year 12. He told me he hadn't finished year 12 either but that if you were over 21 you could get into university through adult entry. Something deep in me stirred and a tiny seed was planted. But I was still too wrapped up in trying to do sex work and keeping up the lies with Chris. After Natalie and I left the party I was still upset at being the raffle prize. I got the feeling Natalie was secretly pleased to see me so humiliated.

On one occasion I got sent to a married couple in their early 30s. I found it really awkward to be fondled by her husband with her watching. I then gave him oral sex and intercourse with her watching. I then did oral on her and she did oral on me. It was the first time I had ever been with a female. I found it a bit strange but she was gentle so it was easier than her husband who had pounded the shit out of me. I felt sorry for her being married to such a sick brute.

One night Natalie took me and another girl, named Lucy, to an outcall. Lucy had been a sex worker for about five years, and looked older than her age. She had blonde straggly hair, and was really skinny. Lucy wasn't very friendly towards me and commented that she wouldn't get work with me around. We arrived at a clubhouse filled with men. I became really scared and said I didn't want to go in. The hairs on my arms were standing up and I felt very anxious. Natalie and Lucy assured me it would be ok because they had been there before.

Natalie drove through an electric gate and we arrived inside the clubhouse. When the gates closed I had a feeling of doom. There was a bar with alcohol and drugs. Lucy and I were taken to a large room with about eight beds in it. Natalie stayed at the bar in the other room. Lucy and I undressed and men lined up to fuck the shit out of us for hours. I was crying on and off but didn't fight back because I was clearly outnumbered. Lucy was handling it better than me and told me to shut up and stop snivelling. That would make it easier. I don't know how many men fucked me and I don't even remember if they used condoms – I know I didn't shower between them. All was just a blur. I dissociated to such an extent I can barely remember anything, but it seemed to go on for a long time. I just closed my eyes and laid there while they emptied their loads into me. But I do remember how terrified I was. I remember Natalie coming in a few times and I said to her I wanted to go and she said I had to "finish the job." She was without sympathy and compassion. Eventually we finished with the animals and went back to Natalie's. Lucy and I were silent during the drive back. When we got out of the car Natalie handed us $100 (what an insult!). I had a long shower and curled up in bed with a sleeping pill. I felt sore and angry with myself for getting into that situation. I had no one to turn to, or to talk about it with, because, after all, I was a prostitute, and getting raped is part of the job description, right? Perhaps I deserved it because I was a prostitute.

A week later Natalie asked if I wanted to go out for a drink with her and Lucy. I took it as a peace offering. I got dressed in jeans, high heels and a normal tank top. The club we went to seemed a bit rough but I had a drink and just told myself to enjoy it. Lucy appeared to be high on drugs. Natalie was encouraging me to drink more but I wanted to stay sober. Some of the men from the clubhouse were there and I started to feel nervous and anxious. I said I was going to the bathroom. As I walked to the entrance, one of the men who had been talking to Natalie came out of a little side room. He grabbed me and told me to get inside one of the rooms. I felt really scared. I looked around the room in panic. It was a long room with a mattress on the floor. On one side was a mirror that looked directly out into the club. You could spy on people in the club but they couldn't see in. There was a couple screwing on the mattress. The man who had grabbed me didn't appear to notice them. I told him I wanted to go and he said I had to fuck him first. He was angry and aggressive and I was so very scared. I started to cry and took off my jeans, underwear and shoes. I asked him about a condom and he said no and that I wouldn't get pregnant. He was getting impatient and frustrated with my stalling and trying to finger me roughly. He pushed me down on the corner of the mattress and raped me like an animal in front of the couple. The couple would have known he was raping me but they did nothing to intervene. When it was over he got up, tucked his dick away and left me there. I was so sore. The couple didn't say a word, and walked out a few minutes later. I got dressed and tried to pull myself together.

I walked out directly to Natalie and told her what had happened and that I wanted to go home. She said not to worry about what had happened, and she would talk to him to make sure he paid me. I couldn't believe it – what money? – I hadn't consented! It wasn't about the pay – I was upset about being raped, about being brutalised, and about being treated worse than an animal. What the hell was wrong with these people? Natalie told me she had decided to stay and Lucy and I could get a lift home with a man she knew well. I said I didn't want to go with him but she assured us it would be ok. I figured if I had Lucy with me it should be ok. I was just so tired and traumatised I didn't have the energy to push it. I agreed to go with the man and Lucy.

Once outside the club, I had a good look at him. There was something cruel in his eyes, and he was seedy and dodgy looking. I said to Lucy that I thought he was bad news, but she said she knew him and it would be ok. But instead of driving us to Natalie's house, he drove us to a motel where he had booked a room. I was filled with dread. I knew I was fucked. My only hope was Lucy. Once inside the room, I started to cry and whine. The man looked at me in disbelief and said to Lucy, "What the fuck is wrong with this skank?" I told him I just wanted to go home because my head was pounding and I felt sick. He said he had something that would make me feel better. Stupidly enough I took the drink he gave me which had something in it. I think it may have been speed. He was getting angry and said he wouldn't take us home unless we had sex with him. I was starting to crack up and couldn't stop crying. I felt like I was in a nightmare and there was no way out. He was getting really angry with me and threatened to hurt me if I didn't shut up.

The man then drove Lucy and me to a high-rise apartment about 20 minutes away. I felt sick, so he wound down the window and I vomited out the window while he drove. I begged him to take me home or to drop me off somewhere but he just laughed and said I would be staying with him as long as he felt like it. Lucy had gone quiet in the backseat and I had no idea what she was thinking. We got to the unit. I had cried myself out and was resigned to whatever came next. Once inside the apartment he demanded Lucy and I fuck him again. We couldn't get him to cum, and by now he was starting to get into a rage, screaming at us and calling us 'dumb whores'. I said I felt sick again and Lucy said she would take me into the bathroom. Inside the bathroom Lucy gave me my handbag and said, "You are too good for this, don't waste your life as a prostitute. Go, I will take care of him." Lucy left the bathroom and distracted him while I took off.

I walked to a phone box and called a cab and after what was the longest, most horrendous night of my life, finally made it home. I was in a state of shock, and showered for an eternity. I felt so dirty. I then curled into a ball for a while before sitting up and rocking backwards and forth, crying on and off for hours. I felt like I was in an exhausted fog and couldn't believe that I had been raped twice in one night by two different men. I also felt guilty about leaving Lucy there, but she knew the man and Natalie would have known where she was. I found out later that he had beaten Lucy brutally and I still feel so ashamed that we didn't both run out. Maybe if I had stayed things may have been different. I just don't know.

After this I moved back in with my parents, I had broken up with Chris and was barely finding the strength to hold things together. They sensed something was really wrong with me. But it was good to feel safe again. I couldn't comprehend what had happened to me and felt completely numb and alone. I don't know how I got through those early days. I slept a lot and didn't eat much. My weight dropped to 48 kilos. Unfortunately, because my mother seemed to be pissed off at the sight of me, I felt that I had to move out of home again. I had no money saved because my new job as a filing clerk didn't pay much. I would sit in archives and file most of the day, or type up documents in a cubicle. I just felt so alone. I still couldn't wear underwear because my vagina always felt sore and scratchy. I had been to numerous doctors (not telling them what I did) and had tests done, but was told there was nothing wrong with my vagina. Perhaps it was just years of overuse.

In order to move out of home I needed money. I was dreading doing sex work again but just told myself to suck it up and do it. Even though I was good at dissociating, I always felt dirty and unclean, and sad and alone. Even just the thought of men touching me made my skin crawl. I avoided eye contact with people and spent my weekends alone and crying. I had no idea what I was crying about. I didn't want to go out to clubs with my old friends (the few I had left) because I wasn't interested in men. In fact, I wasn't interested in anything and wished I could go to sleep and never wake up. I felt like I had no options. The only legitimate work I could get was crappy, low-paying, meaningless work that made me depressed. I couldn't see a better future and just existed in a fog.

One day I met a gorgeous blonde lady about my age called Kate who said she would give me a shift or two a week and take only 30 per cent. It was in-calls only, and I would have a key and see only the clients I wanted to see. I was able to refuse anyone I wanted. Kate sensed I was a bit of an emotional mess and put no pressure on me to work or see clients. She was completely drug free and had a nice apartment. Kate had worked for a few years privately, only taking the odd girl here and there to work for her. She never talked about her working experiences and I didn't see a lot of her as I was always in her apartment alone.

I kept my filing job, and worked Saturdays and Sundays for Kate, telling my parents I was doing extra filing work. I also answered Kate's phone at her mini-brothel. The men ringing asked me the most disgusting questions – like did I have a tight vagina, was I horny (yeah, right), did I like being fucked (you have got to be kidding!), what turned me on, and did I have shaved pussy. The questions really pissed me off, but I pretended on the phone that I just loved being asked them. Some men would call and jerk off on the phone. You would be talking to them and their breathing would get laboured so I would just hang up. Some men repeatedly called and asked disgusting questions but didn't make a booking – I started to recognise sex callers and would just hang up.

I found it really isolating in Kate's apartment; I longed for someone to talk to, other than sex-mad clients. I felt afraid when I saw a new client because I never knew what kind of psycho would turn up at the door. I was also worried about the police showing up and charging me, about the neighbours, and about someone I knew turning up (such as a family friend or an ex-boyfriend), or my parents finding out what I was doing. I became very anxious and jumpy. I started to self-harm as a way to cope with the stress. I hated myself and found it difficult to look in the mirror.

Before I started a shift I had to get myself mentally prepared. I had to sit for a while after I got there because I was anxious and stressed before I even started. I needed half-hour gaps between clients to just rest my brain. I seemed to be in a hyperactive state when clients got through the door. They took this as sexual excitement. It astounded me how many men genuinely thought I enjoyed the 'work'. If I enjoyed having sex with disgusting, dirty strangers why would I charge them money for it? As if a hot young chick would want to have sex with an overweight, hairy, smelly middle-aged man. Some of the young guys were terrible too because they thought they were Casanovas and would try to fuck you as hard and as long as possible to show what studs they were. All I could think of was, "hurry up and cum, moron."

Clients were always asking me out but I had no desire to see any of them in a romantic way. I thought they were disgusting and just after a freebie. One client who saw me weekly was a lawyer who became very fond of me. He started to notice that I was unhappy and asked me why I was a prostitute. I told him I couldn't get a job that I liked and there were no other options for me. He encouraged me to think about studying and we spent quite a bit of our time discussing study options. He investigated the adult entry requirements for university and helped me prepare an application. I asked why he was helping me, and he told me he was falling in love, but understood that I didn't feel the same way.

I couldn't believe it when I was accepted into a university course. I screeched with delight when I got in. I could finally see a way out of the sex industry but still found it hard to believe that I was going to have a proper career. I happily handed in my resignation as a clerk and set off on full-time study. I was initially quite overwhelmed with the timetables, large lectures and all the reading I had to do. I failed my first assignment and was devastated. But I went to see the lecturer who kindly offered to help me. He tutored me weekly on researching and writing assignments. I approached another lecturer because I had failed an early statistics test and she also freely helped me. I will always be grateful to those two lecturers who gave up their time to help me. Once I got a handle on how to study and write I was like a sponge, and ended up finishing the year with top marks! It was very satisfying to see my family and friends' faces at the news I was doing well at university because most of them thought I wasn't too bright.

I was very excited about studying and enjoyed the challenge. I felt like I was doing something worthwhile that would allow me to leave the sex industry for good (because in order to pay the bills I was still seeing some clients). I made friends with a blonde-haired girl about my age. She was lively and very empathic and kind to others. One day some in our group were talking about a TV show on prostitution and she surprised me by saying strongly, "The poor bitches have been through enough with the job." I was surprised by her response because most people spoke of prostitutes only in derogatory terms. As I got to know Lisa better she struck me as one of the kindest and most open-minded people I had ever met. For the first time ever I told someone outside of the sex industry what I did. Lisa didn't judge me at all or question me but just accepted it. It meant so much to have someone like me for the person I was, and not for the work I did. As time went on I trusted Lisa more and more and would frequently offload to her when I had had a difficult client. She was an incredible listener.

There were times when working as a sex worker got me down so much I couldn't get out of bed for days. Lisa understood and took notes for me. I missed pretty much every class but because Lisa would tell me what was happening at university and gave me her notes, I passed with high results. I was still working for Kate but only once a week. Kate was really good to me and we began to get on personally as well. Her background was similar to mine. She never wanted to talk about prostitution and whenever I tried to bring up the fact it was messing with my head, she would change the subject.

I stopped going to classes completely, but luckily Lisa encouraged me not to drop out and kept sharing her notes and research with me. She was such a good friend. Somehow I got through the semester, but my marks had dropped to passes.

I was up and down, and getting more upset about being a prostitute. I really wanted to get out of the industry, but just couldn't seem to be able to stop. Even though I worked only one day a week at Kate's, I found myself dreading it all the other days. I hated being touched and having to pretend I enjoyed it. I talked dirty a lot because it got men off quickly. I hated all the disgusting things I was saying, but I blocked out a lot of it. Kate had begun to slowly lose it. She was working less and less, and had difficulty paying the bills. I tried to talk to her about what was going on, but she didn't want to talk about it. Kate and her fiancé split up and she started an air-hostessing course. She closed down her mini-brothel.

I was living at home again and had saved a lot, so I had six months off. I really was hesitant about working somewhere new. I had heard that a legal brothel had opened in Brisbane. I had never worked in a real brothel before but liked the idea it was legal (I didn't have to worry about being busted) and had proper security. So I rang up the brothel and organised an interview. The man who ran it was an ex-pastor and youth worker, but looked like a seedy leech. Apparently he was running the brothel to 'save the girls'. What a load of shit. He was a pimp making money off our bodies and souls. If anyone needed saving, it was him. I started my first shift a week later and was told I needed to do a minimum of two shifts. The place was like a giant cage. It had a plastic air about it and all the girls seemed tense. It was incredibly busy and the rooms stank like body odour and had a bleach smell from all the semen in the bins.

I found it incredibly stressful. Whenever I heard the buzzer announcing a client I would jump. I found it so degrading to have the men decide which girl to pick. I never got used to it and found it humiliating. I was also worried I would see someone I knew. The clients were rougher and more disrespectful than the mostly regular clients I had been seeing at Kate's. They wanted to pound me as hard as they could. The pimp also took 50 per cent of our wages. The owner of the brothel – the pimp – was constantly hanging around the girls, listening to whatever we had to say. I found this really irritating. I wanted to talk to the girls about clients but couldn't because he was always listening, and we weren't allowed to say anything negative about them. I also didn't find the girls all that supportive. I think the environment of having to compete for clients fostered that. The receptionists looked down on us and would make snide remarks. I wasn't allowed to refuse clients unless they had a STD – and even then I was questioned about it.

The pimp and the receptionists did not care how tired and overworked we were, and the turnover of girls was really high. Every shift went by in a blur because it was busy and I had dissociated to such an extent I didn't even know how many clients I had seen, let alone what they looked like. I didn't even care. The less I remembered the better. I had started to scratch a lot during and after shifts. Again there was no medical reason for it, but I just felt like I had something crawling over my skin. I scratched so much I broke my skin. Parts of my skin became infected, but I didn't care. I noticed I was not getting picked as often as the other girls and realised that I was losing my looks. My hair was stringy, my eyes lacklustre with bags under them, and I was terribly thin. But I didn't really care how I looked.

The years of stress, anguish, dieting, smoking and an unhealthy lifestyle had taken a toll on my appearance.

After a particularly demanding night shift dealing with clients one after the other without any breaks, I felt like I was ready to explode. I told the receptionist this had been my last shift and was abused for not giving enough notice. I just didn't care. That place was toxic and the worst I had ever worked at. I heard sometime later on the news that the 2011 floods had wiped out the brothel and, because it had no insurance, the pimp lost everything and had to close down. Last I heard he was working as a real estate agent.

I did get my degree, but I couldn't get work afterwards. I applied for jobs in my area, but couldn't even get an interview. I became very depressed and despondent, and was having suicidal thoughts. What was the point of all that study, and selling my body to get through it, then to finish study and still have no job? I was so angry. I continued to work as a prostitute.

Because I was no longer really young and wasn't all that pretty anymore, I wasn't getting many clients. So I had to start degrading myself even further. I started to do sick shit I would never have done before. This meant bondage where I beat men until they bled, using strap-ons and fucking and fisting men up the arse. It made me feel so revolting. One time a really old man came in with a catheter. Fucking a man with a catheter is a truly sickening experience.

The biggest sicko I saw was a man in his mid-forties who wanted me first to drop hot wax on his nipples, penis and balls. He kept sniffing amyl nitrate. I then had to thread a needle and 'sew him'. God, my stomach turns as I write this. I had to insert the needle into one side of his nipple and push it hard so it would come out the other side, and then do the same with the other needle. Backwards and forwards I sewed his nipples together and there was blood. I then had to 'sew his balls to his penis'. God help me. He was paying a lot extra so I just did it. I don't know how he could get off with the pain.

The grand finale was when he made me stick a huge needle down the eye of his penis. I remember trying so hard not to be sick. No amount of hand-washing could make me feel clean after that.

By that time I was bitter and hated myself. When clients were really rough with me I would cry or even pray while they were pounding. I didn't even try to pretend with the rough ones anymore. I am not religious but I found comfort in softly praying while a client was pounding the shit out of me. I found praying got my mind off what they were doing to me. Sometimes clients could hear me pray but it didn't stop them brutalising me.

And then, like an act of divine intervention, around this time a friend happened to hear I was looking for work, and by chance she was looking for someone with my qualification who could move to work in the country. She was even offering relocation expenses and subsidised housing. I jumped at the offer. I eventually excelled in the position and moved higher up the ranks. It allowed me to turn my back on prostitution forever. So in the end, all it took was someone to take a chance on me and offer a good, secure job with career opportunities.

Then it was finally *au revoir 'Mademoiselle'*.

'Mademoiselle' subsequently undertook a Masters degree, and graduated with distinction after completing a major research thesis. She went on to have a family, and now lives and works with her husband in regional Australia.

No Life for a Human Being

Autumn Burris

Adult-oriented businesses, such as 'exotic dancing' or stripping, are a gateway to prostitution. They are also a gateway to mental illness, including disassociation. By 'disassociation', I mean the capacity to mentally separate yourself from what is happening to your physical body. Disassociation is necessary to participate and survive in these businesses. Putting myself on stage was preferable for me because it meant I could disassociate through looking up to the ceiling instead of into a sea of eyes. Being 'off the floor' and on stage also meant groping hands were less likely to reach me.

As a survivor of indoor and outdoor, legal and illegal exploitation, I can assure you that all are equally harmful to the soul. Prostitution is routinely violent, psychologically and physically. The transaction means repeatedly having someone you are repulsed by touch you and/or enter your body, causing psychological damage. I wouldn't accept overnight appointments because I couldn't disassociate long enough to get through the night. Disassociation became more normalised over time and with practice – a trick of the trade. I learnt to numb myself by using alcohol and drugs, an important tool in surviving. I coped with all the unwanted sexual exchanges by limiting the amount of time with each sex buyer and instituting non-verbal and/or verbal boundaries – for example, keeping sex buyers away from my face and not allowing kissing.

But the problem with disassociation is that once you exit

a life of sexual exploitation you don't just go back to normal. Disassociation becomes a part of how you operate in daily life. In prevention programs I talk about the possibilities of healing from sexual exploitation, but I have to be truthful that, once you cross that line, you are never the same again. Yes, healing and recovery is possible, but return to a pre-exploitation state is not. It is as if once you cross that line of that first 'date' or 'appointment', something has been done, so the next one and the next one don't really matter. You are already in it, feeling worthless and empty, and never able to return to the person you were before. You are in servitude in the system of prostitution.

When a sex buyer rents your body he often demands more of you than agreed. If you reject him, more often than not, violence ensues. It is common for sex buyers to act out violently against prostituted women. Upon entering prostitution it is immediately clear that there is no such thing as respect for human rights or physical boundaries as soon as a client buys power over you. They live out their fantasies through renting your body. Fantasies they wouldn't think of asking their loved ones for, are requested of you. The demands range from fetishes to different sexual positions to a variety of types of sex. At the point that a sex buyer becomes violent and the Exploited realises there is no way to escape the situation, you become quite compliant, with the only goal being to escape the situation alive. In some cases the primary goal of the sex buyer is to inflict violence on the prostituted person. These men aren't able to accomplish their goal of sexual release until obvious pain is inflicted. Sex buyers are some of the sickest of the sick. Many are criminals, such as serial rapists and killers. You simply have little security or control over what happens behind closed doors or in remote locations. You learn to cope.

The act of having my body purchased for a price was always about vulnerabilities and the need for survival. My early childhood years were centred on money, body image and dependence on men for money. That unintentional grooming process made me a prime candidate for systems of exploitation.

The buyers of sex leveraged my vulnerabilities for their personal gratification. They caused an imbalance of power between my exploited self and the purchaser. Homelessness, substance abuse and a lifetime of grooming by society and my family were my vulnerabilities. Sex buyers know exploited individuals don't choose this life for themselves. The fact I had needle tracks on my arms and other parts of my body, and was obviously impaired by drugs, are indicators that each exchange was only about the sexual gratification of the sex purchaser. After once being beaten beyond recognition – my eyes were black and blue and bloodshot from the blows and my body covered in bruises – I was later that night picked up by men, and not one of them asked me if I was all right or refrained from purchasing my body. While my physical body hurt from the beating, I was rendered emotionless through living prostitution on a daily basis.

While each sexual exchange that involved money for a sexual act and/or the illusion of it was different – a variety of types of men of different socio-economic status and different nationalities/ethnicities – the common denominator was you never knew what to expect from them. The awfulness of each experience happens on a continuum ranging from violation of your lack of desire to be there in the first place, which feels like rape, to actual rape.

The buyer of sex rented my body for a period of time with the expectation that I had no right to reject any acts requested of me. Dignity is denied to the Exploited from the negotiation phase to the completion of the transaction. I can't describe the feelings of degradation that arise when you have to verbalise the sex acts and put a price on what is intended to be priceless, and then know of the personal violations that will soon take place. Then, while enduring all this harm, you realise it is going to happen again, and that you'll be bought and sold again, within an hour or so. The sexual violence continues from the negotiation stage to the completion of the act. The dialogue and negotiation necessary to get the act of prostitution started is the verbalisation stage of sexual violence. The acceptance of cash for the verbalised acts is the agreement to what will come to fruition as a result. The removing of barriers that clothing provides reduces your security and dignity and subjects you to penetration of an organ into your body that you wish more than anything was not anywhere near you. And all the while you have to listen to the comments and noises of someone you not only care nothing about, but are repulsed by, and, in turn, he cares nothing for you. A split second of relief because the act is over is felt as you wash yourself up and dress. But you know that within an hour and for hours on end you will be bought again.

Security is denied because the Exploited essentially has no control over the actions of the buyer. One evening I got into a late-model truck with a man. A few miles down the road it became clear that I needed to jump from the moving vehicle to escape him. I reached for the door handle only to realise I was locked in. The panic I felt, knowing what was sure to come, was unbearable. Prior to being discarded like a piece of garbage on the road I was raped and beaten beyond recognition. I knew I was hurt bad enough that I might not be able to make money. In the mirror I was unrecognisable: black, blue and swollen. Shockingly, I was picked up by another buyer within the hour. This incident was not an isolated one.

I am now a survivor exited from prostitution and other forms of sexual exploitation for over 18 years. Those of us fortunate enough to survive are not perpetual victims, although the recovery journey to healing is a lifelong process. The recovery and healing process is similar yet unique for each exploited human. The journey is like peeling an onion except you are unsure of how, and at what point in your life, another layer will be stripped away. Early on my path to healing I had a boss who was acting 'funny'. I told the late Norma Hotaling, who was my peer counsellor at the time, and she said it was sexual harassment. My question back to her was, how is this any different from the rest of my life? Later on, I was in a relationship with a man who I really cared about. I asked him during sex, "Are you done yet?" I didn't know of any other way of being in the world. After I had been out of exploitation for about five years I was sexually assaulted by an acquaintance in my sleep and then stalked. When I attempted to press charges against the perpetrator I was told by a trusted law enforcement officer that my past prostitution convictions would make a criminal trial difficult for me and my recovery process. I had to weigh up justice and my healing and recovery. When I discovered the perpetrator was a serial rapist of women in recovery with prostitution convictions, I obtained a restraining order and was relocated out of the state for my safety.

When will society understand that the Exploited are human? When will society begin to let go of the lies and learn the truth that prostitution itself is a violation of human rights, and this is not changed by 'choice'? Society can learn this by listening to exited survivors. I stand with my sisters and brothers in the fight to abolish all forms of sexual exploitation. Together we can put an end to the purchasing of bodies for the sexual gratification of men.

Autumn Burris is a dedicated and passionate leading expert with over fifteen years of experience in combating exploitation. Her efforts focus on addressing complexities in a holistic way. As the founder and director of Survivors for Solutions, *she offers direct client services, advocacy, community education and outreach, public policy advocacy, and consultation services to non-profit organizations and various institutions.*

My Pain on Display[1]

Donna

In 2015 an exhibition was held at the Canberra Museum and Gallery (CMAG) in the Australian Capital Territory, titled 'X-Rated: The sex industry in the ACT'. The exhibition was funded by the ACT Government and a Canberra medical centre providing a range of health care services, operating since 1980. It was of particular interest to me because I spent some years being exploited as a prostitute in Canberra in the 1990s. I wanted to see how an industry I have firsthand knowledge and experience of would be depicted in an art gallery. I wondered if it would it be an honest and realistic insight into what actually happens.

I left the exhibition after 20 minutes, feeling sick and numb. I went home and cried. I cried because of the ignorance of those who put the exhibition together. I cried because the exhibition was one-sided – it clearly had an agenda to glamourise the sex industry. I cried because there were no stories of survivors of the sex industry. And I cried because some of the images caused disturbing memories to come flooding back to me – memories that I have spent 20 years healing from. In 20 minutes I went back to that horrible time in my life.

Anyone who has experienced PTSD will understand my experience that day. The exhibition included photos of several brothels across Canberra – I had done some time in just about all of them. Working in a brothel is not like any other job, it's

---

1   This contribution is a slightly amended piece which first appeared at <http://melindatankardreist.com/2015/05/act-sex-industry-exhibition-ignores-the-brutal-experiences-of-women-like-me-prostitution-survivor-speaks-out/>

unbelievably stressful. Generally you don't have any other options for earning money, so poverty is the main driver. It's hard on your body, hard on your mind and hard on your overall wellbeing. You tend to not be able to stay more than a few months in one place.

I was 17 when I first started work in a Canberra brothel. The owner knew I was underage and was fine with that. He knew the younger I looked, the more desirable I would be to punters and the more money I would make for him. There was no duty of care toward me.

Seeing pictures of those brothels brought back to me the many violations that were done to me. The pressure to do anal sex, the extra money offered to go condom-free, the drugs offered in lieu of money, group sex with a football team who treated me like a piece of meat, the call-outs to hotels where I had no idea who I would encounter, and the guys who want to dominate – happy to rough you up to get what they want.

There was also a very large photo of a peep show booth – which is the small black room where men sit alone. They insert coins to make a flap open for them to view a live strip show. The man is unseen by the woman – he leers at her while masturbating into a tissue and calling out vulgar instructions. It is a pretty degrading experience. There was a range of photos showing stills from porn movies. Many showed women receiving oral sex from an attentive man, with the woman depicted with her back arched and her head thrown back in the throes of pleasure. Those pictures did nothing more than glamourise the sex industry: the man paying for the service has the power, not the woman. It's the woman who is normally the one who has a dick shoved in her mouth, whilst the john holds her head, encouraging her to deep throat.

The reality is that in prostitution your vagina is rubbed raw from all the johns you have serviced, often so painful after a particularly aggressive john that you have to use numbing gel to keep working. And all the while being expected to act like a porn star as though the overweight public servant on top of you is the greatest fuck you've ever had.

I was not surprised that the Interchange General Practice would fund this exhibition. It was always the place to get a script for drugs if you weren't coping or to get a Sexually Transmitted Disease certificate signed off on the spot. But for the ACT Government to be funding the exhibition – with the people's taxes – was appalling. The government already taxes the industry, and so keeps vulnerable women suppressed and forced to make a buck from hardship. Does the government really have to compound this by supporting an exhibition so degrading to women? It seems it has bought the ridiculous lie that selling timeshares on our vaginas really is a good thing for women.

This exhibition was devoid of input from survivors; there was nothing showing the sordid, abusive and damaging elements of the industry. It was presented merely as an interesting look at the history of an industry. In writing this piece, painful though it is, I want to give voice to all the survivors who were ignored and disappeared by the exhibition. I know our experiences will never be included in an exhibition like this, but at least you can know of ours, here, in this book.

Donna lives with her family in Canberra and works in the public service.

When You Become Pornography

Christine Stark

One day last spring I was driving my battered green Ford Escort to a Minnesota Indian Women's Sexual Assault Coalition meeting. My car looked like someone had pelted it with rocks the size of dinner plates. I bought it that way four and a half years ago for $1600. It had 93,000 miles when I bought it, now it has over 200,000 miles. The mechanic told me it was not a good deal, that it was overpriced (hell, it looked like shit!), but it's crisscrossed the state with me and my dog seatbelted in it for therapy, speeches, coalition meetings, work, pow wows, and ceremonies. Guess I lucked out.

The meeting was in southwestern Minnesota, USA, where my father's side of the family live. My aunt and cousins are on hobby farms near there. They won't talk to me because my aunt doesn't like that I tell about my father and his father. I miss my cousins, and worry if they're all right, so it's always difficult when I drive through the area. It's hard for me to drive anywhere near the area, and when I know I have to go through it I get anxious. The flat landscape agitates me. Being within a couple hundred miles of the place sends me spiralling into PTSD. It's hard to sit still or concentrate (I just want to get away), thus making our annual coalition excursions to southwestern Minnesota that much more trying.

So I was already somewhat anxious about the drive and I made it worse by opening Melissa Farley's book on prostitution and trauma and reading a section on the internet and child pornography. I have a bad habit of doing things that increase my anxiety when I'm already feeling anxious. (I also have a bad habit of reading while driving, which was not curbed by getting in trouble as a teen for reading while driving. Some anonymous neighbor used to call my father whenever I drove home with a newspaper splayed out over the steering wheel and dash so that I could catch up on the latest happenings while driving along a curvy road near our house.)

So there I was, driving along a winding lakeshore straight out of a Norman Rockwell painting, snatching sentences about child pornography in between stop signs and oncoming cars and curves. Three paragraphs down on page 78 it says 60% of child pornography currently on the web is from the 60s and 70s. My mind flips like a Rolodex spinning through filed and distant memories, clamped down, snapped shut.

Me. Mine. Pictures. Posing. Smile. Me. Everyone can see.

The porn made of me is most likely on the internet, still being sold. I already knew that, but seeing it in black and white marks on paper took it out of my head. Turned it into official words with official statistics and percentages. My thoughts abruptly ended, like a cliff, they dropped into thin air. My emotions flashed to despair and shame so deeply ingrained that they've worn deep brooding grooves, sprouted rivulets and thin spider veins in my body. It's such a part of me I don't notice it unless I poke at it. I don't poke at it much because when I do, I feel it will kill me – the knowledge that my deepest pain and shame can be downloaded and I can never stop it, is more than I can bear. My panic spiked, I slapped shut the book, stared down the glittering grey road ahead of me, and drove that spike deep with one practiced hammerhead.

I regained my emotional balance, avoided taking a dunk in the lake, crunching an oncoming car, a tree, the convenience store where I buy soda and fuel. I once asked the store clerk if he knew of my cousin's husband's family from Willmar. He didn't and I was glad that a momentary lapse in judgment, a lack of emotional discipline on my part, wouldn't be snaking its way to my cousin's husband, then cousin, then aunt, then father.

I drove on. Late afternoon turned to dusk. Then the moon emerged, a hollowed-out pale pumpkin. My day continued, round and round, although at that moment the emotions reared I thought my existence, my consciousness itself, would be obliterated. My life continued, like my tires humming across the grey pavement at 72 miles per hour (cops won't ticket you for seven over), like the film looping reel to reel (I wonder if they transferred those old films of my rape first to VCR then DVD), like my looping psychological response (I call it my hamster wheel).

I don't know how to convey the utter despair of pornography I felt that day in the car – a flash of lightning illuminating the landscape of my soul, then gone. It left because it would destroy me, and since my mind is a good friend to me, it banished that burning, searing awareness to a nether world.

Every single piece of pornography of me is a picture or film of me being raped. Raped as a child. Raped as a teen. Raped as a young adult. And it is for sale. Rape is intimate. It turns you inside out, exposing your pink and bloodied insides, cracked bone, marrow, rivers of hemoglobin, the softness of your pulsing heart, the exchange of fluids between cell walls, the underside of your skin. All things not meant to be seen, not meant to be exposed. Not meant to be public. Rape is violation, taking, stealing, crossing boundaries of another's self. Rape is destruction. It is brutal. It smashes, caresses, smashes, caresses. It takes bits of the body, bits of the mind, bits of the soul. Like Frida Kahlo: a nip and tuck here and there. Each rape bloodies the spirit.

Pornography is not death (unless you are murdered in it). It is a murdering of the spirit, a splitting of the essence of a human, a fragmenting of the mind, a splintering of bone, a deadening of the senses, a deflating of self so profound you are rendered less than everyone and every single thing around you including the dirty dime on the floor next to you. Being made into pornography turns you inside out like rape. It exposes the underside of your skin; it violates, takes, smashes, appears to caress, appears to smile, appears to enjoy, appears to rebel. It does not take bits of the body, mind, soul. It consumes them whole. Each time. So each time you regenerate or you die. In pornography you are not an object. It leaves you less than object. The equation becomes you $<$ object.

Pornography is rape, but it is much more than that. It is endless public rape. The wounds can never close, no matter how tight you pull the stitches, because your rape is still being played, watched, enjoyed, cummed to. There is no closure, no hope of closure. One push of a button, one click of a mouse, and there it is again: the screams, the smiles, the arching back, the whips, the chains, the animals, the stiff leather that smells like chemicals and sweat and dried cum. It's all there, a nanosecond away from making some man smile, again, from making some man cum, again.

No nothing in this world analyses that. No nothing in this world discusses that. No nothing in this world understands it other than the survivors and the spirits of those who did not survive, fluttering about our heads, like tiny birds, red-throated hummingbirds, green cascading chests, tiny, delicate wing beats whispering *please tell, please tell, please tell.*

Please articulate this pain, shame, death of spirit. Please use your voice to speak. Please don't let their gags silence you. Please don't be numb. Please pull up that spike. Please tell the truth of pornography. Please do not let them get away with this without giving voice to the sound of our wings, the words unformed trapped in our brains, never unfolding, curling outward, downward, to the sides, rising up like a flower, passing through lungs, larynx, throat over tongue under teeth to the world.

Please bring our life back into the world of the living, the world we did not belong to, the world that was against us, the world that would not have listened even if we had struggled, struggled so very hard, to create hot pink peonies the size of fluffy softballs, tiger lilies with their long robust orange petals with brown slashes like marks from a pen, their spiky green leaves draped to the ground, red hibiscus unfolding in pure glory then shrivelling and drooping, paying homage with their brilliant bowed heads beneath the passing of one sun.

No nothing has explained it, the demolition of spirit, the loss of joy, the terror, the sense that part of your self is gone yet follows you everywhere, just over your shoulder, trapped, endlessly raped, pain looping, cries looping, fake forced smiles looping. No nothing has explained it, that sense of hopelessness. Of no safety. Of no escape. That the spirit of the rape does not leave. You are haunted, by it, by those dead from it, by your selves, by your fragments. By that spike. The knowledge drilled into your body that you are worthwhile only when you are being hurt. Only when you are being used. The knowledge drilled into your mind that the rape never stops, that many hundreds, maybe thousands, of men will see the underside of your skin, that viscous space between your skin and the meat, your delicate red blood cells. They will laugh, write a check, run a credit card. Buy you. Ejaculate. Moan. Feel great physical pleasure from your torture. Sadism. Nothing explains it, the knowledge that pornography is you being sold into infinity and there is nothing you can do to end it.

So it is up to me to try to do justice for those *manidoog* fluttering about my consciousness at one million beats per second. It is up to me to do this for myself. It is up to me to stop this lack of agency. Three simple words no one can understand in relationship to sexual exploitation unless they've experienced it. *Lack of agency.* Words and phrases to describe damage so profound you no longer know if you have a self. Do shattered bits of mirror, part of an iris here, a lock of hair there, the curve of a tooth, make a self, or is that self gone forever?

Or just for a while. Will it come back? And how? What if your self was never formed – you were a baby, a toddler, a girl of four – and you have revolving bits of jagged mirrors circling, moving up and down like a carousel, you on painted horse after painted horse, swirling, twirling, red, green, orange, a large purple swath on the hip, to fool the world into not seeing you, into not seeing you are shattered, a revolving door of selves you must hide in order to live. And if your self is gone forever, never even got to show up, make an appearance in this lifetime, how will you live? Can you live? Do you want to live? Can they steal you forever?

Lack of agency. Three simple words. You survived, so the therapists say, but now you must deal with no longer knowing if you have a body. Hours of lying somewhere as an adult fifteen years after the assault of you, a girl, a precious baby girl, your child's body bent, broken, twisted, bleeding. You were left, until the next shoot, on the floor, in your crib, on a mattress near a radiator, in the corner of the garage on the dog's blanket. No one cared. No one helped. No one comforted. Ten years after the porn shoot and you are still so disconnected from your physical self that the only way you believe you know you are alive is because you are able to ever so slightly move one pinky one millimeter to the left and then, yes, now you know, that is how you know you are alive. And if someone is there to witness this, the aftermath, you may muster the energy to ask *Am I alive?* because you truly do not know and they say *You are alive* and you feel obliged to believe them and you have conflicted feelings. Is it good to be alive, in this world? Is it good to survive? For back then, every time you survived they crucified you again. However, the other person, the witness, said you are living. They did not murder you. Yet.

In Madison, years ago, when I was 22 I used to walk the streets. Day after day into the nights. For hours and miles through the eastside of town. I could not be still. I could not stay in one place. I could not stop. When I did stop I did not know if I had a body, if I was alive, where I was, who I was. What I would do.

One December afternoon, on my way to therapy, I'd ridden my bike over the sludgy sidewalks rather than catch the bus (which made me feel trapped). When I left therapy it was chilly, snow piled in rough mounds along the edges of the sidewalks, early evening, the last strands of the day co-mingling with the edges of the dark, wintry night. I wanted to avoid being at home so I stopped at a café a block away. I got my drink, sat down by myself, alone as usual, pulled out a book, read some, set it on the table. It was too much to concentrate, usually, but especially right after therapy, the things I'd talked about, felt. I sat there. My drink, closed book, and me. The memories crept up and over me, prickly, vine-like, fast-growing. I went into a stupor. I sat and stared. Became increasingly numb, dissociated, I gave my body over to the memories, the horror, my ever-present survival skills.

I'd been reading a little about pornography. How the women in it are objects. At the café they had tiny purple flowers arranged on the centre of each table in bottles of Orangina. I remember the tables were round; the purple petals were round; the bottles were fat and round at their bases. It's strange, the things a person remembers while being traumatized – the first time around, second time, it doesn't matter. I remember the pattern of circles in the room, the fatness of the bottles reminded me of the belly of the *Venus of Willendorf*, it was dark outside, the building had enormous windows almost the size of the walls themselves. Indeed, other than the warmth in the building, there did not seem to be a separation between the inside of the café and the downtown street scene – parked cars, European style buildings, the deep blue of the evening, mystical streetlights shimmering over dirty snow. It was a time people were returning to their homes, families, loved ones. All things I longed for. The scene reminded me of a Pissarro, a place and time I would surely never visit, except in my imagination, a place where I was not alone, where I could have connection not of pornography, but of beauty, mysticism, transformation, transportation to a world different from my own, a world of imagination where I did not worry about living on the streets, in the cold, in the dark where I did not wonder how I would manage to live, not just money, but live in my body, with a spirit so rendered. 'Drink me' the Orangina bottle said in cursive writing across its fat belly in that Madison coffeehouse, and I was struck by horror at how I was utterly immobilized, utterly unable to act or think as much as the smallest animal who at least must think of food, safety, how to get them, ever-watchful, alert. I could not think. I could not act. My mind had ground to a halt. I watched from a distance, from the past, from a place removed by 15 years and 500 miles. Everything was above me, beyond me, the men would do what they wanted with me, even though I was in a café, there was no separation, and there was nothing I could do to change that, nothing I could do to protect myself, nothing I could do to keep them off me, as a child, or as a young woman in my mind in a café. In that café I knew those writers had it wrong, as I experienced horror, unreality, a dripping Dali painting, the man clasping his head with his mitten hands in Munch's 'The Scream'. I had no agency when they turned me into glossy 8 × 11s and I felt it that night at the café, like it was happening again: no agency, not an object, but less than object, less agency than the bottle because the bottle had a voice. I had none. It had life. I had none. It had a message. I had none. It said something: *drink me* and as sadomasochistic as that is, it was more power than I had at that particular moment in time and space, an extension of the horror of being turned into pornography, a painting could perhaps do some justice to that feeling, that lack, that negative space where a person should exist – me – that living horror trailing through the streets as if she were alive. Words fall far short.

But interestingly, now, as I write this and as I remember it,

that horror, and as I feel it, that café and that moment serve as
a connection, a living connection, a sound connection between
me, the middle-aged adult, and that youth I was, so alone, so
lonely, so powerless, so terrified, so sorrowful. So very, very
frightened, unsure of whether I would survive the memories,
whether I would right myself someday, return to the world as
I knew it, as others experienced it, as a person with agency, as
a person who belonged in the world with other living beings,
with the ability to make decisions to affect one's own life, strike
a balance between the here and now with the past – the past,
ever present and ready to rear into, tear apart, take over my
life. A bridge between my two selves, a great white corpus
callosum, a remembrance of a me I have great compassion for,
a me I have great respect for, a me who had great perseverance
and determination although she did not know it at the time, a
me who was a survivor and then a bridge to another time and
place rendered by the imagination of an artist a century ago
on another continent, a stranger. The time and change that
has passed between us, if we were to touch fingertips, travel
back to Michelangelo, he god, me a lifeless Adam, strangers,
our lives bookends, and all the little things that have happened
since then that we call life and history and memory, and all
the deaths, and all the sufferings and inequities and terrible
losses, and yes, the justices, too, no matter how small, we
cannot forget them. It is at our peril that we forget them. And
this man, this artist with the evening blue palette that matched
the color of the night air outside that Madison café when I was
22, he and I and our imaginations are as one and for that I am
deeply appreciative as it makes it possible for me to know life
has gotten better for me. At least the nightmares ebb and flow
now, I have some respite, the peace of his painting and the
peace of my memory of that evening, as if I am there now, a
spirit, flying above, hovering over that young woman, so alone,
so tired, such shock pervading her mind – I am there with her,
whether she knows it or not. That connection is my brain in all

its plasticity growing again, rebuilding, rekindling neurons to ease the pain, the loss, the terror, to connect one split self with another, right to left, left to right, to be less split, less fragmented, more whole, in my mind and memory, more human, not less than an object, not beneath an Orangina bottle, not a throat stuffed with penises, making me less communicative than a bottle, cursive writing generated by a computer, chosen by a graphic designer, stamped on paper, spit to glass with glue, read by many, thought about by few, but at least read.

And that connection between our selves and our imaginations seems almost sacred to me as I sit in a small town I hate, lonely and alone, the dark evening rising up out of the ground, tenuously employed, unsure of what to do next, riddled with weeks of flashbacks like the stop signs shot at on country roads, bent, flayed, holed, but less so now than then and less so now that I have written this and felt those connections, deeply and fully comprehending the power of art, of representation, of passing along, of giving, of imagination, of communication, of extending beyond the boundaries of self and time and space to connect in a meaningful way with another, with another self, with myself, with the blues and reds of a Parisian moment so long ago painted on a canvas by one now dead. But in death there is life and in life there is death.

Pornography is not really death, although some die from it. With death comes mercy and release. When you become pornography and your heart does not stop and oxygen continues to cascade through your bloodstream there is no mercy. There is no transformation into a delicate, shimmering spirit bird. There is only forgetting and moving on, as dead as you are, as best you can. Or there can be remembering. But if you remember, go back to the horror, there are raw loops of pain, photos of welts, of debasement so extreme many will not believe and most will not care. If you look to others you might not make it, but if you look to yourself, that girl you were, ripped anus, semen coated mouth, the one pinned to the stinking floor by pain and exhaustion and despair, and you strike a deal with her, no one will or can do this for you, and no matter how terrible the day or how splendid, you are alive and that is a gift, to be grateful for, though you may not be able to feel that or know it. No one knows how long you will have this life in this particular form and way and possibilities, so you strike a deal, go back and find that girl, make a pact and that pact is you will help her and she will help you, then you can make it, split apart, the two of you can come together, because her body continued, the oxygen pumped, even if her mind stopped, even if time and place stopped, she survived, her body became yours, and now you can survive too.

And that's how it works, this life, this survivorhood. It's a crapshoot. A minefield. A car pelted by plate-size rocks that keeps on running. One second you're an adult on your way to present at a conference, the next you're 30 years back. It's that moment on your walk from the gas station to the car when your eye catches, fleetingly, the sun strike the side of your car at just the right angle releasing thousands of light particles from stars a billion light years away into the atmosphere, your atmosphere, your eyes, your brain, stitching together nanoseconds of green hummingbird glory.

Christine Stark grew up in Minnesota. Her writing has been published in numerous anthologies and periodicals. Her first novel, Nickels: A Tale of Dissociation, *was a Lambda Literary Finalist. She is a co-editor of* Not for Sale: Feminists Resisting Prostitution and Pornography *and a co-author of* Garden of Truth: The Prostitution and Trafficking of Native Women in Minnesota. *In high school she was an All-State athlete in soccer and played college soccer in the Big Ten. For over twenty-five years she has been a grass roots activist and speaker. Currently, she teaches writing at a community college and university in the Twin Cities. She is studying for a Masters in Social Work and in her spare time runs, writes, draws, and spends time with friends. Christine has American Indian and European heritage and lives in Minneapolis with her partner, April, and their dog and cat. For more information: www.christinestark.com.*

And They Call This 'Sex Work'?

Simone Watson

The massage parlour's reception was clean, almost stark. White walls and one tasteful rug on the floor, a sofa, green plants in the corners, and a shelf full of expensive herbal teas. A brass plaque with a buzzer adorned the door on the ground floor of a business building right in the middle of the city. The johns were directed to an apartment one floor below a penthouse where the madam lived. The adjacent apartment was where we, 'the girls', stayed, until an intercom buzzed one of us from across the hallway for a 'client'. As the 'nice girls' – also known as 'sheep brains' by the madam – we wore white uniforms, minimal makeup, and clear nail-polish. Under the uniforms was the lingerie the men were anticipating when they got us into the room. There was no lining up in a row for the johns. They didn't even see us before we were called. The madam had a keen sense for what type of girl a john wanted and she was rarely wrong. If you did well, you got a regular. I soon realized they made up any image for us that they liked. As a thin brunette, I was also sometimes referred to as 'voluptuous', or a 'sexy red-head', or any number of stereotyped combinations they liked once we were in the room alone together.

Inside the rooms, and in contrast to the fresh reception, red and gold dominated the walls. Ornate mirrors gave the man a view of me from almost any angle. Each room had a sparkling ensuite which we cleaned after every client used it. First, when he arrived, and always before he left. We straightened ties, we made sure there was no trace of us on him. That was called being professional. We had Dettol to remove every trace of him we could.

I hated those mirrors. It wasn't just hard looking in the mirror at the end of the day for 'moral' reasons, it got to the point, within only a few weeks, that it was hard to identify myself. Being told I was tall, short, petite, buxom, red-haired, or a dark temptress all day by different men is a strange part of being prostituted. It may seem like a small thing, considering the repulsion I felt actually having sex with these men, but the mirror baffled me in this way, and I avoided it except to quickly tidy my hair, or check my make-up. It was functional, as mirrors are supposed to be, but I couldn't see who I was looking at.

While there was no expense spared on making the sex rooms decadent, and the reception expensively understated, cheap lubricating oil was used. More than twenty years later I am nauseous at the scent of baby oil.

When young men came in, I was acutely aware that I was the same age, and probably no more or less attractive than any of the young women they were dating, or would be interested in as a girlfriend. I was also aware that because of where I was, the idea of me being their friend, girlfriend or even fellow student, never entered their heads. The older men were mundane creeps, the young men rude, brash and conducted themselves as though I were an anthropological subject – at the same time, of course, they, like the old creeps, wanted the sex.

I started benzodiazepines the first moment I could get to a doctor for a script after my first day. Panic attacks were a constant plague and while we were not allowed to drink at work, I made up for it at home. I spent the money I earned as quickly as I could – on books, gifts for friends, anything that would make me feel better momentarily. I was a generous friend to have at that time. I admit enjoying that. I also admit that the car I was saving for never materialised, the down payment on a house never happened, the trip overseas remained just a dream. My university degree was repeatedly postponed because mentally and emotionally I was wiped out and a world apart from anything as useful, or as normal as, university. But is this all there is haunting me from my time in prostitution? Does it sound so bad?

I want to tell you a little of what it is like to be in prostitution and to be a prostitution survivor. As you've heard, I worked in 'higher-end' legal and illegal brothels. I was in the 'safer end' of the industry. I did street prostitution only once. Sometimes I wonder which is worse: the prostitution I endured – which I insisted was my 'choice,' a requisite of the 'job' – or having to listen to people defend it now. The prostitution itself – the men, one after the other, after the other, after the other, with their sad and lonely stories (but they wanted the sex), with their entitlement (they had a right to the sex), their hostility (they demanded the sex), the violence, (they paid more to hurt me for sex or just hurt me in the course of it). All men from different walks of life who believed they had a right to me because, well, I was there. On top of me, inside me, around me, touching me, grabbing at me, trying to kiss me, ignoring me if I was exhausted or upset and doing it anyway, some even apologising to me, but doing it anyway. Some complaining about me (oh and I suffered for that!) but coming back to do it again anyway, or finding another woman who hadn't forgotten to take her valium that day like I had – but who had just enough valium to dissociate but not look like she had, and most importantly, remembered to smile.

And they call this 'sex work'?

Attempts have been made, overwhelmingly now by the pro-prostitution lobbyists, to make this a term of dignity for the prostituted. However, whose dignity does it really serve? We are prostituted. The word is ugly and visceral. Put simply, it is truthful. This is why the pimps and johns don't want us to use it, and why the general public may not want to hear it. We do not owe dignity to the pimps and johns.

Yes, those memories linger whether I am meeting with politicians, or trying to be heard among the cries of 'sex worker rights' in the media. Or the intellectuals who calmly look at me as an interesting subject – who view it all as a sociological phenomenon of interest. Rather than violation. Rather than agony. Rather than urgency. And when travelling all the way, with the resultant PTSD, to meet politicians in my own or another state in fear and desperation that another generation of human beings will endure what I went through, and telling them I am a survivor. Then going back to a hotel room to sleep and being woken several times sweating and suffocating. Feeling weights on me. Crying, then feeling stupid. Checking the internet for news from home and finding another person telling me they hope I die and that I am feminist scum and a man hater and too ugly to fuck. That I needed to get raped and that would sort me out.

This is my life. Would I do this if I thought prostitution was just another job I once had? If being prostituted was 'sex work'? It costs money to travel even when almost everything is paid for. Having done it at least nine times last year, I often risk losing my rented home, in one of the few places I feel vaguely safe, because I 'chose' to risk it (sound familiar?), just for the opportunity that someone, anyone, who has sway, might listen: I mean really listen. Not listen and put it in the 'opinion' basket. Not listen and say that full decriminalisation is somehow bringing us into the 21st century when it is the most oppressive form of sex inequality on the planet. Not listen and then ignore the truth about New South Wales, Victoria and Queensland, as well as Germany, the Netherlands and Brazil. Not listen and then give free rein to the pimps, procurers and profiteers, the very ones who made their fortunes off my body and stole my life away. This is the life I have now. Writing emails and going broke, telling people I was in the sex trade, breaking it to my family. Because, like the other women trying to get people to understand what prostitution really is, I care about my life, and I care about other women. I am hoping that you will listen.

Simone Watson is an indigenous woman living in Western Australia, and the Director of NorMAC (Nordic Model in Australia Coalition). See <http:// normac.org.au/>

Incest Was the Boot Camp for My Prostitution

Jacqueline Lynne

If ever I am asked what is the one moment of my feminist life of which I am most proud, I would say, without a doubt, it is the moment in which I drew a deep breath, mustered up courage, and spoke up from the inside out; the moment when the personal became political. My story of surviving male sexual violence is not unique. Countless Indigenous women have survived this same violence. Tragically, countless other Indigenous women have not.

I know the things that have hurt me most in my life, as a Metis girl growing up in Canada, have happened to most other Native women and our loved ones. In telling my story, I hope you will gain a deeper understanding of the extreme levels of male sexual violence directed towards brown women and girls every day. I also hope, after reading this, you will be spurred to action. I ask you to join with Indigenous Women Against the Sex Industry (IWASI) in our fight for freedom, and for the re-instatement of our full rights as human beings.

It is impossible to tell you my life story so I'll give a few snapshots to show how I got 'groomed' for prostitution in my home, and how my experiences of being prostituted mirrored my experiences of being sexually abused. And then how I got out of prostitution. I will also discuss a pioneering country that fused political hope with political will to stop male sexual demand for prostituted women.

I am a proud Metis woman descended from the Cree Nation on my mother's side. Originally, my family was from the Red River Settlement, but we fled west to South Saskatchewan during what is known to my people as 'The Reign of Terror', and we settled around the Fort Qu'Appelle area. My mom was born and raised in Regina. During World War II, she moved to Vancouver. After overcoming her claustrophobia (she felt the mountains were hemming her in), my mom fell in love with the west coast. So she stayed, and that's how I came to live here.

It's no accident I look white. My grandma wanted her future children to not suffer the racism she experienced growing up Native on the prairies. So, she had white men's babies. These babies grew up and they had other white men's babies, too. So, I look white because of multiple generations of breeding-out which is nothing more than the slow genocide of my people. My grandmother hated the Indian blood in her – that's no accident, either. That's racism's intent. My mom tried to turn around the tide of generational internalized racism. She told me stories of our culture, and of our Nation's hero, Louis Riel. She told me to be proud of who I was, and of our history as Metis people. I was proud until other kids started name-calling. I can still hear my mom saying, "Never be ashamed of the Indian blood running in your veins, my girl!" Too late, it had only taken one humiliation by my peers to silence me for decades. I have had the privilege of 'passing' as white all my life. I've been invited to laugh at racist jokes, or to complain about 'how good the Indians got it'. When challenged, I'm usually made to feel as if I'm the problem. I'm told "it's just a joke," or "I'm way too serious," or some such drivel.

When I was a toddler, my mom married a man, a very violent man. He was a head-injured ex-professional boxer who loved alcohol, and hated women. He beat my mom. He beat my brother. He beat our animals – some to the point of death. I was told that I 'got the better end of the stick' compared to my brother because I didn't get beaten. For years, I believed this family lie – I needed to. When drinking, my stepfather's violence was especially brutal. He and my mom drank a lot. When I was three we lived in a house on the corner of Jackson and Hastings streets. One day I was outside playing when I heard the screen door slam. I looked up to see my stepfather coming down the stairs with a German shepherd pup lying limp in his arms. My stepfather seemed dazed and didn't notice me. I watched as he walked over to the garbage cans by our fence. He dumped the puppy into the garbage. I think a vital part of me went into the garbage can that day. Our animals cowered. We all cowered. Looking back, I view my childhood home as a war zone. My brother was my protector and my refuge.

My mom left this first stepfather when I was eight. Years later, as an adult, I asked my mom how she worked up courage to leave. She told me of one instance when she and I were lying in bed together, and I said, "Mom, I'm afraid if you don't leave Daddy, he's going to kill Donnie." Donnie is my brother. Shortly after separating, my stepfather paid mom this compliment: "Verna, you're one tough cookie. Every other woman I've ever lived with is either dead or in a vegetative state!" This is the type of fear I lived with growing up – knowing me, or my brother, or my mother, could be killed. This fear of being killed is very real for Native women and children.

When I was ten another violent man entered our lives. He was my third stepfather. We moved to Terrace. One day my brother came home from playing hooky, yet again. Our new stepfather knew because the school had called. He beat my brother so bad that he ran away. At the age of 12, in the middle of a Terrace winter night, he hitchhiked to Vancouver – never to return. He had taken his last beating. My stepfather issued my mom with an ultimatum: choose between me, or your son. This was a calculated step in a series of steps strategically orchestrated, over time, to gain sexual access to me. My mother chose my stepfather. She lived to regret her decision for the rest of her life.

As you can imagine, by the time my third stepfather entered my life, I was not a trusting girl. It took him two years to win me over. With my trust gained, he started to groom me. There were so many times I was left alone with him. I didn't know I was being snared. I craved healthy male parenting – it had been sorely missing from my life. He knew this, and he used it to his advantage. In other words, I was a sitting duck for his abuse. His 'affection' grew increasingly sexual over time. I was scared. I was confused. I didn't know what to do or who to turn to. Sexual abuse was not talked about in the 1960s. I sure couldn't tell my mom. I'd break her heart with that kind of news. Even if I had told her, maybe she wouldn't have believed me. Maybe she would have given me away like she had my brother. Our family would have fallen apart for sure.

My solution to all of these fears was to take myself out of the picture. I asked if I could go to a private girls' school outside of the city. That way I'd be out of harm's way. My heart sank when I was told I couldn't go. I lived with a growing sense of impending doom.

From ages ten to 12, my stepfather worked on me. He gave me his time and his attention. He showered me with gifts and affection. He told me he had a special love for me that the rest of the world wouldn't understand. In fact, he could go to jail for how he felt about me. I was 13 and starting grade eight when my stepfather told me he had to have me. I felt trapped, defenseless. One morning, while lying with my stepfather, he aroused me. It confused and frightened me – I had never experienced this arousal, ever. In an effort to stop him, and to tell him what I needed, I sat on the edge of his bed saying, "I don't want you to love me like this. I want you to love me like a father." He said, "I do love you like a father, but a stiff prick has no conscience." With his one comment, rape was to become both a synonym for love, and a blueprint for sex.

Another time, when lying with him in his bed alone, he was naked. At one point, he put his leg between my thighs. My body responded again, only this time, stronger. I felt utterly overwhelmed, I felt like my body was betraying me, and I didn't want it to. I didn't want him to do what he was doing to me. The only way I could make him stop was to not feel anything. I sensed a click in my head. Then I froze. I thought, "You can do what you want to me. I'm not going to let my body respond any more. I won't feel anything. I won't be here." I dissociated.

The day of my first rape, my stepfather carried me in his arms, 'over the threshold', to his bedroom. I was terrified. My body stiffened as he laid me on his bed. My closed legs were my only resistance. He pried them open, and he raped me. I felt the physical pain of my hymen being broken, but the rest of me was numb. Afterwards, he held me close, and told me he loved me. I remember standing in the shower, in a state of shock. I looked through the open bathroom door to see my stepfather standing naked in his bedroom. In that split second, with my blood flowing down my legs, my world as I knew it was shattered.

For the next four years my stepfather raped me every chance he got. I was his captive 24/7. He trained me to please him. His abuse of me came shrouded in 'romance'. I became his girlfriend, and his rapes only proved how much he loved and desired me. Over time I began to believe that sex was really all I was good for.

When I was 16, I became pregnant for the second time by my stepfather, but this time I went to full-term and gave birth to a daughter. I gave her up for adoption. Her adoption papers did not show her Native ancestry – I was advised by the hospital social worker that my baby would have a hard time finding a family if I mentioned she had any Native blood in her. Today, my daughter knows she's Metis, and she's proud of it. When my daughter was 21, we both placed ads in the same newspaper looking for one another. A savvy typesetter placed our ads together, and shortly thereafter our reunion began. Recently, she's begun learning Cree. So much for trying to erase the red skin! She is the only beauty I can make of what happened to me.

Andrea Dworkin once said that incest is the boot camp for prostitution. Deep in my bones, I know this to be true. I was my stepfather's fuck-doll – albeit, a frozen one. I moved in all the right places, I said all the right things. I moaned. I groaned. I gave sexual performances worthy of Oscars. I told my stepfather how good a cock he had every time he raped me. He trained me for every trick I would turn in my life. All those men needed to be reassured that their cocks were the very best, too. Do you have any idea of all the orgasms I've faked in my life? Countless! At what cost to me? It's inestimable.

The first trick I turned was old, fat, and white – just like my stepfather. Turning this trick was no different from being raped by him. I performed. I did all the things to this trick that I had been trained to do to my stepfather. Within minutes, it was all over. I left the room with money in hand. I thought this was 'easy' money. I felt free, unencumbered. I had a sense of pseudo-sexual empowerment. At least I didn't have to pretend I was in love. I was not trapped in an ongoing abusive relationship, or so I thought. After decades of help from trauma counselors, I have come to understand that every trick I turned re-enacted my stepfather's rapes. I've been raped repeatedly, in my home, and in prostitution. I started doing heroin to cope with the pain of living in a world that had reduced me to being every man's fuck-doll.

The last trick I turned was in December 1972. While sitting in a bar I swallowed a handful of pills. Time to go to 'work', I thought. I was no longer able to turn tricks unless I was high. It was a dangerous thing to do, but I didn't care anymore.

As I was leaving the bar, a trick came in. He and I negotiated. As we were making our way to his hotel room, I slipped on the ice. Down I went. Not once, not twice, but three times. I tried, but I couldn't get up. Immediately, my winter boot started to swell. I asked the trick to flag me a cab. I told him it was only a sprain, and that I'd tend to it when I got home. He told me it wasn't a sprain, it was broken. He knew because he was a first-aid attendant in a logging camp, and he had seen such things before. He seemed genuinely concerned. I couldn't bear weight, so he helped me to his room. The pills I had taken quickly wore off and I was in great physical pain. But as soon as we got to his hotel room, it became clear the trick had no intention of calling an ambulance. He started to run a bath instead. Then he started to undress me. I couldn't fight. I couldn't stand. I couldn't run. I begged. I pleaded. I cried for him to let me go. My protests, my tears didn't matter to him. I didn't matter to him. What mattered most to this trick was his erection. All I was to him was a dirty whore who needed cleaning up before raping. He helped me into and out of the tub. He helped me to his bed. He raped me. Then, he called his father. He laughed and joked with his dad about what he had just done to me. After dressing me, he helped me to the lobby. I was relieved to be alive, and thankful that he had *only* raped me.

I had broken my ankle and was in a non-walking cast for five months. After being discharged from the hospital I never returned to the streets. I couldn't see myself turning tricks on crutches, especially after what I'd just been through. That's how I got out of prostitution. In 1972 there were no exit programs to leave prostitution. There still are no comprehensive exiting programs in Canada today. I crawled out of prostitution, transferred my heroin addiction to alcohol, and muddled into mainstream society as best I could – hiding a shamed, and splintered self. How many other Native women crawled out like me? How many didn't make it out? The numbers are too high to count.

Twenty years later, I began volunteering at a drop-in center for prostituted women. I was shocked at what I saw. Most of the women in the room were of Native ancestry, and most of them looked like death camp survivors. Why were so many brown women in this drop-in center, devoid of the basic necessities of life? Why were so many here on these streets of Canada's poorest postal code? This question haunted me. It would become my research question when I went back to school.

In 1998, I learned that Sweden was about to enact groundbreaking legislation. Sweden was the only country in the world, at that time, which said prostitution was not 'work'. Instead, Sweden viewed prostitution as one form of male sexual violence, on a continuum of male violence, directed toward women and girls. Sweden wanted the violence that is prostitution to end. The whole aim of this approach was to create Sweden as a zero-tolerance zone. The law, in combination with public education, awareness-raising campaigns, and a whole range of preventive and tertiary social supports (such as affordable housing, medical and dental care, trauma counseling, employment training, and child support) sought to create a society where women and girls could live lives free of all forms of male sexual violence.

In reading my story, it is my hope you will understand the connections between incest and prostitution. Indigenous women here in Canada and throughout the rest of the world know that incest truly is boot camp for prostitution. We do not want sexual subordination – we want sexual freedom; we do not want defilement – we want dignity.

Jacqueline Lynne is a social worker based in Vancouver and co-founder of Indigenous Women Against the Sex Industry. She has co-authored a range of research articles on the topic of Aboriginal women and prostitution. She is a contributor to Not For Sale *edited by Christine Stark and Rebecca Whisnant, (2004).*

WARNING:
Prostitution Destroys
Your Soul

Geneviève Gilbert

I was a shy young girl. My gymnastics training helped me beat the boys at sport. I loved drawing and everything creative. Raised Catholic, I was gregarious and a book lover. I didn't 'choose' prostitution: a mixture of the culture I lived in during the 1990s, 'sex-positive' feminism and a longing to be loved by my biological papa who had abandoned my siblings, mother and me, chose it for me. Poverty chose it for me. Anger chose it for me. Wanting to be loved chose it for me.

I fooled myself into believing that if I was having sex, then I was being loved. With this faulty thinking, my secret transition to prostitution was relatively easy. Before entering prostitution I could go clubbing, pick up any man I wanted and get my sex fix. So I thought if I could have one-night stands and 'friends with benefits', why not be paid for it? I was going to make all the men pay for the child support money my father never provided. If I couldn't sue the Canadian government for failing to track down *mon papa*, I would make all taxpayers pay for it. Sex became not only a substitute for love but a way of exacting revenge for the faults of my father.

Yet in making men pay to use me, while thinking I had the upper hand, I allowed them to destroy me, to degrade my desire for real intimacy and to sacrifice a decade of my life that

I could have instead spent as an emerging painter, editor and video artist.

I had not heard of prostitution until I was 18. A French girl I befriended in the Quartier Gay of Montréal confided that she had done it a few times to pay bills. I clearly remember the moment, sitting with her in the front seat of her beige Lincoln Continental. I felt deeply sad and shocked. She looked fragile and lonely yet I wasn't able to be of any help to her. Worse, I was to follow her down this destructive path, justifying it as being fearless and daring – aren't artists supposed to be open to everything?

Over the course of my hidden life in prostitution I had flashbacks about my father's behaviour. Once, when I was about seven, I had looked inside some black plastic bags in our basement, hoping they might contain a present for me. Instead I was confronted with photographs of men and women doing things I didn't quite understand. I had stumbled on my father's secret stash of pornography.

When I was eleven, my father boasted on a visit with us that he'd had sex with child prostitutes from the Caribbean and South America. He reminded us that there were children in worse situations than us; that we would be doing all right without him and without his money. We had the pension, after all.

His statement about using child prostitutes confused me. I had not yet had sex and didn't really know what sex was. Similar to many Québécois people who want to avoid the harsh Canadian winters, he lived in Miami, Florida for half of the year. This state and city are the hottest hubs for sexual trafficking in the USA. It was much later when I already was in prostitution that I remembered the inappropriate content he shared with his innocent daughter. Maybe I reminded him of a child he had sex with. What a scary thought!

My mother mentioned to us that my father had, in a drunken rage, threatened to kill us all. Many times. In the early 80s, there was little media debate about domestic violence and words such as 'alcoholic', 'drug addict' or 'violent' were not part of my mother's vocabulary. But my father was all of these. But this did not quell my desire to please him, nor dampen the pain I felt after he left us.

During the completion of my Master's Degree research project in Interactive Media in Montréal – in debt, disillusioned and unhappy about the job prospects for women in the competitive world of IT and programming – I called an escort agency. My thoughts were: maybe I didn't have to have sex? Maybe I could just take part in a staged romantic dinner for lonely men, and fake a girlfriend experience where only conversations took place? I was good at that, talking. I longed to learn English by travelling or studying overseas and I needed money.

I met with the owners of the escort agency at a secluded train station. That first night I was put in a white, spotless van to be driven to men's houses or hotels. My first client pounded me for two hours without looking me in the eyes. *Sans-arrêt*. It was at his house in a leafy suburb of Montréal. I was left alone with him until the driver from the agency came to pick me up. It was my experiment as an artist: an *in situ* performance. It was the start of the performance of my life: my demise, my double-life and secrecy surrounding illicit sexual transactions.

That summer, I made CAD $20,000 offering my body as a 'ripe cherry' – as I wrote in my notes at the time – and then left the gritty, unforgiving, unkind world of visual arts in Montréal to study in Melbourne for a year. My dream of escaping Canada and learning English was coming true. I imagined that Australia was going to transform my life. What I didn't know was that unhappiness would follow me … until I found new hope in God.

After I finished a multimedia degree in Melbourne I tried to find a job in my field. It was extremely competitive and

I felt at a disadvantage as in my whole life I only had part-time jobs as an arts teacher, museum guide and a two-year position as a fundraising coordinator at my university. I finally managed to be selected for a one-week training program, but a mobile phone and a car were required. What was I going to do? I walked to an Internet café and typed into the search engine: 'escort agency prostitution Melbourne'. Three days later, I started day shifts selling my body for money. Again.

So within a year of arriving in Melbourne, I was back in prostitution. The lure of a high-class lifestyle was strong. Men were ready to pay prostituted women hefty amounts of money and coming from a life of material poverty as I did, that held its own attraction like sweet lollies to a child. My plan was to pay off my university debt through prostitution just for a short while and then run my business. Leaving prostitution afterwards is another story … it became impossible. It was not so much about financial need; it was how the money made me feel. I was still compensating for being abandoned and rejected by my father and for being bullied at school for my shabby clothes. I thought I was getting revenge on all those who had wronged me. If only they could see me now in my designer clothes!

I got what I had never had by way of material things. But I lost so much of myself.

For the next seven years 'I put on my face' – the expression us 'girls' used when we applied our make-up before our shift – my wig, and my personae. I was Jane, then Paris, Marina, and Trinity. I had acts I would charge extra for, and outfits to help with the fantasy the punters were buying.

We lied to our friends and family about what we did. I ran a real web and graphic design business. As soon as a contract was completed and I had no further work, I was back at *The Boardroom.* What a hypocritical name to suck all of us in.

If RhED, Scarlet Alliance, Swop or SIN were representing 'sex workers' in Australia and safeguarding our rights, then why didn't they tell me about the dangers of 'sex work' within the five-star brothel in South Melbourne I was sub-contracted to? Did any of these organisations provide me with this information? Did they offer me exit programs between 2001 and 2010? *Pas du tout!* Melbourne's first state-funded exit program was launched in 2010 just as I was leaving the industry. I was one of the first to successfully complete it with a wonderful social worker who took care of me. But how ashamed I felt to need a social worker! Prostituted women always think that they have it all together and do not need help. I certainly thought I was on top of the world. I didn't know we had the right to receive accurate information about the 'job' and its consequences.

The 1994 Victorian *Sex Work Act* states that assistance should be provided for "organisations involved in helping sex workers to leave the industry" and for "the dissemination of information about the dangers (including dangers to health) inherent in sex work, especially street sex work." But I never heard of any assistance offered to exit prostitution during my seven years at the legal Melbourne brothel.

I had to sign a lousy three months' contract requiring us to behave and not take business outside of the brothel. We even had to pay a $5 administration fee for signing this contract. What a joke.

Brothels look like nightclubs where popular music is blasting interminably on repeat. No place for classical tunes in there. Trust me, this does your head in. There is porn on flat screens around the lounges day and night. I felt sorry for every one of us having such an emotionally tough role in this forced theatre of the absurd, being touched by strangers and fulfilling the schoolgirl fantasies of deranged clients. It was so depressing and I had to get out! Yet I could not separate being prostituted from my life any more. Not on the inside of me, not in my head, not in my heart. The spiritual damage was endemic.

Even when I tried to dissociate during those countless paid rapes, I found it hard to separate what was happening to my

172

body from my real self. During the hour-long-bookings I could at least play gentle Québec singer Ariane Moffatt. I can't listen to the album *Aquanaute* now without it taking me straight back to the brothel's luxurious stone-walled room with state-of-the-art Jacuzzi, rounded bed and royal blue satin sheets which, like the designer clothes, were the trappings of luxury which competed with my growing sense of despair.

I also still have recurring flashbacks each time I go to the supermarket at night. There were so many times when after my shift I would dash to a store to fill up on groceries on the way home. This is PTSD and it may linger for the rest of my life. I learnt to live with those memories and accept them. I learnt to be gentle and patient with myself.

Most of us were warned to never give our phone numbers to clients. It didn't take long to break that rule. This means you end up on your own, managing men's every demand. Between 600 and 1000 men a year and many private bookings later, I wondered, hey, is this really 'a job like any other'? Am I really appreciated for giving so much of myself? Why am I doing this for men who see me as nothing but the entertainment they buy? I never dreamed of such a 'job' when I was little!

In prostitution, people are simply used. The money earned is an illusion of power. Real power is found in mutual respect, compassion and giving to others. These values do not exist in the world of prostitution. Giving a blow job to a man is not helping his sex addiction. The money men give us is not helping the disadvantage we face and which continued when we started prostitution. All people need to address women's and girl's oppression in our society.

A quiet mild-mannered Russian client asked me out during the first months when I 'worked' at the South Melbourne brothel. He said he wanted to help me get out of prostitution. I believed him. I had never been proposed to before so I thought, wow, this man must be really serious about me! Looking back I didn't think I had ever been that gullible. We got married three months later and I continued to earn a living from prostitution. I still thought this relationship was serious and only later realised he was marrying his fantasy – and becoming my pimp as well! Less than two years later, I had to seek support from a domestic violence service. Twice, he tried to kill us while behind the wheel. There are photos which still haunt me, of us smiling over a glass of wine at a Tasmanian winery. I had bruises on my arm; it was the day after the car accident we had on Christmas Day 2004. When, like a thief, I left our shared apartment overlooking palm trees on St Kilda beach, I fell into a deep depression and became suicidal. I had always taken pride in keeping fit and healthy, yet now even my health was being taken away by someone who had not only tried to kill me but insisted I continue to service other men.

In 2003 I began attending church. I knew it was wrong that I was in prostitution yet I could not confide to pastors. I felt no one could fully understand me and I didn't want to be judged. I stayed in prostitution but really wanted to get out. After many years living this heavy double-life, I grasped at every bit of hope I could find in people crossing my path. So I started dating another client who seemed to be a very spiritual and clever single Hong Kong businessman. He began attending my church and booked himself in to get baptised. He also promised a 32 per cent return on my investment in his currency exchange scheme. He delivered. I stayed away from prostituting myself for one year in 2007, living on the earnings of his exchange scheme.

However, he too had a violent temper. Our relationship began to be a constant drama: he yelled at me on Toorak Rd in front of gobsmacked passers-by after imagining I was having an affair. He wanted to pay me $10,000 to have a child, which was not a sign of love but of his possessiveness, using power over me just like he had done paying me for sex. He had escaped criminal charges – I learnt this from another client, a police officer who did an illegal search on him – for reselling computer equipment from the warehouse of a company he used to work for. A criminal. When a friend of mine who had also invested money in the same scheme blamed me and said I now should give him back the money he had lost, I fell into a state of total depression. For two weeks I drank alcohol every night. I could not sleep as all of this was doing my head in. I was waking up in the morning in a state of panic. I was imagining I was a mentally unwell patient in a psychiatric ward. I was beginning to be detached from myself. I could sense myself becoming crazy. I wanted to die.

'The subject' as I now called him – as even just mentioning his name made me nauseous – ended up disappearing with one hundred thousand dollars cash of my hard earned money.

I went back into prostitution as I was going to lose the small unit I had purchased. Three years of legal battle, many headaches and long, stressful days making frantic phone calls later, I managed to retrieve 87 per cent of my money. I even got to meet his real wife and kid. It was the shock of my life to learn from his partner in his ambitious IT networking start-up that "it might be good for me to know that his son goes to Scotch College." I didn't even know he was married! My psychologist told me his behaviour was similar to those who suffer from Borderline Personality Disorder. He was truly nuts!

During my years in prostitution the violence was sometimes underhand, sometimes direct. I was gagged, choked, gang raped, pushed, pulled by the legs, shoved, yelled at, threatened, lied to, anally raped, filmed and photographed naked with and without my consent. I had to put up with foul-smelling clients, obese clients with flabs of skins completely hiding their penis (and you have to find it), nervous, dangerous men on hard drugs, men who drugged me without my consent. For example – and this shows how naive I was – one of my regular clients liked to take cocaine in the room and constantly offered me some to get high with him. I always refused. But the shifty ones would put some powder on their tongue just before going down on me. The drug travelled through the skin into my blood vessels and a short time later I was not myself anymore. I lost control: the drug had kicked in. I felt nervous and stressed. I didn't like the feeling of derailment of my thoughts that these drugs often provoked.

I had sex with guys who were just out of prison or on remand: rapists, drug dealers, perpetrators of violent assaults with convictions and crimes committed that I had never heard of. I was such a 'good girl', ignorant and impressionable. Some didn't say why they came to a brothel but they boasted that they missed their missus. Some looked normal and fashionable, some looked as if they'd had a rough life. Hippy or high-on-drugs couples who wanted the lesbian experience were also sent my way from reception. I was taken to swingers' parties and had young, trendy, private clients. I took anything: what was important to me was that my act, each time, was convincing so I could get the most money from them.

I was abused by old men who took me on so-called 'sailing holidays' where I had to have sex all day long on a small boat. The dream beaches and pristine turquoise water I saw could have been imagined in my head. The unsavoury 'holiday' memories eclipsed the beauty of the nature I witnessed on the Great Barrier Reef. Big-shot millionaires who own famous Australian businesses ordered me around like a submissive dog in training. One had pancreatic cancer and could not ejaculate, but I still had to get him off. He needed so much arousal that he always asked for two women. I had to fake orgasms, fake love, be 'the girlfriend experience' those losers were longing for.

Losing seven years of my life being a hole for men's pleasure is violence.

I came down with many sexually transmitted diseases, including herpes, which I caught in 2005. It is incurable but thankfully I only have mild recurrences now. I also at some stage got hooked on sleeping pills, very common amongst us anxious prostituted women unable to switch off at night.

During my last year within this lifestyle I went to the brothel only about once a month. I didn't want to be there. I wanted to be dead rather then going there. And I hated myself for being unable to leave. But I could not find another source of income which made me enough money to keep my unit. I became an Australian citizen in 2007 but refused to go on the pension. I would not be doing what my father did and live at the expense of the state.

Eventually I found the strength to exit the industry. A large part came from finding God. The peace it brings is priceless. Still, regaining my integrity was a long process after transitioning out. Some people who claim to 'rescue' women from the sex industry to this day cannot understand how difficult it was for me upon exiting. And although my Christian friends have been a big support after I started sharing my story with them individually, not all Christians are able to forgive. I read that many people withhold the truth out of fear; to be killed, to be badly hurt, to lose something important. Remember why you lied the last time. Most people do. In prostitution, it is compulsory to the trade. We do not report when we are conned or violated – it is part of 'the job'.

I gained great strength when by accident I came across Sheila Jeffreys' book *The Idea of Prostitution* in 2009.[1] All of a sudden I understood the deeply dehumanising nature of the sex industry. Everything fell into place; Sheila's view of feminism was 'radical': she analysed the root cause of women's oppression.

Through secular organisations' support I found a mainstream job in 2009. Intense, regular prayer and counselling sustained me. 2010 was the year I became prostitution-free. When I finally managed to turn my back on prostitution for good, I was determined to help other women exit this vicious, life destroying industry.

---

1   *The Idea of Prostitution* by Sheila Jeffreys. Published by Spinifex Press, North Melbourne (1997, reprinted 2007).

I decided to start Pink Cross Foundation Australia, a charity whose volunteers visit brothels and offer support.[2] My healing continues as I assist others in their marathon effort to transition out of prostitution. It takes the strength and perseverance of an athlete to succeed. All successful athletes have a team behind them. I want to do that for prostituted people.

I realise my story may shock some and outrage others. But it can't be any other way. It was difficult to write down and reveal that prostitution had become such a big part of me. I would rather you knew about my art which I have kept going. In artspeak, I am conducting relational art and performative projects with the community. I have reinvented myself both as a social worker and an executive.

As I volunteer for Pink Cross Foundation, I speak to many former or current prostituted people and addicts as well as those who call themselves 'sex workers'. Some say they love their job. I caution them that it may look glamorous at first, but that the ongoing abuse of our body without consideration for our mind and soul is extremely destructive for a person's life. I want every woman leading this life to know that there is support – and other options – available instead of having to sell sex in order to survive. I want everyone to thrive. It is a challenge because we live in a porn-saturated world that is manipulating young boys and girls, robbing them of the understanding of the real meaning of love, sex and intimacy. Australia has some of the worse prostitution laws in the world. Legalising this industry oppresses women even more. I meet so many women who lost twenty years of their lives in legal brothels. Nothing on the resumé to find a job at forty something! Talk about disadvantage.

I am thankful that my mother continues to love me unconditionally. I owe her my good values, resilience, determination and creativity. I owe her my love for children, for disabled people such as my adorable sister Mélanie who

---

2   <http://www.pinkcross.org.au>

has Down's syndrome. To my dad, I say that I have forgiven him. This is why I can now thrive; before, hatred held me back. Since I accepted God as a father, his son Jesus is now my role model as he showed compassion to everyone: prostitutes, punters and pimps.

As for the 'adult entertainment industry', what is needed are practical solutions to the inherent violence associated with it. We need to aim to achieve a gender-equal society and the sex industry is the furthest away from equality for women. All citizens have to take part in this conversation and realise that this violence is happening in our midst, every day. Women and girls are trafficked right next door and we don't see it.

We need to shift our focus to the buyers and ask: Why do they buy? How can they break free from this entitlement to buy women? Without being paid, a woman would not have sex with them! We need to create support programs to change their attitudes (John's Schools like they exist in the USA). We have to expose how men use their financial power over women to get non-consensual sex.

Those who have been prostituted are in urgent need of our support including receiving therapy. This soul-destroying industry claims too many lives. It has to stop.

Geneviève is a visual artist. She founded Pink Cross Foundation Australia in 2010 and it became incorporated as a charity in 2013. She provides support to people in the sex industry wishing to leave.

I Was Worth More

Charlotte

"Bar staff wanted," the ad read. "I can do that," I thought. I'd been looking for a job for weeks and it didn't seem as though the search was going to end any time soon. I didn't have any experience behind a bar – not having my alcohol serving qualification made it difficult – but the ad assured me all training would be provided. My heart sank when I recognised the name of the bar – one of the local gentlemen's clubs in Queensland, Australia. "Don't be so fussy," my inner voice hissed. After all, I'd applied for close to a hundred jobs only to be met with a handful of generic, 'You're overqualified' replies. "You will probably get bored," they would say. Bored? When you need money to put food on the table, a job with a huge interest factor isn't high on the list of priorities.

I replied to the number listed and a few days later was heading to the interview. 5pm on a Tuesday afternoon – right after my weekly scheduled appointment with my psychiatrist. I didn't tell him where I was headed.

I arrived at 5pm on the dot only to be met with words that felt like a punch in the stomach – "We don't actually have any bar positions left, but we do have dancing positions if you want to try out for one of those?" Lightbulb moment – so that's how they lure girls in (there never were any bar positions, I later found out). "Sure," I replied. Why didn't I just say no and get the heck out of there? The truth is, although I was terrified, for the most part I didn't care. Using my body to lure a bunch of strangers to pay money for the privilege of looking meant nothing to me. I had no self-worth. From the ages of four through to seven I was the victim of commercial sexual exploitation – with a family friend pimping me out to his friends, strangers, and anyone else interested. Instead of learning that my body was private, mine, something special to treasure and look after, I learned that it was a commodity to be used exclusively for the pleasure of men in exchange for money or goods. A concept that even all these years later I was yet to unlearn.

Even as a small child I knew this was something to keep secret from my family. I didn't want to cause them pain. And the main abuser told me there would consequences for me, like killing my family, if I told them. He also told me everything that was happening was my fault, and my family would leave me if they found out, because I had 'been so bad'. I sometimes wonder if my family did actually know but didn't want to confront the bitter reality. They all know who I was abused by, though, I told them last year.

Just like cattle, those of us who had agreed to trial as dancers were paraded in front of the club owner, an old man in his 70s, in a private room at the back of the club. We were asked to take our clothes off and stand single file while he walked up and down the line, inspecting our bodies and interrogating us. He stopped in front of me: "What is your weight like at the moment?" I told him it was fairly stable and he responded by asking how quickly I thought I could lose another five kilograms. Many years into an eating disorder, the answer rattled off my tongue – "I could lose that in a couple of weeks." "You'll do," he grumbled. "Pick a stage name." And just like that it was done. I was hired. The rest of the night was largely a blur. Hair down, makeup on, kitted out in the highest pair of heels you've ever seen and a dress with so little material it hardly fit the definition. I was deemed ready to hit the floor and start reeling in the customers. Each girl was expected to go on stage and dance on the poles at the whim of the floor manager. The club had a three song rule – the first song was dress on, dress off during the second song and by the third song it was mandatory that you were dancing with all clothes and underwear removed (it was one of only a few 'full nude' clubs in the city). At the end of the shift I gathered my things and flew out the front door as fast as I could. Before I began the long train ride home I threw up several times – the result of having memories of my sexual abuse flood back and the copious amounts of alcohol consumed during the night. You'd be hard pressed to find a sober girl working at that strip club. As one of the dancers told me, "I couldn't do this job if I wasn't drunk."

I knew I wouldn't be returning to the club. I wouldn't be receiving any of the money I earned that night – pay was withheld from dancers until they returned to the club for subsequent shifts. I needed a job where I was more in control. Feeling trapped and defeated, I decided the only way to get myself out of financial difficulty was to return to what I had done all those years ago – selling my body. Trained to use my body from the age of four, it was something I turned to sporadically over the years, particularly as a teenager when I would trade sexual favours for money, alcohol, or whatever else I needed. It was a secret I had kept well-hidden.

It was then that I got into the world of 'web-camming' – being paid for performing sex acts live on video via the internet. Many people still don't know this world exists but it's a big industry with big money to be made. I really thought I was clever. I thought I had found the perfect job – I could choose the hours I wanted, remain apart from the customer through a computer screen and earn a large amount of cash in a very short time. I was so wrong. Sure, it was a great feeling being able to pay all my bills on time and have more than enough cash to splash around afterwards, but the damage began to show. It was only ever supposed to be a short-term thing – something to help me keep my head above water for a couple of months while I found another job. But I had no idea it would be so hard to walk away from. The cash – and the blackmail – kept me there for two years.

Who were the men who wanted me to perform sexually on camera? They were young single guys in their 20s and US soldiers on deployment. A lot of guys were in relationships or married – more than half. I seemed to get men mostly in the 30–50 age bracket. A few were quiet but the majority was very aggressive. I came across way too many men requesting I pretend to be their daughter, to dress and act like a young girl and call them daddy (I refused). One guy got me to write degrading words all over myself with a marker – whore, slut etc. He wanted me to hurt myself too. He and other customers threatened to expose me to family and friends if I ever stopped giving them what they wanted. Could they actually do that? I had taken all the precautions I knew about, but I was so young and naive and terrified of being caught out, not least of all because these activities were illegal where I lived. As the weeks passed by I fell further into a rabbit hole. Soon I was also making and selling private photograph and video collections along with used underwear and other item to clients who found me through third parties like Craigslist and Backpage.

Some local clients who had purchased video and pictures started harassing me to meet them in person. I decided to start work in a local 'massage parlour' – the ones operating under the guise of offering 'non-sexual massages' – what a lie. The parlour advertised me as aged 19 or 20 and, though I was older, that's what the customers believed – many thought I was in high school. The owners actually thought it was great for their business that I looked underage – they knew it would bring in a lot of customers. Every girl there offered sexual services for money, myself included. You wouldn't last long if you didn't. The clients knew what was going on, they went there wanting sexual services. No one requests you unless they can get their 'happy ending'. There are message boards where people discuss and rate local massage parlours (and in turn the parlours advertise their girls) and they don't want the bad publicity. A customer can easily go online and say 'don't choose this girl, she doesn't put out'. As the only Caucasian I was in high demand, even more so for my young age and even younger looking appearance. Many clients happily thought I was a minor.

Why didn't I just walk away? After all, no one was holding a gun to my head, right? But the gun doesn't always have to be physical. It can be psychological. And that is every bit as persuasive and threatening.

As a former victim of sexual abuse, at no time did it occur to me that I deserved anything better. The words of past abusers rung in my head – "this is all you are good for." Words I believed with every part of my soul. Threats of exposure, of arrest and jail-time, and the huge influx of cash, were other psychological chains that bound me to the sex work.

I did eventually make it out of the sex work industry – more than a decade after starting to prostitute myself casually. It certainly wasn't easy and even today I still have times where I think about going back to those jobs to 'just help me get through the next couple of months'. But I know now it is never a temporary thing. You don't walk away from these things so easily and you certainly don't walk away unscathed. In the end it was the love of my partner and best friend that helped me get away from that insidious world. Both of them are survivors of childhood sexual abuse and my best friend in particular has special insight, having worked in the sex industry for a long time.

I first thought that I didn't want to return to the massage parlour when I was on an extended holiday back home one Christmas. I confided in my best friend who told me how much her own life had improved since she had left the industry. She assured me that I deserved, and could achieve, the same level of happiness and freedom she had. Around the same time I began dating my partner. We had met many years earlier at university. I was upfront about my work in the sex industry. My relationship with these two very special people has allowed me to slowly learn that I have value and worth as a human being, no matter what I have or haven't done during my time on this earth. They have been patient and kind with me, taking the time to explain how and why I deserve to be safe and happy. They have helped me see that I am so much more than just my body and being able to trade sexual favours with men. That I am loved.

I made the decision to end all of my involvement in the industry. I still have a long way to go to recover not only from my childhood abuse but also from my time spent as a sex-worker, but I know I will get there. I am free now, and I will fly higher than I ever thought possible. To anyone reading this who is still involved in the sex industry – you are so much more than your body and your ability to provide sexual gratification. You are worthy, important and loved. You deserve so much more. The world is out there waiting for you. You will survive this.

Charlotte, 27, lives on the east coast of Australia. Since leaving the sex industry she has become a passionate advocate for other survivors of commercial child sexual exploitation (CCSE) and works to raise awareness about the increasing prevalence of CCSE within the Australian community. Through this work she has discovered a love of teaching and is currently completing tertiary study in Education.

Keep the Faith

Rebecca Mott

I am feeling lost,
     waiting to cry
I am an atheist,
     but my spirit is crying
I wake to my tears,
     move day-to-day in my tears
tears long hidden
     tears land in my stomach, frozen
tears of finding myself
     not understanding the route home
tears that know too much pain,
     too many ways to torture a prostitute,
tears of a body
     remembering what no-one should know.
These tears make me believe myself.
These tears are giving me back a faith.

I am confused
     not understanding how to be truly human
     by the simple ways to stay alive
     without constant reminders of a hell I have left.
I am confused
     when they say no harm is done to the prostituted
     rape is a crime,
     torture is a crime,
     lack of freedom is a crime,
     murder is a crime –
     but not when done to the prostituted.

I am confused by the acceptance of the term 'sex worker',
    it makes male violence ok
I am confused to come away from the sex trade,
    only to find that I am sub-human.

Confusion is the backbone of my fight for real change,
    confusion fuels my faith.
I am hurting from a past never forgotten,
    a present of fighting to stay standing up,
    a future that may be unreachable but so worth having.
I am hurting from having penises,
    objects, hands and mouths
    polluting all my body.
    Leaving no hole unfilled,
    no cell not invaded.
I am hurting from a past no one should know
    a past made of gang-rapes,
    of being alone with men who see nothing
    but an object to destroy,
    of wanting to die but fighting to stay alive.
I am hurting even now
    as my body vomits knowledge
    knowledge it must abandon
    must know to salvage some kind of humanity.
I am hurting with exhaustion
    carrying extreme trauma
    carrying so much poison
I am hurting as I dream of a future with no sex trade,
    a future where prostitution is forgotten,
    remembered only
    so as never to make that mistake again.
I hurt knowing it is beyond my reach.

My hurt is vital to my knowledge of my truths.
My truths feed my faith.

My faith is strengthened not weakened
by the truths inside my hurting.
This prose-poem is prayer to whatever my spirit is.
The prayer of an atheist is odd,
      but I am praying to push my spirit into never giving up
        when pain, grief and confusion is saying – Stop.
My prayer is entering where words have little or no meaning.
My prayer is sending slow and calm healing
      to all the pain and terror that punters put into me.
My prayer rises from grief
      sunk deep into my stomach,
      eases the constant pain inside my throat,
      reminds my heart can mend.
My prayer reaches to my teenage soul,
      my broken twenties
      holds those times without judgement,
      without frustration –
      only love that refuses to let go.
My atheist prayer is a gift and a prize
      for staying alive.
So as in my love of Northern Soul –
      I will Keep the Faith.

Rebecca Mott is an exited prostituted woman living in England. She writes a blog that she uses to express what it is to live with extreme trauma after prostitution, and to campaign for the abolition of the sex trade. She writes that it is a human rights issue, for the prostituted live in conditions of torture. She will never call herself a sex worker.

My Canvas, My Pain, My Healing

Suzzan Blac

I have composed a series of 42 paintings over a four-year period. The images depict my story of abuse. I painted them purely for myself. I needed to get pain and madness out of my head and onto a physical canvas I could see, something tangible, so that I could better process my torturous inner trauma. But, because sexual abuse and rape are so stigmatised, and because of shame, guilt, condemnation, isolation and abandonment, I hid my paintings for over a decade. In 2011, I decided to show them to the world. I realised that a contributing factor in the continuation of sexual abuse and rape is silence. Silence impairs victims and empowers perpetrators.

One piece portrays the time I was held captive by sex traffickers in 1977 when I was sixteen, after answering an ad asking for models. I was duped by a man claiming he owned a modeling agency in the UK. At the interview he gave me a contract that my mother had to sign, because I was a minor. She did so without question. She had taught me from the youngest age that my beauty was all that mattered. Though I grew up in abject poverty, I was dressed to attract attention and told I had to use my appearance to attract men. Within a week I left Birmingham and headed to London with this important and successful man. He was courteous, charming, kind, respectful and very flattering. He told me I was beautiful, photogenic and could make really good money in London and on the continent. I was really impressed and very excited.

I was also extremely poor, naïve and a victim of past child physical, emotional and sexual abuse. I was ripe for predators, and mother's parenting skills were faulty to the point where she had signed me away to a strange man without question. This wonderful man. This hoofed devil. He led me into the depths of absolute fear and vile depravity. No adult should experience that, let alone a child. I found myself captured inside a run-down, boarded-up old hotel, and in the presence of several men who reeked of malice and evil. Within an hour I was told to take my clothes off. I was then violently raped by the man who had brought me. While raping me he forced me to tell him I loved it. He then ordered me to get dressed. As I did so, he forced me against a wall and held a knife to my ribcage. Seething, he whispered, "I've killed bitches that misbehave before, you fucking hearing me?" As I begged him to please not kill me, he withdrew the knife, pointed it at me and burst into laughter: "You should see your face, it's priceless." I was then locked inside a small room with a bed. As my frozen, paralysed mind and body began to thaw, my emotions gave way. I curled up into the foetal position and broke into a million pieces. Later that night, one of the other men came into my room. He sat down on the bed and asked if I was okay because he had heard me crying. As I relayed what had happened to me, he lifted my chin so I could look into his eyes, as he quietly spoke to me, "You know, you look just like my dead wife, and I'm going to fuck every orifice that you have."

These rapes were my introduction to the terrifying, threatening and evil world of forced pornography and prostitution. I had no phone and no money. I didn't even know where I was. I saw five other girls, and I heard a lot more female voices. I called one painting 'Pornographic Meat' because that's how I and the other girls, who were also in this hellhole, were treated. We were like scared cattle held in an abattoir for human consumption. We huddled in the corner of a huge room after being ordered to choose some exotic lingerie from a large basket to put on prior to being filmed in a room full of men, video and lighting equipment, two Alsatian dogs and sex toys. We didn't talk to each other, we didn't even make eye contact or acknowledge each others' presence. We were frozen in fear, in time. We were locked inside of an outer shell of heavily made-up faces. We were no longer human beings. We were fleshed robots obeying our captors.

They told us to sit down on some filthy sofas next to a large coffee table that was covered in hard core pornographic material, which included children and animals. One of the men laughed and said, "We are going to watch a picture show, I'll go get the popcorn." As I watched in absolute horror at sadistic and animal porn movies, my mind began to give in. I had succumbed to whatever they were going to make me do, or do to me. They had already broken me, like an abused, captive animal. They were in control and all I could do at this point was to go through the motions and try to function in a sterile, detached and impassive way. I wasn't being brave or courageous, it was merely a case of having no choice. I had to do whatever they wanted or I could be killed. Although sometimes, when unwanted clarity intervenes and I became somewhat lucid in the reality of my predicament, I wanted so much to die. And, yet, in other moments, I truly didn't.

They ordered us to perform sexually in front of a video and a still camera. I tried to comply, like an un-dead actress, obeying an insane director's commands. At one point he said he wanted 'butcher shots' but I didn't know what he meant. He laughed and said, "You're meat! Open your fucking legs darlin'!" I hesitated, then tried for a while. But the utter degradation swallowed me up and turned me inside out. The tears flowed out, which enraged my captor to the point of whacking me around my head and whispering into my ear, "You know what will happen to you if you don't." I cried even more as he shouted and swore at me. Until, finally, like a demented diva, he threw his arms into the air and screamed, "FUCK OFF BACK TO YOUR ROOM!" I sat on my bed, smoking and rocking back and forth for hours, waiting for the next sick instalment.

So, here I was, a small, sixteen year old girl locked in a room where men would come to threaten, beat and rape me or take me to other men who would pay to rape me. My life had ended that first day, my mind had completely shut down. My free will had been ripped out of me. I would now do as I was told – without question. My despair was overwhelming. I prayed to God, but he wouldn't answer me. I prayed that I would fall asleep forever, but I kept waking up. I would awake to only to stare into the dead eyes of men who had no right to walk amongst the living.

I eventually escaped from the sex traffickers who had abused and exploited me, but my mind was still incarcerated inside the darkness of utter desolation. Riddled with guilt, shame and self-blame, I spiralled into drug dependency, anxiety, depression and attempted suicides. At 18 I sought medical help. One doctor offered Valium, another molested me. In the following ten years I suppressed my inner trauma, but it sometimes manifested in violent outbursts.

At twenty-eight, I gave birth to a baby girl. She gave life to me. My daughter was the catalyst for me to recognise my past abuse and understand that motherhood involved uncon-ditional love, devotion, nurture and protection. I married and had a second child. As a survivor, though, I still felt like an outcast – made to feel uncomfortable, strange, defective and dysfunctional. I worried about consequences and reverberations that could jeopardise myself and my children. An abused person should never have to hide their pain, anxiety and distress out of fear of being re-victimised.

In the years 2000–2004, I felt compelled to paint. It was an antidote to this 'psychological poison' that was slowly killing me. A decade later I finally brought them out of hiding and into the world. My images are a social message depicting the sexual conditioning and exploitation of women. They depict the moulding of young girls who are groomed to become mere ornaments and sexual objects to appeal to and gratify males. They also depict my demonic pornographic torture. Pornography is 'filmed prostitution'. Pornography fuels disrespect, degradation, subordination, oppression, privilege, entitlement, power and wealth, sexual assault, psychopathies and sexually motivated murders, and my paintings reflect this.

After I posted my paintings online I began to receive messages from other survivors. They said I was a voice for them, in their inability to express their own trauma and pain. They said I inspired them. The truth is, they inspired me. I was no longer silent. Now I was going to shout out about my abuse and the abuse of others. And, so, in these most fortunate days, when I am seated inside a large room of empty seats waiting for another group of social workers to arrive for one of my seminars about child sexual abuse and trafficking, I know I have completely turned my life around. I have turned all of my bad into good.

Suzzan Blac is an English surreal artist who paints images of physical, mental and sexual abuse. Her art is shown in galleries around the world. Her memoir The Rebirth of Suzzan Blac *was published in 2012 (Bettie Youngs Book Publishers, USA). Her website can be found at* <www.suzzanb.com>

COMMENTARIES

I Was a Pimp

Jacqueline Gwynne

I was a receptionist at a 'high class' brothel in Melbourne, Australia, for two years. My job title was 'receptionist'. I had a brothel manager's licence. But in reality I was actually a pimp. I had to sell women.

I suffered Post Traumatic Stress Disorder (PTSD) for a few years afterwards and was really angry at the world because the job forced me to dwell in the dark, seedy underbelly of life.

One of the main causes of PTSD for me was exposure to hard core porn that I could not escape. Shifts were 13 hours long, so that's a lot of porn. Porn wasn't just in the introductions area, it played on big screens in every room. The whole building was lit with red lighting which made it even more eerie and unnerving. I was quite oblivious to what was in porn because I had never watched it before then. It was violence against women on film where the women are verbally abused, degraded, treated roughly, choked, and their hair pulled. There were never condoms.

The brothel had a 'no drugs' policy but the reality was most of the women took drugs and had addictions to either street or prescription drugs. Ice was common; others took heroin. I saw many girls start in the brothel who were perfectly healthy, fit, happy and then quickly deteriorated in a matter of weeks, becoming very thin, withdrawn, sick, depressed and addicted to drugs. Drug dealers would come in pretending to be clients and then supply drugs to the girls.

It is not a nice job, certainly not glamorous like you see on TV shows like *Satisfaction* or movies such as *Pretty Woman*.

The women took drugs to survive the work, numb themselves and to forget what they did. I was studying at the time and needed work and couldn't find anything sustainable. My background is Visual Arts which is a very difficult field to get work in. Some of the other receptionists also came from an arts background. There is generally always work in the sex industry because it is awful and not many people want to do it. The majority of sex work is night shift. You don't socialise at the same time as people in the normal world.

Even though I was only a receptionist there is still stigma attached to it. My mother wouldn't talk to me about it and if I did tell friends or family about things that happened at work they would shut down and did not want to hear about it. I keep in touch with a few of the receptionists that I have become really good friends with. It's great to catch up because they are the only people I can talk to openly about what happened because no one else gets it. I haven't been able to keep in touch with any of the sex workers – their work environment is so extreme, many of them come from backgrounds of abuse and dysfunction and have major trust issues.

It has taken me a long time to recover from PTSD. I've always thought of myself as open-minded, streetwise and not easily shocked. But each shift there would be something that would have you thinking: WHAT? You are exposed to the absolute depths of human depravity. Stuff that would truly make your skin crawl and being completely sober made it all the more excruciating. Every night there would be an incident of abuse or violence. Girls were spat at, bitten, verbally abused and treated roughly.

When I started, I was pro-porn and pro-sex work. At first I thought it was cool and exciting. I had read many books and watched films about the sex industry. It is glamourised in the media. But, in reality, the men are mostly fat, ugly, mad, old, creepy, have poor social skills, very few sexual skills and appalling personal hygiene. They generally can't have normal relationships with women because of these reasons and they also have no respect for women. Any man that walks in to a brothel has no respect for women. I heard some revolting stories, one in particular of a guy with his pants filled with diarrhoea! I mean how on earth do you feel in the mood when your pants are filled with shit? The girl made him shower three times before she started the booking. Men who frequent prostitutes have a sense of entitlement. They feel entitled to abuse and use any woman, whenever they want.

To support these industries is to be in denial. The work chips away at you. At first I found it fascinating and exciting but it's like tiny pinpricks over and over that become deflating. No woman should have to resort to prostitution. Although some tell themselves it's a choice, it is more that they are in denial that is a survival strategy that gets you through the night. Another survival strategy is humour. Many of the women were hysterically funny and we'd get ourselves through the night by making jokes about it.

The main brothel that I worked at was just outside of the city centre. It was marketed and presented as a classy venue. The clients ranged from university students, international students, taxi drivers, business men, lawyers, tradesmen, retired men, drug dealers and musicians. The men came from different cultural backgrounds; there were a lot of Indian, African, Middle Eastern, Greek and Asian men. The majority of clients were white Australian men. There were religious men too, Catholics and Muslims. They came in dressed in plain clothes. I would check their identification details from their drivers' licences and you could see in their photos that they were religious men because of their head wear or a priest wearing a collar. I could tell that they looked really uncomfortable when I checked their details. The temporary marriage ceremonies that were annulled at the end of the booking were a practice of some Islamic men.

There were some men from certain cultures that the girls would refuse to be introduced to. They'd look at them through the security camera and I would have to tell the men that all the girls were busy. These men were considered to have no respect towards women and rough and aggressive, with 'octopus hands'.

The basic service was for sex, oral and massage. The way for the girls to make more money was from extras. Extras were services including anal sex – which no woman I met enjoyed – kissing, fantasies and perversions. Fantasies or perversions could include pissing, bondage and discipline, paedophile fantasies, lesbian double fantasies, stripping, lap dances, transvestites and any other weird request the client had. I had to explain the basic service to the clients and anything extra they would discuss with the girls.

Paedophile fantasies were the worst. There was this total creep who would get a girl to pretend she was his six-year-old sister. After such a booking the girl would be physically sick and had to go home.

Brothels in Victoria don't allow alcohol but you have no control over what goes on in the rooms or what clients bring in. Many of the men would come in drunk, especially on a Friday or Saturday night when I worked. The girls would meet them and it was up to them whether they wanted to go ahead with the booking. But when you're broke and your rent is due or you have kids to feed, you do what you have to do.

Introductions would usually take place in the 'porn room' or if it was a busy night in the lounge or by the pool table. I told the clients a bit about each girl, and what they looked like using descriptions like young, blonde, slim, large breasts, hot legs, petite, exotic, Asian, brunette, voluptuous, mature, sensuous, extroverted, wild and any other words that came to mind. To give them the impression that there were lots of girls to choose from, we'd make some up. Each girl has a working name, usually a flashy, tacky name drawing inspiration from porn stars, movie stars or models. These names are alter egos, not an alias to protect their identity as I first thought. They were like stage names to help them slip into character and escape themselves. Some guys would play with themselves as I was talking to them while staring at the porn. I'd break up large groups into smaller groups of no more than three at a time. Coordinating large groups of drunk men in a brothel is not easy.

Every room had a surveillance camera and I would watch from reception as the girls introduced themselves in the porn room. I could see the clients try and feel the girls up. If they decided to wait for a girl that was unavailable they would just sit and watch the porn. Guys would wait for a girl that didn't exist which was awkward for me as they could wait up to two hours. I'd see them with their hands down their pants on the surveillance cameras and I would go and interrupt them to ask if they wanted a drink. They had no clue that ten women would be laughing at them on a screen in another room. It was a really sleazy and intimidating environment, especially when I had several groups of bucks' parties, or 18th and 21st birthdays. Music was always pumping loud just like a nightclub environment so I had to yell to project my voice. I'm actually quite a shy and softly spoken person so it was way out of my comfort zone. I suppose I took on another persona as the madam/door bitch. After the girls had finished introducing themselves I would go back in and ask the clients which girl they would like to go with. If some girls hadn't had many bookings that night I would talk them up to persuade the client to go with them.

I've heard that most brothels have security or a bouncer but I was it! I was the manager, the receptionist, security, a pimp and the bouncer. I was only allowed to call the police if a client got angry about the service he received. I could have called the police numerous times, but abuse, intimidation and sexual harassment were all just part of the territory. The owner didn't want us calling the police. We were expected to handle it all on our own.

There were lots of weird prank phone calls. It is a very extreme working environment where you are subjected to sexual harassment all night. The phone is ringing constantly and I was expected to be a phone sex service provider. A game that some guys would play would be to try to persuade the receptionist to have sex with them. This would happen on most shifts.

The owner of the business was quite mad. There were surveillance cameras all around the place and he would sit in his Brighton mansion and watch everything that went on. Being watched like that is very unnerving and I could never fully relax. He could be very charming but I just never knew when he would snap and become aggressive so I was constantly walking on eggshells.

A male friend of the owner ran a business organising sex parties which were held in a large room upstairs. He'd arrive to greet the participants for the party which were scheduled to go for two hours and often only lasted an hour or less. People would sign up over the internet and pay a fee. There were couples that came along to the sex parties, some young couples, students, young professionals, tradesmen, middle-aged men. I had to let them in and show them where to go. They were probably quite surprised to find themselves at a brothel. I guess it looked like a hotel and a nightclub on the inside. Most of the time there weren't enough women so the sex workers at the brothel were invited and had to pretend they had signed up over the internet. The girls were paid to participate but were instructed not to let on that they were prostitutes.

One night there was only one woman and around ten middle-aged men at a sex party. They decided on a gang bang fantasy but the woman only lasted ten minutes because the men were rough, aggressive and unpleasant. She freaked out and literally ran out the door. I guess they didn't look like what she imagined. You'd never see the same people twice with the sex parties as many of them probably wished they just kept it as a fantasy.

At the brothel there was a woman who was really beautiful, intelligent and creative, but addicted to prescription drugs. She told me she would dissociate during her bookings. Having sex with men you don't want to have sex with was so unpleasant that she would leave her body to cope with the pain and trauma. She was one of the most popular girls there, but it all depended on her mood. If she was feeling low she could not disguise her anger and would get no bookings. Prostitution is all about being a good actress. The most popular girl at the brothel had the most beautiful natural long blonde hair (many wear wigs) and was a charmer with the clients, but she actually hated sex.

Another girl invented a fake career to tell her family because no family wants their daughter in prostitution. She built a website and had business cards printed with a pretend business name. There were some really intelligent, interesting women that ended up getting trapped in the industry because their partners had left them and they had to bring up children on their own. Most of them live a double life and don't tell their family or friends where they are really working. They'll tell them they are working night shift as a cleaner or something. The tragedy is that this job is something that you really need to talk about because it is so awful. This is why many women turn to prescription or street drugs. Living a lie like that must really mess with your head.

It messed with my head the way clients talked to me about the women. I'm sure they talked to the girls differently but they would complain to me about their 'quality', like they were slabs of meat. It would make my blood boil but I had to keep a smile on my face and be courteous to these men who were scum of the earth. They would complain that the women were too fat, too old, had hairy vaginas, didn't provide anal sex. The men would request exactly what they had seen in porn and wanted the girls very young and blonde. They would request to pay extra for no condom: that would happen every night. I have no idea if any girls did, there were rumours of it happening. When you haven't had a job all night, can't pay your rent, it's 4am and some guy offers you $500, what do you do?

I really liked a lot of the girls. Many are very intelligent and wise women. I would talk to them all the time, in between bookings. Sex work is not as lucrative as many would imagine. I was actually quite surprised that there isn't a lot of money in it, certainly not for the working girls. There were a few girls who would see up to ten clients a night but most saw two or three and it wasn't uncommon for girls to get no bookings at all. It would make me feel really sad for them, they would sit there for 13 hours and not get one job. Dating sites like Tinder have girls giving it away for free so guys don't need to pay for it. Also internet porn has guys just staying at home and masturbating.

Girls would come and go; some would only last one night. Some of the girls would work at other Melbourne brothels. There were girls that started out in stripping but actually felt safer and more respected in prostitution. In stripping they are among mobs of drunk men who yell abuse at them and sexually assault them. Stripping is more like porn on stage. They felt more in control in prostitution. There were women who also did escort work, they would try to talk it up and call themselves 'high-class call girls'. Escort work is actually more dangerous than street prostitution because girls were often trapped in strangers' houses with no escape. They are exposed to more violence, rape, abuse and drugging. They also have no idea what they will have to deal with when they arrive at the client's house. You never knew if there was just one man, or ten hiding in the next room.

Many of the women are really good actresses – they had to be – and had double personalities. To interest the men, they would have to be charming and happy so they would really play it up. You have to pretend that you like them, pretend that you are interested in them, fake that you are enjoying the sex and fake an orgasm.

A girl who I became close to told me that all sex workers have addictions. She didn't have an addiction that I was aware of so I asked what hers was. She said she was addicted to the lifestyle: fancy wines, restaurants and jewellery. Most were addicted to drugs, some gambling, others shopping.

Being paid for sex is not what I think of as consensual sex. If you met these guys elsewhere you would not want to have sex with them. Prostitution is virtually paid rape.

A very young girl who worked in the brothel was six months pregnant. She told everyone she had some condition like irritable bowel syndrome that caused her stomach to bloat. We found out months after she left that she had actually been pregnant. It makes me really sad to think about her. I don't know what happened to her.

Statistics say that 75% of sex workers in Victoria are single mothers.[1] There has to be better choices for women, equal pay, equal opportunities and better pay for female-dominated fields. No woman should have to resort to sex work.

There is a high rate of depression and suicide among sex workers, and there was one fatality while I was there. This girl came from tragic circumstances and was just out of jail for armed robbery. She had lost a child and I was close to her for a while because I was the first one to take her in and show her kindness. I did drawings of a few of the girls and she wanted some to give her boyfriend. I was shocked at some of the poses she wanted me to draw which were quite pornographic. Coming from dysfunction, mental illness, drug addiction and working in this industry really warps your sense of what is normal. She said she had bipolar disorder. She was probably taking heroin or ice. It was unclear if her death was a deliberate

---

1   <https://www.tasa.org.au/wp-content/uploads/2015/03/Maher-JaneMaree.pdf>

suicide, accidental or murder by her boyfriend. I was really upset when we got news of her death and it affected me deeply at the time.

I stopped working because my partner at the time was not happy about it. Working night shifts puts a strain on relationships. My Mum wasn't happy about me working there either.

Before taking on the role as Secretary for Pink Cross and writing this piece I hadn't had to analyse the situation much. It only dawned on me recently that I was not just a receptionist but it was also my job to sell the women to make money for the brothel. During my training, the women were referred to as 'service providers' and we were in the business of 'renting rooms'. Realising that I was a pimp doesn't sit well with me. At the time I was just doing my job, trying to survive it and probably in denial about what was really going on. Before entering the sex industry I really knew nothing about how degrading and exploitative of women it truly is.

You do things in your life that you don't even realise you're doing or why. I have had issues with alcohol and a tendency to binge drink to block things out. I've been practising Buddhism and meditation which have provided me with useful tools for dealing with struggles in my life and the bad memories. It is only recently that I have sought out therapy with a psychologist and hypnotherapist to manage my drinking habit.

I would like to see prostitution abolished in my lifetime. I don't think it is safe for any woman, physically, mentally or spiritually. While prostitution continues to exist, I believe that no woman in the community is safe.

Jacqueline Gwynne is a Melbourne-based artist. She has worked in various roles as an arts educator. Jacqueline is currently the Secretary of Pink Cross Foundation Australia*, a not-for-profit organisation that helps people transition out of the sex industry.*

The Men
Who Buy Women
for Sex

Caitlin Roper

"Why do newspaper articles about the sex industry almost always feature a picture of a woman as if prostitution were a buyerless transaction?" This question was posed by *The Economist's* Simon Hedlin in 2015.[1] Hedlin's comment points to just how effective attempts by the sex industry to obscure the realities of prostitution have been. In an industry fuelled by male demand, the sex buyers have all but disappeared from the equation. The pro-sex lobby goes to great lengths to reframe the purchase of female flesh by men not as exploitation and abuse, but as an exercise in women's choice and autonomy. It doesn't ask why men purchase economically disadvantaged women and girls for sexual exploitation, or examine why male buyers do what they wish with women's bodies. Instead, we often see clients painted as respectful and simply seeking female companionship.

Radical feminist activist and writer Samantha Berg points out that, "People quibble over what percentage of prostitutes 'choose' it while ignoring that 100 per cent of johns choose prostitution."[2] It is primarily men buying mainly women and

1   <https://twitter.com/simonhedlin/status/637685010099798016>
2   <http://worldnewstrust.com/stomping-johns-the-demand-side-of-prostitution-mickey-z>

children. According to Detective Inspector Simon Haggstrom of the Stockholm Police Prostitution Unit, in the 15 years since buying sex has been criminalised in Sweden, in 1999, police have not detected a single woman paying for sex.[3]

While the media tends to depict lonely and often disabled men as looking for companionship through prostitution, or even just someone to talk to, a major international study, 'Comparing Sex Buyers with Men Who Don't Buy Sex' by Melissa Farley and colleagues,[4] debunks these myths and finds that over half of the buyers are already married or in de-facto relationships. One exited woman in Canada shared her insights on why men in committed intimate relationships purchase sex. Speaking to *Sun News Network,* she said, "I spent 15 years servicing men and allowing them to use me any way they saw fit. I've had clients confess that the things they paid me to do were things they would never ask their wives, whom they respected, or their 'child's mother' to do."[5]

The 'Comparing Sex Buyers' study reveals that men who pay to sexually exploit women are aware of the harms they inflict. It found that, "Two thirds of both the sex buyers and the non-sex buyers observed that a majority of women are lured, tricked, or trafficked into prostitution," and that "41% ... of the sex buyers used women who they knew were controlled by pimps at the time they used her." This awareness, however, did not stop them: "The knowledge that women have been exploited, coerced, pimped or trafficked failed to deter sex buyers from buying sex." While knowledge of harm done to women in prostitution was not a sufficient deterrent for the men surveyed, they did agree that the most effective deterrent

---

3   <http://www.newstatesman.com/politics/2014/11/why-paying-sex-legal-so-many-countries-because-laws-are-made-men>

4   <http://www.catwinternational.org/Home/Article/212-comparing-sex-buyers-with-men-who-dont-buy-sex>

5   <http://www.nationalnewswatch.com/2014/07/10/former-prostitute-blasts-media-for-misunderstanding-issue/#.VhYTiEKBhSk>

to buying sex would be being placed on a sex offender registry, being exposed in public, or having to pay significant fines and go to jail.

Sex buyers tend to regard the women they buy as less than human, and as solely existing for their sexual use and enjoyment. Men who purchase sex are quite open about their belief that their entitlement to sex should take precedence over the wellbeing of the women they buy. Sex buyers express contempt for the prostituted women they use, both in research studies and on customer review websites where they detail and rank the 'services' of the women they buy. Common themes emerge among these candid reviews.

One theme is that sex buyers regard the women they buy as mere objects for sexual gratification. The online Canadian Invisible Men Project, which collates postings made by sex buyers on prostitution review websites, records buyers as making comments about individual women such as, "She's a sad waste of good girl flesh,"[6] and "If you want an attractive receptacle for your semen she will do." [7] At the same time that buyers appear to despise the women they buy, they require of these women absolute compliance and submission to sex acts demanded of them. Sex buyers have been recorded in *The Guardian* newspaper[8] as expressing opinions such as, "I don't want them to get any pleasure. I am paying for it and it is her job to give me pleasure. If she enjoys it I would feel cheated." In her 2007 book *Making Sex Work*, Mary Lucille Sullivan writes that, "The [sex] buyer's economic power means he determines how the sexual act will be played out. Buyers believe their purchasing power entitles them to demand any type of sex they want."[9]

6   <http://the-invisible-men.tumblr.com/post/66211778026>

7   <http://the-invisible-men.tumblr.com/post/57795772092>

8   <http://www.theguardian.com/society/2010/jan/15/why-men-use-prostitutes

9   Mary Lucille Sullivan, *Making Sex Work, 2007*, p. 285, p. 287

The 'Comparing Sex Buyers' study crucially finds that, in systems of prostitution, sex buyers are motivated by the opportunity to control and dominate a woman so that they can perform degrading sex acts against her that female partners would refuse. Farley and colleagues recorded statements from buyers such as, "If my fiancée won't give me anal, I know someone who will,"[10] and "You get to treat a ho like a ho ... you can find a ho for any type of need – slapping, choking, aggressive sex beyond what your girlfriend will do – you won't do stuff to your girlfriend that will make her lose her self esteem."[11]

This sense of entitlement to treat prostituted women worse than girlfriends does not change even when buyers realise the women they are buying are unwilling participants. The Invisible Men Project documents sex buyers as expressing opinions such as, "I wish she had loosened up or pretended to be into it more. She grimaced as I came on her which was a turn off ... Would recommend for those interested in ethnic girls, big boobs ... just wish she'd lighten up a bit,"[12] and "She had the gagging expression on her face ... again she just lay there and complained about it hurting."[13]

Perhaps worse still, sex buyers are able to recognise signs of trafficking among the women they use, but this awareness appears to be no impediment to their behaviour. The Australian prostitution review website *Punter Planet* features a posting by a buyer expressing the sentiment that, "the sex ... was the best part as Hana was tight and able to take instuctions [sic] well. Her English is non existant [sic] in April but may be better

10 <http://www.catwinternational.org/Home/Article/212-comparing-sex-buyers-with-men-who-dont-buy-sex>

11 <http://www.catwinternational.org/Home/Article/212-comparing-sex-buyers-with-men-who-dont-buy-sex>

12 <http://the-invisible-men.tumblr.com/post/76352163428>

13 <http://the-invisible-men.tumblr.com/post/75511499318>

now. Lucky for me i was able to converse in some Korean with her."[14]

Psychologist Melissa Farley and her colleagues have conducted years of research into men who buy women for prostitution and their motivations. The factors driving men to become 'customers' of the sex industry aren't too different from those leading them to become rapists. Just like rapists, prostitution buyers are disproportionately pornography users, they resent women's refusal to do things they want them to do (such as sex acts), and they see their sexual behaviour as not particularly harmful of others. This self-interested, self-centred approach to others and society manifests itself in the worst behaviours of male sexual entitlement, but it is an entitlement shared by most men, even if each individual man doesn't buy a woman for prostitution or target a woman for rape. Pornography users might be understood as coming a step closer to this extreme model of male sexual entitlement, which is concerning if we think about the currently high rates of pornography consumption by men all over the world. The expectation that women will comply with men's desire to re-enact sex acts they've seen in pornography, and some men's willingness to buy women in prostitution if their girlfriends refuse to submit to pornographic sex acts, shows an escalation in the power of male sexual entitlement which is being fuelled by the global sex industry.[15] More than any group, prostituted women, such as those whose testimonies are included in this book, know about the sexual violence against women and girls that is escalating as a result of the global sex industry.

---

14 'Might and Power' article <http://www.punterplanet.com>, accessed 19 June 2011.

15 Farley, M., Golding, J., Matthews, E.S., Malamuth, N., Jarrett, L. (2015) 'Comparing Sex Buyers with Men Who Do Not Buy Sex: New Data on Prostitution and Trafficking.' *Journal of Interpersonal Violence* (August, 2015) pp. 1–25. Available at <http://prostitutionresearch.com/2015/09/01/men-who-buy-sex-have-much-in-common-with-sexually-coercive-men-new-study-shows-4/>

It is a difficult fact to confront that sex buyers are more concerned with the quality of the 'sexual service' they receive than the fact that women they pay to exploit are not there by choice and are gravely harmed by being prostituted. As long as men prioritise their perceived right to the bodies of impoverished women and girls over women's basic human rights in this way, the prostitution industry will continue to thrive. It is only when men are held accountable for their abuse of women in the sex trade that we will see meaningful progress.

Caitlin Roper is an activist and campaigns manager for grassroots campaigning movement Collective Shout: For a world free of sexploitation. *<www.collectiveshout.org/>*

Ten Myths about Prostitution, Trafficking and the Nordic Model[1]

Meagan Tyler

Whenever the Nordic Model is raised in public discussions there is a set of predictable objections raised by those who oppose it. Many of these responses rely on a variety of misconceptions about, and misrepresentations of, prostitution, sex trafficking, and the Nordic Model itself. These falsities and fabrications will be familiar to anyone who has written or said anything that publicly criticises the sex industry. The same claims, usually without reference to relevant evidence, are repeated so frequently in certain spheres that they have practically become mantras. It appears as though some people believe that if you simply say something often enough, it will become a sound basis for policy.

Increasingly, the most heated public arguments about the sex industry are occurring online, in particular, on social media. These forums are often not the most conducive to reasoned engagement and debate but they do demonstrate the monotony with which the same arguments are used by sex industry supporters to shut down survivors, feminists and other

---

1   This list originally appeared at *Feminist Current* in December 2013: <http://www.feministcurrent.com/2013/12/08/10-myths-about-prostitution-trafficking-and-the-nordic-model/> It has been edited and updated for this collection.

advocates of the Nordic Model. In the interests of being able to offer more than 140 character responses to these predictable pro-industry lines, I have compiled a list of rejoinders to some of the most common criticisms I have come across.[1]

1. I'm a sex worker, I choose sex work, and I love it.

This is one of the most popular retorts *de jour* and it is treated by many who use it as a sort of checkmate argument, as though any one person stating that they enjoy 'sex work' makes all of the other evidence about violence, post-traumatic stress disorder and trafficking in prostitution,[2] magically disappear.

The callous individualism of arguments like this was succinctly skewered by Maud Olivier, a Socialist MP who first introduced a Bill to prohibit the purchase of sexual services in France in 2013. She slammed the hypocrisy of such assertions, asking her fellow National Assembly members: "So is it enough for one prostitute to say she is free for the enslavement of others to be respectable and acceptable?"[3]

That an individual experience does not invalidate structural analysis should be obvious but the persuasive power of the 'I love sex work' refrain endures largely because it is seen as nullifying the claim by radical feminists and others that systems of prostitution are harmful to women.

The idea that claims of prostitution's harms are disproved by an individual claiming to personally enjoy prostitution relies on fundamental misunderstandings of radical politics, the concept of structural oppression and tired old debates about false consciousness. Just because you like something

---

2   For a useful (and easily accessible) overview of this evidence, see Melissa Farley's website, *Prostitution, Research and Education*: <http://prostitutionresearch.com/>
See also: Maddy Coy (Ed) (2012) *Prostitution, Harm and Gender Inequality.* London: Ashgate.

3   BBC News (2013) 'France prostitution: MPs debate ban on paying for sex.' *BBC* News, 29 November. Available from: <http://www.bbc.com/news/world-europe-25118755>

---

does not mean that it cannot be harmful, to you, or to others. Radical feminists, for example, often criticise beauty practices as harmful[4] and some women stating that they enjoy wearing high-heels and make-up does not make the critique wrong. Nor does it mean radical feminists hate women (as is sometimes claimed) for wearing high heels and make-up, or for being in systems of prostitution.

Similarly, when anyone practicing radical politics points out that free choice is a fairy tale, and that all our actions are constrained within certain material conditions, this does not equate to saying that we are all infantilised, little drones unable to make decisions for ourselves. It only means we are not all floating around in a cultural vacuum making decisions completely unaffected by structural issues like systemic economic inequality, racism and sexism.

2. Only sex workers are qualified to comment on prostitution.

This myth is often used in tandem with the first and while this may be part of a wider problem of attempting to spuriously employ personal experience to trump research and disprove wider social trends (the 'sexism doesn't exist because I've never seen it!' excuse), there is more to these interactions in the context of prostitution. Repeating that only current 'sex workers' are qualified to talk about the sex industry is an attempt to a) silence survivors' voices, and b) pretend that the consequences of prostitution apply only to those in prostitution.

The growth of vocal prostitution survivor groups in recent years has clearly been threatening to sex industry profiteers. Organisations such as *SPACE International, Survivors for Solutions, Organisation for Prostitution Survivors* and *Sex Trade*

---

4   Sheila Jeffreys (2015) *Beauty and Misogyny: Harmful cultural practices in the West.* 2nd edition. London: Routledge.

101[5] have mobilised to make survivor voices heard and to advocate for abolition and policies that target demand. To try and reduce the impact of groups like this, it is common for industry supporters to claim survivors cannot speak as 'sex workers.'

As Helen Lewis explains, this argument operates to excise survivor voices from the conversation altogether:

> Unsurprisingly, women who experience prostitution as little more than paid rape will do everything they can to leave the trade. But that means they're not sex workers any more. So – hey presto – their opinions can be discounted. We end up in a 'no true Scotsman' situation that skews the answers we get; only people with an overall positive view are permitted to talk about that industry. It's as if the Leveson inquiry had only heard from *News of the World* journalists.[6]

Indeed, her central point is that it would be considered absurd in other policy areas to ignore those who are most harmed. The same should be true of prostitution.

It is also true that much feminist opposition to prostitution has focused specifically on the harms to women in prostitution, and rightly so, these harms are serious and endemic.[7] But, as advocates of the Nordic Model point out, the existence of systems of prostitution is also a barrier to gender equality. As long as women (and, yes, there are men in prostitution, but using the word 'people' here would only obfuscate the fact that the vast majority of those in prostitution *are* women) can be bought and sold like commodities for sex, this will be

5   For further information see: SPACE International –<http://spaceinternational. ie>, Survivors for Solutions – <http://www.survivors4solutions.com>, Organisation for Prostitution Survivors – <http://seattleops.org>, Sex Trade 101 – <http://www.sextrade101.com>

6   Helen Lewis (2015) 'Listen to the sex workers – but which ones?' *The Guardian*, 9 August. Available from: <http://www.theguardian.com/ commentisfree/2015/aug/09/listen-to-sex-workers-but-which-ones>

7   Melissa Farley (2013) Prostitution, Liberalism and Slavery. *Logos: A journal of modern society and culture*, v12(3): 370–386.

an issue for all women. The Swedish government recognised this when the first Nordic Model legislation was introduced in 1999.[8] An understanding that systems of prostitution are an impediment to gender inequality was a key element of the framework underpinning the laws banning the purchase of sex. Unsurprisingly, this is an element of the Nordic Model often ignored by its detractors.

3. All sex workers oppose the Nordic Model.

Firstly, it is important to point out that for every 'sex worker' rights organisation that opposes the Nordic Model, there is a survivor-led organisation that advocates for it. The idea that every woman with any experience in the sex industry detests the Nordic Model is tactical claim by a number of these organisations around the world and it relies heavily on myth number two. This claim is, more often than not, followed by links to various 'sex worker' blogs which prove, or so we are told, that all women in prostitution hate the Nordic Model and would prefer full decriminalisation.

It is clear that there are a number of very vocal opponents of the Nordic Model within the sex industry who have a significant platform, but it can hardly be said that these organisations represent all women in prostitution, all around the world. Indeed, it is important to question how representative these organisations are, especially in light of investigations by Julie Bindel and Kat Banyard that have exposed pimps in important roles in a number of prominent sex worker rights organisations such as the Global Network of Sex Work Projects.[9] Nor can

---

8 Gunilla Ekberg and Kajsa Wahlberg (2011) The Swedish Approach: A European Union country fights sex trafficking. *Solutions Journal*, v2(2): n.p.

9 Julie Bindel (2013) 'An Unlikely Union'. *Gaze: A modern review*. April, n.p.
Kat Banyard (2015) 'Why is a pimp helping to shape Amnesty's sex trade policy?' *The Guardian*, 23 October. Available from: <http://www.theguardian.com/commentisfree/2015/oct/22/pimp-amnesty-prostitution-policy-sex-trade-decriminalise-brothel-keepers>

it be said that the odd blog post (light on references or other evidence) *proves* that the Nordic Model is a failure. We need more independent research into the experiences of women who wish to exit prostitution and we need to amplify the voices of survivors who speak out about the harms they have endured.

4. The Nordic Model denies sex workers' agency.

One of the things that critics seem to find so difficult to comprehend about the Nordic Model is that it is actually about restricting *buyers,* not about restricting those in prostitution. That is why it *decriminalises* prostituted persons. The Model does not discount the possibility of prostitution by 'choice' but rather establishes that the buying of women in systems of prostitution is something that the state should actively discourage.

It is pretty simple. The Nordic Model acknowledges that less demand for prostitution, and less demand for trafficking, equates to less prostitution and less trafficking, thereby reducing the number of women exposed to these particular types of abuse and creating a better chance of achieving gender equality.

If you think that the state should encourage the growth of the prostitution industry and treat it as a form of gainful employment for women, then you are bound to disagree, but that does not mean the Model denies anybody's agency.

5. The Nordic Model conflates prostitution and trafficking.

Many proponents of the Nordic Model adopt the understanding of trafficking advanced by the United Nations Protocol to Prevent, Suppress and Punish Trafficking in Persons Especially Women and Children (see Article 3a). This is a more nuanced understanding of trafficking than the 'people moved across international borders at gun point' version that is popular in much of the mainstream press. Perhaps this is where the confusion sets in.

Even in employing the more realistic, UN-endorsed understanding of the mechanics of coercion and trafficking, however, the Nordic Model does not assume that every woman in prostitution is necessarily trafficked. What the Nordic Model *does* do is recognise that there is a *connection* between the markets for prostitution and sex trafficking or, more specifically, that the demand for sexual services fuels sex trafficking. So, if you want less sex trafficking, then you need to shrink the market for prostitution. This logic has been further supported by a comprehensive study of 150 countries, conducted by economists in the UK and Germany, showing that "the scale effect of legalised prostitution leads to an expansion of the prostitution market, increasing human trafficking."[10]

6. The Nordic Model does not work/ pushes prostitution 'underground'.

The contention that the Nordic Model has not reduced demand for prostitution is one often repeated without supporting evidence, but occasionally it is claimed that the Swedish government's own review of their legislation showed the Nordic Model to be a failure. As legal scholar Max Waltman has demonstrated, it did no such thing.[11] Research commissioned by the Swedish government for its official review showed that street prostitution had halved as a result of the changed laws.[12]

In response to this, some claim that the study employed a flawed methodology and that prostitution has merely gone underground. Perhaps, but that overlooks other sources,

---

10 Seo-Young Cho, Axel Dreher and Eric Neumayer (2013) Does Prostitution Increase Human Trafficking? *World Development, v41(1): 67–82.*

11 Max Waltman (2011) Sweden's Prohibition of the Purchase of Sex: The law's reasons, impact and potential. *Women's Studies International Forum,* v34(5): 449–474.

12 Government Offices of Sweden (2010) The Ban against the Purchase of Sexual Services. An evaluation 1999-2008. English Summary. Available from: <http://web.archive.org/web/20131113102557/http://www.government.se/content/1/c6/15/14/88/0e51eb7f.pdf>

including research indicating the number of people in Sweden buying sex has fallen and that police report having intercepted communications from traffickers declaring that Sweden is a 'bad market'.[13]

It is also worth considering what 'underground' is supposed to mean in this context, as in legalised and decriminalised systems, like some in Australia, 'underground' is taken to mean street prostitution. So if prostitution has moved off the streets, where has it gone? Online and indoors, is the assertion of critics, which is quite odd given that advocates of legalisation frequently tout the benefits of indoor prostitution.[14]

7. The Nordic Model deprives women of a living.

This myth is the most intriguing because it is actually an admission that the Nordic Model works, directly contradicting myth six. The Model can only deprive women of a living if it does, in fact, reduce the demand for prostitution. Moreover, comprehensive exit programs are a critical part of the Model, involving access to a wide variety of services including retraining and employment support.

Hashtags like #nothingaboutuswithoutus (used by a number of groups, not exclusively sex industry organisations) regularly appear alongside this claim as though the only satisfactory option available is for everyone to accept a flourishing prostitution market because some people want it that way. Not just any people though, of course – workers – if you buy the line that 'sex work is work'. Leaving aside the problems with the

---

13 Kajsa Claude (2011) *Targeting the Sex Buyer: The Swedish example.* Stockholm: The Swedish Institute.
Kajsa Wahlberg (2010) Speech given to the Third Swedish-Dutch Conference on Gender Equality: Trafficking in Human Beings and Prostitution at the Swedish Embassy den Haag, The Netherlands. 6th December.

14 See for example Ronald Weitzer (2005) Flawed Theory and Method in Studies of Prostitution. Violence Against Women, v11(7): 934–949.

concept that prostitution is a job like any other,[15] if we accept this premise, then the argument does not follow: workers in any given industry do not get to unilaterally determine whether or not that industry continues.

Take the brown coal or forestry industries in Australia, for example. These are sectors that have been deemed by governments to be harmful in a number of ways and that, as a result – while they are still potentially profitable – they no longer have a social licence to continuing operating uninhibited. Workers in these industries are often, understandably, incensed at seeing their jobs threatened, which is why unions advocate for 'just transitions'.[16] That is, unions push for providing retraining and facilitated access to social and employment services for affected workers. For the most part, these unions have given up arguing that the harmful industry in question should continue simply to avoid employment disruption for workers. Funnily enough, these 'just transitions' sound an awful lot like the exit programs proposed by those recommending the Nordic Model.

If 'sex work' is work, and prostitution is just another industry, then it is open for wider public discussion and policy changes like other industry, including the possibility that governments will no longer want it to function.

8. The Nordic Model has made prostitution unsafe.

First things first, prostitution *is* unsafe. To suggest that the Nordic Model is what makes it dangerous is disingenuous. Such declarations also ignore research showing that traditional

---

15 For useful sources on why this is problematic see: Mary Sullivan (2007) *Making Sex Work: The failed experiment of legalised prostitution in Australia.* North Melbourne: Spinifex Press. Also: Janice Raymond (2013) *Not a Choice: Not a Job: Exposing the myths about prostitution and the global sex trade.* North Melbourne: Spinifex Press.

16 See for example: Jim Young (1998) Just Transition: A new approach to jobs v. environment. *Labor and Society*, v2(2): 42–48.

forms of legalisation and decriminalisation do virtually nothing to protect women in prostitution from very high odds of physical and sexual violence as well as psychological trauma.[17]

Secondly, systems of legalisation foster greater demand and create an expanding illegal industry surrounding them, so it is a fallacy to pretend that in localities where prostitution is legalised, all women are actually in legal forms of prostitution. In addition, rates of trauma are similar across legalised, decriminalised and criminalised systems of prostitution.[18] Sadly, even the Nordic Model is not capable of fully protecting women still in prostitution from many of these conditions – as long as there is prostitution there will be harm – but the idea that it makes conditions worse is spurious.

Thirdly, the 'more violence' claims mostly relate to a widely cited ProSentret study which found that women in prostitution had reported an increase in certain forms of violent acts from johns, including hair pulling and biting, after the introduction of the Nordic Model in Norway.[19] What is often left out from these accounts, however, is that the study also found women reported a sharp decline in other forms of violence, including punching and rape.[20]

Finally, as to women in prostitution not being able to access adequate social services: this may well be a problem on the ground. If so, it absolutely needs to be addressed, but this is an issue of implementation rather than a flaw in the Model itself. The original version of the Nordic Model, introduced

---

17 See for example: Melissa Farley (Ed.) (2003) *Prostitution, Trafficking and Traumatic Stress*. Harworth Press: New York.

18 Melissa Farley (Ed.) (2003) *Prostitution, Trafficking and Traumatic Stress*. Harworth Press: New York.

19 Ulla Bjørndahl (2012) *Dangerous Liaisons: A report on the violence women in prostitution in Oslo are exposed to*. Oslo: Pro Sentret.

20 Samantha Berg (2013) 'New research shows violence decreases under Nordic model: Why the radio silence?' *Feminist Current*, 22 January. Available from: <http://www.feministcurrent.com/2013/01/22/new-research-shows-violence-decreases-under-nordic-model-why-the-radio-silence/>

in Sweden, was part of the *Kvinnofrid* reforms to funnel more government money and support to a variety of services tackling violence against women, including specifically in prostitution.[21]

9. The Nordic Model is (de facto) criminalisation.

During the last few years, the Nordic Model has come under serious consideration in an increasing number of jurisdictions across the globe. Again, this has posed a threat to the sex industry. One of the latest ways to try and discredit the Model in this context has been to claim that it threatens the safety of women (linked to myth eight) because it has the same outcomes as full criminalisation: where there is criminal sanction for both male buyers and for prostituted women. Sex industry advocates frequently use this misrepresentation, but it has also been taken up by researchers, especially those working in criminology.[22]

It should be readily apparent that any criminologist claiming a legislative framework where those in prostitution are *decriminalised,* and offered targeted social services and exit programs as victims of crime, is the same as one where those in prostitution can be fined or incarcerated as perpetrators of a crime, is being intellectually dishonest. But some have adapted the argument to assert that the Nordic Model works as *de facto* criminalisation. This modified claim suggests that because buyers are criminalised, prostituted women are unlikely to report violent assaults and other crimes to police.

As a number of prostitution survivors have argued, however, this is counter-intuitive. In legalised and decriminalised systems it is often extremely difficult for prostituted women to secure

---

21 Gunilla Ekberg (2004) The Swedish Law That Prohibits the Purchase of Sexual Services: Best Practices for Prevention of Prostitution and Trafficking in Human Beings. *Violence Against Women,* v10(10): 1187–1218.

22 See for example: Rebecca Hiscock (10 August 2015) 'Celebrity activists get it wrong on Amnesty International's sex work policy.' *The Conversation.* Available from: <http://theconversation.com/celebrity-activists-get-it-wrong-on-amnesty-internationals-sex-work-policy-45863>

convictions against buyers for sexual assault, or even to have police and prosecutors take such cases seriously. Whereas, under the Nordic Model, a buyer can be charged automatically, simply as a result of having paid for sex.

Furthermore, the *de facto* argument is exposed as almost entirely disingenuous by the fact that many using it favour the model of full decriminalisation found in New Zealand. If it is women's safety we are concerned about – and indeed we should be – then full decriminalisation has not been found to offer any great police protection. The New Zealand government's five-year review of the Prostitution Reform Act showed that "a majority of respondents felt that decriminalisation made no difference with respect to the violence of johns [buyers] in prostitution," that "few" prostituted persons "reported any of the incidents of violence or crimes against them to the Police."[23]

Last, but certainly not least, if we are to apply this same *de facto* logic to other legislative and policy options, the proponents of full decriminalisation and legalisation are in trouble. We know that full decriminalisation and legalisation lead to an increase in demand and in trafficking inflows (see myth five). So, if we are to judge and label these approaches only by a particular outcome, then proponents of full decriminalisation and legalisation will have to accept that they therefore support the *de facto* decriminalisation of trafficking.

10. The Nordic Model is really a moral crusade in disguise.

Despite the evidence-based policy of the Nordic Model being introduced by a number of progressive and socialist governments, the notion persists that this is some kind of underhanded religious or conservative attempt to curtail sexual expression, rather than an effective way of tackling trafficking and violence against women.

---

23 New Zealand Government (2008) *Report of the Prostitution Law Review Committee on the Operation of the Prostitution Reform Act 2003*. Wellington: New Zealand Government: 14, 57, 122.

Maybe this all depends on how you define 'moral crusade'. If you view the movement for women's equality as a moral crusade, then I suppose it is. If you are determined to dismiss all of the evidence in support of the Nordic Model and instead want to debate this on a 'moral' level, then by all means do. Those of us who think violence against women is a bad thing are bound to win that argument.

Meagan Tyler, PhD, is a Vice-Chancellor's Research Fellow at RMIT University, Australia. Her research interests are based mainly around the social construction of gender and sexuality. Her work in this area has been published in Rural Studies, Women's Studies International Forum *and* Women and Therapy *as well as several edited collections including* Everyday Pornography *(Boyle Ed, 2010),* Prostitution, Harm and Gender Inequality *(Coy Ed, 2012) and* Freedom Fallacy: The Limits of Liberal Feminism *(Kiraly and Tyler Eds, 2015).*

RECOMMENDED READING

Barry, Kathleen. (1979). *Female Sexual Slavery.* Englewood Cliffs NJ: Prentice Hall.

Barry, Kathleen. (1995). *The Prostitution of Sexuality: The Global Exploitation of Women.* New York: New York University Press.

Barry, Kathleen. (2011). *Unmaking War, Remaking Men. How Empathy Can Reshape Our Politics, Our Soldiers and Ourselves.* North Melbourne Spinifex Press.

Bindel, Julie. (2016). *The Pimping of Prostitution: Abolishing the Sex Work Myth.* Basingstoke: Palgrave Macmillan.

Bray, Abigail. (2013). *Misogyny Re-loaded.* North Melbourne: Spinifex Press.

Brown, Louise. (2001). *Sex Slaves: The Trafficking of Women in Asia.* London: Virago Press.

Coy, Maddy. (Ed). (2012). *Prostitution, Harm and Gender Inequality.* London: Ashgate.

Dines, Gail, Robert Jensen and Ann Russo. (1998). *Pornography: The Production and Consumption of Inequality.* Florence, Kentucky: Routledge Publishing.

Dines, Gail. (2011). *Pornland: How Porn Has Hijacked Our Sexuality.* Boston: Beacon Press; North Melbourne, Spinifex Press.

Dworkin, Andrea. (1979). *Pornography: Men Possessing Women.* New York: Pedigree Books.

Dworkin, Andrea. (1988). *Letters from a War Zone.* London: Secker & Warburg.

Dworkin, Andrea. (1991). *Mercy.* New York: Four Walls Eight Windows.

Dworkin, Andrea and Catharine A. MacKinnon. (1998). *Pornography and Civil Rights: A New Day for Women's Equality.* Minneapolis: Organising Against Pornography.

Ekis Ekman, Kajsa. (2013). *Being and Being Bought: Prostitution, Surrogacy and the Split Self.* North Melbourne, Spinifex Press.

Farley, Melissa. (2007). *Prostitution and Trafficking in Nevada: Making the Connections.* San Francisco: Prostitution Research and Education.

Farley, Melissa. (Ed). (2003). *Prostitution, Trafficking and Traumatic Stress.* Binghamton: Haworth Press.

Farr, Kathryn. (2005). *Sex Trafficking: The Global Market in Women and Children.* New York: Worth Publishers.

Griffin, Susan. (1981). *Pornography and Silence. Culture's Revenge Against Nature.* New York: Harper & Row.

Herman, Judith L. (1994). *Trauma and Recovery: The Aftermath of Violence from Domestic Abuse to Political Terror.* New York. Basic Books.

Hester, Marianne, Liz Kelly and Jill Radford. (Eds). (1996). *Women, Violence and Male Power: Feminist Activism, Research and Practice.* Buckingham: Open University Press.

Hicks, George. (1994). *The Comfort Women.* New York: W.W. Norton.

Hoigard, Cecilie and Liv Finstad. (1986). *Backstreets: Prostitution, Money and Love.* Philadelphia: Pennsylvania University Press.

Itzin, Catherine. (Ed). (1992). *Pornography: Women, Violence and Civil Liberties.* Oxford and New York: Oxford University Press.

Jeffreys, Sheila. (1997). *The Idea of Prostitution.* North Melbourne: Spinifex Press.

Jeffreys, Sheila. (2009). *The Industrial Vagina. The Political Economy of the Global Sex Trade.* Florence, Kentucky: Routledge Publishing.

Jackson Katz. (2006). *The Macho Paradox: Why Some Men Hurt Women and Why All Men Can Help.* Naperville, Illinois: Sourcebooks Inc.

Kiraly, Miranda and Meagan Tyler. (Eds). (2015). *Freedom Fallacy: The Limits of Liberal Feminism.* Ballarat: Connor Court Publishing.

Levy, Ariel. (2005). *Female Chauvinist Pigs: Women and the Rise of Raunch Culture.* New York City: Free Press.

Lewis, Sarah Katherine. (2006). *Indecent: How I Make It and Fake It as a Girl for Hire.* Emeryville, CA: Seal Press.

MacKinnon, Catharine A. (1989). *Towards a Feminist Theory of the State.* Boston, MA: Harvard University Press.

MacKinnon, Catharine A. and Andrea Dworkin. (Eds). (1998). *In Harm's Way: The Pornography and Civil Rights Hearings.* Cambridge MA: Harvard University Press.

Malarek, Victor. (2009). *The Johns: Sex for Sale and the Men who Buy It.* New York: Arcade Publishing.

Mathews, Paul W. (2010). *Asian Cam Models: Digital Virtual Virgin Prostitutes?* Quezon City: Giraffe Books.

Millett, Kate. (1971/1976). *The Prostitution Papers: A Quartet for Female Voice.* New York: Ballantine Books.

Monzini, Paola. (2006). *Sex Traffic: Prostitution, Crime and Exploitation.* London: Zed Books.

Moon, Katharine. (1997). *Sex Among Allies: Military Prostitution in U.S.-Korea Relations.* New York: Columbia University Press.

Moran, Rachel. (2013). *Paid For. My Journey through Prostitution.* Dublin: M.H. Gill & Co; North Melbourne: Spinifex Press.

Norma, Caroline. (2016). *The Japanese Comfort Women and Sexual Slavery During the China and Pacific Wars.* London: Bloomsbury.

Oakley, Annie. (2007). *Working Sex: Sex Workers Write about a Changing Industry.* Emeryville, CA: Seal Press.

O'Connell Davidson, Julia. (1998). *Prostitution, Power, and Freedom.* Ann Arbor: University of Michigan Press.

Ostby, Anne Ch. (2013). *Town of Love.* With a Preface by Ruchira Gupta. North Melbourne: Spinifex Press.

Qiu, Peipei, Zhiliang Su and Lifei Chen. (2013). *Chinese Comfort Women: Testimonies from Imperial Japan's Sex Slaves.* Vancouver: University of British Columbia Press.

Raphael, Jody. (2004). *Listening to Olivia: Violence, Poverty, and Prostitution.* Boston: Northeastern University Press.

Raymond, Janice, G. (2013). *Not a Choice, Not a Job: Exposing the Myths about Prostitution and the Global Sex Trade.* Lincoln: Potomac Books-University of Nebraska Press; North Melbourne, Spinifex Press.

Rogg Korsvik, Trine with Ane Stø. (2013). *The Nordic Model.* CreateSpace:

Independent Publishing Platform.

Russell, Diana, E.H. (1993). *Against Pornography: The Evidence of Harm.* Berkeley, CA: Russell Publications.

Russell, Diana, E.H. (Ed). (1993). *Making Violence Sexy: Feminist Views on Pornography.* New York: The Athene Series, Teachers College Press.

Russell, Diana, E.H. (1998). *Dangerous Relationships: Pornography, Misogyny, and Rape.* Thousand Oaks, CA: Sage Publications.

Stark, Christine and Rebecca Whisnant. (Eds). (2004) *Not For Sale: Feminists Resisting Prostitution and Pornography.* North Melbourne: Spinifex Press.

Stark Christine. (2011). *Nickels: A Tale of Dissociation.* Ann Arbor: Modern History Press.

Sullivan, Mary Lucille. (2007). *Making Sex Work: A Failed Experiment with Legalised Prostitution.* North Melbourne, Spinifex Press.

Stiglmayer, Alexandra. (Ed). (1994). *Mass Rape: The War Against Women in Bosnia-Herzegovina.* Lincoln: University of Nebraska Press.

Tankard Reist, Melinda and Abigail Bray. (Eds). (2011). *Big Porn Inc. Exposing the Harms of the Global Pornography Industry,* North Melbourne: Spinifex Press.

Tea, Michelle and Laurenn McCubbin. (2004). *Rent Girl.* San Francisco: Last Gasp.

Yoshiaki, Yoshimi. (1995). *Comfort Women.* New York: Columbia University Press.

ACKNOWLEDGEMENTS

If the women whose personal accounts you, the reader, absorb in these pages, had not been willing to write them, *Prostitution Narratives* would have ended as merely an idea. We owe you such gratitude for being vulnerable and brave and for allowing us to share your stories with the world in this book. We hope you find consolation in the solidarity of other survivors and in knowing your raw and potent words make a difference.

When the idea for this book first came to me, I knew it could only happen if Caroline Norma whom I highly regarded as an academic, valued as a sister in a new global uprising for the right of women to live free of violence (in all its forms), and prized as a friend, agreed to work on it with me. Caroline is a leading authority on trafficking and prostitution in Australia and a frontline expert globally. I am so grateful you said yes. It has been wonderful to work with you on a project so close to your heart and mine and now to see the fruit of our partnership.

And, of course, a book idea is nothing without a publisher. Thank you to my long-time collaborators at Spinifex Press, the world's leading feminist publishing house. Publishing books by women writers around the world is a work of love and passion for them. As with my other works, they have been involved in all the details of the process and the book is better for it. Pauline Hopkins, for editing and compiling the manuscript – and keeping us to deadlines. Renate Klein and Susan Hawthorne, for your wise editing and sound advice. And beyond all this, for being a source of endurance and strength and backing me over so many years now.

There were other collaborators. Helen Pringle generously imparted her prodigious intellectual might, mind-bank of historical and legal knowledge and remarkable editing abilities. Helen, I cannot thank you enough. Laura McNally for critical advice and editing suggestions, gratitude as well. To our esteemed endorsers, we were so humbled and encouraged by your gracious words! Thank you for believing in this book. To my co-conspirators at Collective Shout especially Caitlin Roper, Melinda Liszewski and Coralie Alison. You are always available to supply advice, encouragement, support, often multiple times a day. My work is so much easier with you in it. My other friends closest to my heart who have upheld me in tough times, thank you.

And to my family for bearing with me through another book and for believing in my work.

Melinda

Melinda Tankard Reist shows all her typical traits of humility and altruism in this generous inscription, and there will be many of us who are deeply grateful for it. In truth, it is Melinda's own drive, persistence and commitment that is deserving of such kindly expressed sentiment, many important feminist events and actions would never have happened in Australia without them, including this book. It was Melinda's can-do spirit and sense of mission toward social justice for women that brought it about. Thanks recorded here as published words is the very least expression of gratitude I can offer to her on behalf of all of us.

With her, and with me, in this project from start to finish have been the survivor contributors of the book's testimonies. These women and their words are the beginning, middle and end of anything we might do towards the end of prostitution, and it has been a privilege to be entrusted in a small way with them in this project.

Caroline

INDEX

addictive behaviours, 31, 35, 40, 41–2,
44, 48, 53, 54, 56, 79, 84, 166, 197,
205
agency, 148–9, 151–2, 218
AIM (Adult Industry Medicine) tests,
101, 104
alcohol abuse/addiction, 45, 50, 61,
69, 79, 86, 102, 136, 166, 175, 182,
206
Amaya, Barbara, 12
American slave trade, 9–10
Amnesty International, 18
anal sex, 36, 37, 52, 118, 142
anti-slavery abolitionism, 9–10
anxiety, 53, 64, 79, 84, 86, 99, 112,
129–30, 145, 192
Apne Aap, 17
Asian women, trafficking and sexual
enslavement, 46–7, 55
attention, addiction to, 35
Attention Deficit Disorder (ADD)
medication, 35, 43–4

Banyard, Kat, 217
Barry, Kathleen, 14
Berg, Samantha, 207
bikini waitresses, 72
Bindel, Julie, 18n38, 217
The Boardroom brothel, 171–2
bodily autonomy, 72
bondage, 134
brothel owners, 55, 109
brothel receptionists, 20, 52–3, 55,
133, 197, 198, 200–6
brothels
conditions in, 33–4, 35, 36, 38,
39, 44–5, 46, 51–3, 55, 116–18,
129–30, 132–4, 134, 141–3, 172–3
high-class brothels, 79
medical care, 39
payment of women, 34, 35, 44–5,
52, 204

pornography in, 36, 172, 197, 200,
201
security, 201–2
Burris, Autumn, 14

Canberra
exhibition on sex industry, 141, 143
regulation of sex industry, 67–8
underage prostitutes, 67, 68
child abuse/neglect, 32
child pornography
on internet, 145, 146
survivors of, 145–54
child prostitutes, 169
childhood sexual abuse, 50, 59–60,
64, 75, 82, 83, 105, 163–4, 180–1,
184
Cleland, John, 9
Coalition Against Trafficking in
Women (CATW), 5, 12
cocaine, 53, 54, 175
Collective Shout, 20
'comfort women', 13, 14–15
commercial child sexual exploitation
(CSSE), 185
Comparing Sex Buyers study, 208–9,
210
competition, between prostituted
women, 34, 35–6, 40, 53–4, 56,
124–5, 133
condom use, 34, 35, 52, 107, 142, 204
cosmetic surgery, 31, 40, 41, 53
crime, normalisation of, 43
criminalisation of sex buyers, 223–4
crystal methamphetamine ('ice'), 41,
45, 197

de Faoite, Mia, 12
decriminalisation, 18, 27, 158, 217,
222, 224
Deer, Sarah, 9
demand for prostitution, 219–21

Index

conditioning of men, 62
connection with prostitution, 8n17,
33, 102, 193, 211
as endless public rape, 147
forced pornography, 190–2
re-enactment of, 36, 45, 203
and violence against women, 36,
45, 211
websites, 102–3, 104, 145
Post-Traumatic Stress Disorder
(PTSD), 46, 56, 65, 77, 86, 141,
144, 173, 197, 198
poverty/prostitution trade-off, 25–6,
100, 106, 142
power
prostituted women's illusion of,
107, 173
of sex buyers, 142, 174, 209
Priesley, Sara, 8
private clients, 40–1
prostitution
demand for, 219–21
as paid rape, 205
as sexual assault, 7
sexualisation of, 8–9
as social problem, 84
true nature of, 4–5
prostitution laws
in Australia, 178
in Canberra, 67
in New Zealand, 224
in Norway, 222
in NSW, 74
in Queensland, 74
in Sweden; 167m, 217, 219–20, 223
in Victoria, 16n33, 172
Prostitution Reform Act (NZ), 224
prostitutors *see* sex buyers
psychological trauma, 31, 46, 48, 53,
56, 63–4, 65, 77, 86, 99, 136, 141,
144, 173, 187–8, 192, 197, 198
Punter Planet website, 210

racism, 161
rape
by 'clients', 46, 107, 118, 125,
126–8, 139, 166, 222

by pimps, 38
and child pornography, 145, 146–7
experienced in childhood or youth,
50, 70, 74, 75, 97, 145, 146–7
pornography as, 147
as theft, 27
Raphael, Jody, 7–8
Raymond, Janice, 5
rehabilitation, 41, 56
Resourcing Health and Education
(RhED), 16, 171
right-to-prostitution groups, 1–2
Rohypnol, 118
Roper, Caitlin, 20
rough sex, 45–6, 117, 124, 133, 135,
142
Ruhama, 12

sadomasochism, 134–5
Scarlet Alliance, 19, 51, 56, 171
schizophrenia, 47
self-harm, 70, 71, 75, 76, 130
sex, as a service, 27
sex buyers
attitudes to women they prostitute,
209
criminalisation of, 81–2
denialist mentality, 28
descriptions of, 20n41
exoneration by 'sex work'
ideology, 24
knowledge of harm done to
women, 208
media depictions of, 208
military men, 36
motivations, 210, 211
online 'communities', 24–5
pro-sex lobby depiction of, 207
re-enactment of porn, 36, 45, 203
as reason for prostitution, 84–5
relationship status of, 208
responsibility for prostitution of
women, 20, 64–5
self-delusions of, 87–90
sense of entitlement, 199, 209–12
violence perpetrated against
prostitutes, 80–1, 137

Index

sex industry
  denial of violence and exploitation, 2
  difficulty of escaping from, 35, 41–2, 47–8, 56, 84, 94, 108–10, 132, 177, 182–3, 184
  in 'first-world' industrialised countries, 15–18
  glamourisation of, 8–9, 141, 142, 198
  myths about prostitution, trafficking and the Nordic model, 5, 214–25
  representation of prostitution, 1
  women's 'choice' to enter, 56, 71–3, 79, 82–3, 111, 140, 157, 168, 170, 199, 214–15
sex industry *see also* exit programs
sex parties, 202–3
Sex Trade 101, 216
sex trafficking, 46–7, 55, 189–92, 218–19
Sex Work Act 1994 (Vic), 172
'sex work' ideology
  as dehumanising force, 27–8, 186–7
  denialism of, 23–8, 157–8
'sex worker rights', 158, 172
sexual assault
  experienced during youth, 82
  of prostitutes, 106–7
  prostitution as, 7, 138–9
sexual assault *see also* rape
sexual autonomy, 72
sexual enslavement, 14
sexual exploitation
  healing and recovery from, 137, 139–40
  vulnerability to, 62, 68, 69–70, 138
sexualisation of prostitution, 8–9
sexually transmitted diseases, 103, 106, 176
SIN, 171
single mothers, 205
slave narratives, 9–10
sleeping pills, 35, 53, 176
social isolation, 94, 97, 116, 128–9

social media, 24
Space International, 12, 215
Spears, Libby, 18n37
spiritual damage, 172–3
street prostitution, 79, 157, 219–20
strip bars/stripping, 75–6, 136, 180–2, 204
subjective reality, erasure of, 27–8
suicide/suicidal thoughts, 76–7, 86, 97–8, 103, 108, 110, 134, 174, 192, 205–6
Sullivan, Mary Lucille, 209
Sumner, Charles, 10
survivors
  attempts to silence voices of, 215–16
  dangers of speaking out, 6–7, 85–6, 158
  political action by, 11–15
Survivors for Solutions, 215
survivors' testimonies
  growth of, 215–16
  motives for, 15, 78, 158–9, 177–9, 189, 192–3
  publication of, 8, 10–11
  value of, 7–8
Sweden
  prostitution laws, 167, 217
  reforms to tackle violence against women, 223
Swop, 171

Tiffany's brothel, 34
Tinder, 204
topless waitressing, 73
trafficking
  meaning of, 218–19
  sex trafficking, 46–7, 55, 189–92
trust, and intimacy, 61, 62
12 steps program, 41
Tyler, Meagan, 21

underage prostitutes, 44, 54, 67, 142, 183, 184

OTHER BOOKS FROM SPINIFEX PRESS

Not For Sale:
Feminists Resisting Prostitution and Pornography

Christine Stark and Rebecca Whisnant (eds)

Debunking the assumption that 'sex work' is harmless entertainment for men and liberating work for women, *Not For Sale* argues that prostitution and pornography cause harm to those involved and undermine movements for human equality and meaningful sexual relationships.

Not For Sale analyses the connection of pornography and prostitution with broader social issues, such as racism, poverty, colonisation and globalisation, unbridled corporatisation and militarism.

... Not for Sale *offers an eclectic range of voices and writings that challenge and contest the normalization of the sex industry.* Not for Sale *is a must read for all – from long-standing radical feminists to those just coming into their feminist consciousness.*

– Garine Roubinian, *Rain and Thunder*

Rights: World
ISBN: 9781876756499
eBook: available

Making Sex Work:
A Failed Experiment With Legalised Prostitution

Mary Lucille Sullivan

Can a prostitute be raped? Are pregnancy and STIs an Occupational Health and Safety issue? What sort of society buys and sells women and children for sex? Does legalisation solve the dangers of 'sex work'? Sex worker advocates have argued for many years that legalising prostitution is the way to make the industry safer both for workers and clients. In 1984, the State of Victoria did just that.

Making Sex Work shows with great clarity that the legalisation of prostitution backfires. It further hurts prostituted people and encourages illegal sex industry activities that grow at three times the rate of the legal industry.

... *the evidence is compelling* ... *prostitution is male sex right in action, and this is where we need to start.*

– Grazyna Zajdow, *Arena Magazine*

... *a vital resource for anyone concerned with plans to legalise prostitution anywhere in the world.*

– Anna Krohn, *The Record*

Rights: World
ISBN: 9781876756604
eBook: available

Big Porn Inc:
Exposing the Harms of the Global Porn Industry

Melinda Tankard Reist and Abigail Bray (eds)

The mainstreaming of the global pornography industry has transformed the sexual politics of intimate and public life. Yet challenges to the pornography industry continue to be dismissed as uncool, anti-sex and moral panics. Unmasking the lies behind the selling of porn as 'just a bit of fun' *Big Porn Inc* reveals the shocking truths of an industry that trades in violence, crime and degradation. This fearless book will change the way you think about pornography forever.

... A landmark publication sure to help open the eyes of the public to the modern scourge of porn and amplify the call for greater decency and respect. Because without them, there can be no true liberation.
　　　　— Clive Hamilton, Professor of Public Ethics at Charles Sturt University

Rights: World
ISBN: 9781876756895
eBook: available

Not a Choice, Not a Job:
Exposing the Myths about Prostitution
and the Global Sex Trade

Janice G. Raymond

A generation ago, most people did not know how ubiquitous and grave human trafficking was. Now many people agree that the $35.7 billion business is an appalling violation of human rights. But when confronted with prostitution, many people experience an odd disconnect because prostitution is shrouded in myths, among them the claims that 'prostitution is inevitable', and 'prostitution is a job or service like any other'. In *Not a Choice, Not a Job*, Janice Raymond challenges both the myths and their perpetrators.

After many years as a government minister and activist in Sweden, I read this book with great enthusiasm ... Janice Raymond gives us new arguments, better knowledge, and further hope that another world is possible.
　　　　— Margareta Winberg, former Deputy Prime Minister, Sweden

Janice Raymond has uncovered, analyzed, and exposed one of the biggest legislative scandals since the slave trade – that of state-sanctioned prostitution. Her research is impeccable, and her conclusion – that the international sex trade be seen as a human rights atrocity – should be taken on board by every politician, policy maker and law enforcer around the world.
　　　　— Julie Bindel, journalist, author and social commentator

Rights: ANZ
ISBN: 9781742198682
eBook: available

Getting Real:
Challenging the Sexualisation of Girls

Melinda Tankard Reist (ed)

Getting Real puts the spotlight on the sexualisation and objectification of girls and women in the media, popular culture and society.

Girls are portrayed as sexual at younger ages, pressured to conform to a 'thin, hot, sexy' norm. Clothing, music, magazines, toys and games send girls the message that they are merely the sum of their body parts. The effects of prematurely sexualising girls are borne out in their bodies and minds, with a rise in self-destructive behaviours and mental ill health.

Getting Real: Challenging the Sexualisation of Girls *is a necessary and confronting look at consumer targeting of young girls and its adverse effects.*

— *Bookseller & Publisher*

... an incredibly confronting but important book ... It's a terribly bleak but necessary look at how we are eroding what was once the sacred space of childhood with a bombardment of appalling imagery and sexually suggestive ideas aimed at children, particularly at girls.

— Mia Freedman, *MamaMia*

Rights: World
ISBN: 9781876756758
eBook: available

Being and Being Bought:
Prostitution, Surrogacy and the Split Self

Kajsa Ekis Ekman

Grounded in the reality of the violence and abuse inherent in prostitution – and reeling from the death of a friend to prostitution in Spain – Kajsa Ekis Ekman exposes the many lies in the 'sex work' scenario. Trade unions aren't trade unions. Groups for prostituted women are simultaneously groups for brothel owners. And prostitution is always presented from a woman's point of view. The men who buy sex are left out.

Ekis Ekman argues that the Self must be split from the body to make it possible to sell your body without selling yourself. The body becomes sex. Sex becomes a service. The story of the 'sex worker' says: the Split Self is not only possible, it is the ideal.

... If you've ever wondered how to respond to those who say there are no victims in prostitution or what to say when someone proposes surrogacy as a solution to childlessness – this book is a must-read.

— Melissa Farley, Executive Director of Prostitution Research & Education, San Francisco

Rights: World English Language
ISBN: 9781742198767
eBook: available

Misogyny Re-loaded

Abigail Bray

Misogyny Re-loaded is an explosive manifesto against the resurgent sexual fascism of the new world order. By exposing the casual acceptance of snuff pornography in 'gore' culture through to the framing of rape as slapstick, Abigail Bray links the celebration of sexual sadism to the rise of an authoritarian culture of militarised violence. Arguing that a meaningful collective resistance has been scattered by the mass destruction of genuine social and economic security for ordinary women, *Misogyny Re-loaded* presents a scathing critique of the political drool of mainstream billionaire-friendly feminism.

An angry, passionate and polemical book that draws connections between pornography, the pharmaceutical industry, self-help culture and social media to launch an inflammatory attack against patriarchal capitalism.
— Rosalind Gill, Professor of Social and Cultural Analysis,
City University London

I feel like I am riding a speeding bullet headed right for the heart of patriarchy ... I'm reminded of Andrea Dworkin and Valerie Solanas, who never apologized for telling the truth about women's lives. Bray could bring back radical feminism all by herself, with this one enthralling, desk-slapping, hyper-ventilating account of what it is like to be a woman in the new world order. If she doesn't she should get a medal for trying. I dare you to read this book and emerge without a readiness to take a stand!
— Jennifer B Bilek, *Amazon Review*

Rights: World
ISBN: 9781876756901
eBook: available

Unspeakable: A Feminist Ethic of Speech

Betty McLellan

Is pornography just a matter of free speech? *Unspeakable* answers this and other questions by focusing on how women are silenced in every nation on earth: through violence, subordination and exclusion. The author's hope is that radical feminism will continue to be a "feminism of dissent" and that radical, political feminists will continue speaking against the silence.

Be assured that Betty McLellan has not been silenced by the dynamics and forces she describes so cogently in this rethinking of the last – what is it? – nearly forty years of women moving. ... Anyone who may have wondered where the women's movement went, need look no further. Treasure this undying, undaunted voice.
— Catharine A. MacKinnon, Elizabeth A. Long
Professor of Law at the University of Michigan Law School

Rights: World digital
ISBN: 9781742194929
eBook: available

The Idea of Prostitution

Sheila Jeffreys

There are (at least) two competing views on prostitution: Prostitution as a legitimate and acceptable form of employment, freely chosen by women; and men's use of prostitution as a form of degrading the women and causing grave psychological damage.

In *The Idea of Prostitution*, Sheila Jeffreys explores these sharply contrasting views, examining the changing concept of prostitution from White Slave Traffic of the nineteenth century to its present status as legal. The book includes discussion of the varieties of prostitution such as: the experience of male prostitutes; the uses of women in pornography; and the role of military brothels compared with slavery and rape in marriage. She disputes the distinction between 'forced' and 'free' prostitution, and documents the expanding international traffic in women.

This is a thought-provoking, courageous and important scholarly work. For any scholar of feminist studies of sexuality, violence and social and political theory, this text is essential reading.

— Anita Harris, *Australian Journal of Political Science*

The Idea of Prostitution *is controversial, yet compelling. It is for me one of a few seminal works that are truly radical and have left an indelible imprint on my thinking. The book questions liberal notions about what it means to be a woman in today's society in which certain practices are still tolerated or have been normalised.*

— Stieve DeLance, *Chiaroscuro*

Rights: World
ISBN: 9781876756673
eBook: available

Pornland: How Porn Has Hijacked Our Sexuality

Gail Dines

Pornland takes an unflinching look at pornography and its effect on our lives, showing that today's pornography is strikingly different from yesterday's *Playboy*. As porn culture has become absorbed into pop culture, a new wave of entrepreneurs are creating porn that is ever more hard-core, violent, sexist, and racist.

Pornland *takes a quantum leap beyond the tired pro-porn vs. anti-porn debates of recent decades. It will now be the starting point for serious discussions about how porn shapes and distorts social and sexual norms. Gail Dines understands both the economics and cultural power of the pornography industry ... This is accessible and grounded social analysis at its finest.*

— Jackson Katz, filmmaker and author of *Macho Paradox*

Rights: ANZ
ISBN: 9781876756871
eBook: available

Town of Love

Anne. Ch. Ostby
Afterword by Ruchira Gupta

They call them 'women of love', but the lyrical beauty of the term has a hidden dark side: a workforce of very young girls tasked with feeding their families by offering up their bodies for sale. The girls belong to the Nat which includes some of India's very poorest. For centuries, the Nat men have sent their daughters, sisters, and wives into sex trafficking. Baby girls are welcome arrivals in these towns of love – everyone knows that one day, they will be the breadwinners. As a Nat, you are untouchable, despised by Indian society. How would anyone dare break free of this legacy of prostitution, when it also would mean being shunned by your entire family? *Town of Love* is a raw and gripping story that is guaranteed to leave you breathless.

Having personally met the survivors of trafficking about whom this is written, I know that Anne Ostby's novel deserves world attention. It is the essence of a terrible truth that must be exposed.

– Gloria Steinem

The ambition and sensitivity of Ostby's vision open the mind to the plight of a society demeaned by how it treats its most vulnerable members.

– Cameron Woodhead, *The Age*

Rights: World English Language X India
ISBN: 9781742198477
eBook: available

Lupa and Lamb

Susan Hawthorne

The history of Rome is littered with stories of rape, torture and prostitution, from the origin stories of rape to the mass rapes of the Sabine women organised by Romulus. In the Christian era, Popes were renown for their reliance on the incomes of prostitutes. Young women were martyred and, like Saint Agnes, they were dragged naked through the streets to brothels and later killed. These poems have much to tell us about violence at the heart of Western culture.

In this triumphantly inventive excursion into feminist revisionism, Hawthorne is fully mistress of language and genre as she brings her Roman women into view in the diverse roles – lover, poet, prostitute, martyr – and the sometimes dark fates that await them as living instances of she-wolf and lamb.

– Jennifer Strauss AM

Rights: World
ISBN: 9781742199245
eBook: available

Paid For. My Journey through Prostitution

Rachel Moran

When you are fifteen years old and destitute, too unskilled to work and too young to claim unemployment benefit, your body is all you have left to sell.
Rachel Moran grew up in severe poverty and a painfully troubled family. Taken into state care at fourteen, she became homeless and was in prostitution by the age of fifteen. For the next seven years Rachel lived life as a prostituted woman, isolated, drug-addicted, alienated.

Rachel Moran's experience was one of violence, loneliness, and relentless exploitation and abuse. Her story reveals the emotional cost of selling your body night after night in order to survive – loss of innocence, loss of self-worth and a loss of connection from mainstream society that makes it all the more difficult to escape the prostitution world.

You'll laugh, cry and become enraged as you read this clearly difficult-to-pen memoir, as she details her endurance of substance, physical and mental abuse, extreme poverty, great loss and loneliness.
– Felicity Kirkpatrick, *The Examiner*

A brave woman steps out from Ireland's dark side and gives a clear-eyed account of the violence that is prostitution.
– Susan McKay, former Chief Executive of the National Women's Council of Ireland

Rachel Moran has wrought out of the depravity of the 'prostitution experience' an inspirational and brilliant memoir. Courageous and tender; ultimately her story is a searing indictment of men who buy sex.
– Kathleen Barry, author of *Female Sexual Slavery*

Rights: ANZ
ISBN: 9781742198620
eBook: available

*If you would like to know more about Spinifex Press
write for a free catalogue or visit our website.*

SPINIFEX PRESS
PO Box 212 North Melbourne
Victoria 3051 Australia
www.spinifexpress.com.au